THE RESTORATIVE SOCIETY

How Healing Justice Can Transform Our World

DR. MAXWELL SHIMBA

Published in Manhattan, New York by Shimba Publishing, LLC.

Shimba Publishing LLC

Table of Contents

Introduction

Overview of Restorative Justice

Restorative justice is not merely an alternative approach to conflict resolution; it represents a fundamental paradigm shift in how humanity understands and responds to harm, wrongdoing, and the very nature of justice itself. As you embark on this journey through these pages, I invite you to set aside preconceived notions about justice that have been shaped by centuries of punitive thinking. Imagine instead a vision of justice that heals rather than hurts, that restores rather than destroys, that builds bridges rather than walls.

At its core, restorative justice is a philosophical and practical framework that moves away from traditional punitive systems—which ask merely "What law was broken, who broke it, and what punishment do they deserve?"—toward a profoundly different set of questions: "Who has been harmed, what are their needs, whose obligations have arisen, and how can we address the harm while repairing relationships and rebuilding community?"

This approach, as we will explore throughout this book, is rooted in ancient wisdom that predates modern legal systems, has evolved through centuries of human experience, and has gained remarkable traction in contemporary societies worldwide. The principles you will encounter in these chapters are not abstract theories confined to academic discourse; they are living, breathing practices that are transforming schools, workplaces, communities, and justice systems across the globe.

Understanding Restorative Justice

When we speak of restorative justice, we are describing a comprehensive alternative to the conventional criminal justice system, which has long focused on punishment and retribution as its primary responses to wrongdoing. The traditional model, which most of us have internalized as simply "the way things are," operates on a relatively straightforward premise: when someone breaks a rule, they should suffer consequences proportional to their offense. This retributive approach, while intuitively satisfying in its simplicity, often fails to address the complex web of needs and relationships that crime and conflict create.

Restorative justice, by contrast, emphasizes the restoration of relationships, the rehabilitation of offenders, and most importantly, the healing of victims. It recognizes that when harm occurs, a ripple effect spreads outward from the immediate victim to affect families, communities, and even offenders themselves. Addressing this harm requires more than punishment; it requires a thoughtful, inclusive process that brings together all those affected.

The restorative process typically involves direct or indirect communication between the victim and the offender, with the active support of the community. This is not about confrontation or blame, but about creating sacred space where truth can be spoken, pain can be acknowledged, and pathways toward making amends can be discovered together. As we will see in later chapters, this process draws on deep psychological insights about human healing, theological understandings of forgiveness and reconciliation, and philosophical traditions that recognize our fundamental interconnectedness.

Key Components of Restorative Justice

Let us examine more closely the essential elements that make restorative justice distinct and powerful:

1. Inclusion of All Stakeholders

Restorative justice operates on the fundamental conviction that those most affected by harm should have the opportunity to participate in its resolution. This means victims, offenders, and community members all have a place at the table. Their voices are not merely heard but respected; their perspectives are not merely noted but integrated into the search for resolution. This inclusive approach stands in stark contrast to traditional justice systems, where the state effectively hijacks the conflict, leaving victims as witnesses and offenders as passive recipients of punishment.

The psychological wisdom embedded in this approach is profound. When people are excluded from processes that profoundly affect their lives, they experience what psychologists call "procedural injustice"—a sense that the system has failed to treat them with dignity and respect. This perception often compounds the original harm, leaving victims feeling re-victimized and offenders feeling alienated from the very community they need to rejoin. Restorative justice, by ensuring meaningful participation, addresses this psychological dimension while honoring the philosophical principle that human dignity requires agency in matters that concern us.

2. Focus on Repairing Harm

Rather than asking "What punishment does this offense deserve?" restorative justice asks "What needs to be healed?" This shift in focus is not merely semantic; it represents a fundamentally different orientation toward justice itself. The primary goal becomes repairing the harm caused by the offense, which requires understanding that harm in all its dimensions—physical, emotional, relational, and sometimes material.

This focus on reparation draws on deep theological traditions that understand justice not as retribution but as *shalom*—a Hebrew concept encompassing peace, wholeness, and right relationship. When the prophets of ancient Israel spoke of justice, they were not primarily concerned with punishment but with the restoration of right order within community. Similarly, Christian theology understands the work of Christ as restorative—reconciling humanity to God and to one another, making whole what was broken.

3. Accountability

In restorative justice, accountability means something far richer than "accepting punishment." It means offenders are encouraged to take genuine responsibility for their actions and to understand—truly understand—the impact of their behavior on others. This understanding is not imposed from without but develops through direct engagement with those who have been harmed.

The psychological depth of this approach cannot be overstated. Research in moral development consistently shows that genuine behavioral change requires more than fear of punishment; it requires the development of empathy and the internalization of pro-social values. When offenders come to understand, through direct encounter, the real human consequences of their actions, they are far more likely to experience the kind of moral transformation that leads to lasting change.

4. Voluntary Participation

Unlike traditional justice processes, which are coercive by nature, restorative justice typically requires voluntary participation from all parties. This voluntariness is not merely procedural preference; it is essential to the integrity and effectiveness of the process. Genuine engagement and authentic commitment to resolution cannot be compelled; they must be chosen.

This emphasis on voluntariness reflects deep philosophical commitments to human freedom and dignity. It also has practical significance: when people choose to participate, they are far more likely to take ownership of the outcomes and follow through on agreements. The theological dimension here is equally important—many religious traditions understand that genuine repentance cannot be coerced but must arise from the free will of the individual.

5. Facilitated Dialogue

The restorative process is typically guided by a neutral facilitator whose role is not to impose solutions but to create conditions for safe, constructive conversation. This facilitator ensures that all participants have opportunity to speak and be heard, that the dialogue remains focused and productive, and that the emotional intensity of the encounter is managed in ways that promote healing rather than additional harm.

The facilitator's work draws on sophisticated understandings of communication, conflict resolution, and trauma-informed practice. As we will explore in later chapters, effective facilitation requires not only technical skill but also deep wisdom about human nature and the dynamics of healing.

The Origins of Restorative Justice

The story of restorative justice begins long before the term itself was coined. Indeed, its origins can be traced to the earliest human communities, where justice was understood not as abstract rule-enforcement but as the practical work of maintaining community harmony. These ancient practices, preserved in indigenous cultures around the world, offer profound wisdom that modern restorative justice continues to draw upon.

Indigenous Traditions

Native American Practices

Among Native American tribes, justice was traditionally understood as the work of restoring balance within community. When harm occurred, the response was not to isolate and punish the wrongdoer but to bring the community together in processes designed to heal relationships and restore harmony. The peacemaking circles practiced by many tribes, which have directly influenced modern restorative circle processes, created space for all affected parties to speak from the heart, to be heard with respect, and to participate in finding pathways forward.

These practices were grounded in a worldview that recognized the profound interconnectedness of all things. When one person caused harm, the entire community was affected;

therefore, the entire community had a role in healing. This understanding, which we might now call an ecological or systems perspective, is increasingly validated by modern psychological and sociological research.

African Justice Systems

Across the African continent, traditional justice systems have long embodied restorative principles. The Gacaca courts of Rwanda, which we will examine in detail in later chapters, represent a modern adaptation of ancient practices. Following the 1994 genocide, Rwandans faced the impossible task of adjudicating hundreds of thousands of cases through a conventional justice system that had been destroyed. Their response—revitalizing traditional community-based courts—demonstrated the enduring power of restorative approaches.

Central to many African justice traditions is the philosophy of *Ubuntu*, captured in the phrase "I am because we are." This understanding of personhood as fundamentally relational has profound implications for justice. If human identity is constituted through relationship, then harm damages not only individuals but the relational fabric itself. Justice, therefore, must be concerned with repairing that fabric.

Maori Practices in New Zealand

The Maori people of New Zealand have contributed one of the most influential restorative practices to the modern world. The Family Group Conference, now a cornerstone of New Zealand's juvenile justice system, emerged directly from Maori traditions of collective decision-making and community responsibility for addressing wrongdoing.

In Maori understanding, justice is not something done *to* an offender but something achieved *through* the community. When a young person causes harm, it is not merely an individual failing but a breakdown in the web of relationships that should have supported and guided them. Response to harm, therefore, must involve not only the offender but also their family, their extended kin network, and the broader community.

Biblical and Theological Foundations

For readers approaching restorative justice from within the Judeo-Christian tradition, it is essential to recognize how deeply restorative principles are woven into the biblical narrative. Far from supporting primarily retributive interpretations of scripture, a careful reading reveals a God whose character is consistently oriented toward restoration and reconciliation.

The Old Testament Vision

When the Hebrew prophets spoke of justice, they used the word *mishpat*, which encompasses far more than retribution. The great prophetic calls for justice—from Amos's demand that "justice roll down like waters" to Isaiah's vision of a righteous society—are calls for the restoration of right relationship, for the protection of the vulnerable, for the healing of community.

The concept of *shalom*—often translated simply as "peace" but carrying the richer meaning of wholeness, completeness, and flourishing—represents the biblical vision of how things ought to be. When harm occurs, *shalom* is broken. The work of justice, therefore, is the work of restoring *shalom*, of making whole what has been fragmented.

The Torah itself contains numerous provisions that reflect restorative rather than purely retributive principles. The cities of refuge provided sanctuary for those who caused accidental harm, recognizing that justice must distinguish between intent and accident. Restitution requirements for theft and property damage emphasized making the victim whole rather than simply punishing the offender. The Year of Jubilee, when debts were forgiven and land returned to original families, institutionalized regular restoration of right relationship.

The New Testament Fulfillment

Jesus's teachings consistently challenge retributive interpretations of justice. When he instructs his followers to turn the other cheek, to go the extra mile, to forgive not seven times but seventy-seven times, he is not advocating passive submission to injustice but rather offering a radical alternative to the violence-begets-violence cycle. His teaching in Matthew 18 outlines a process for addressing harm within community that bears remarkable similarity to modern restorative practices: go directly to the person, engage them privately, if that fails bring others, and only as last resort involve the larger community.

Perhaps most significantly, the cross itself can be understood as the ultimate restorative act. In Christian theology, Christ's death is not about satisfying an abstract demand for retribution but about reconciling humanity to God—restoring relationship, making peace, healing the breach caused by sin. The apostle Paul captures this beautifully when he writes that "God was in Christ reconciling the world to himself, not counting their trespasses against them, and entrusting to us the message of reconciliation" (2 Corinthians 5:19).

Ancient Justice Systems Beyond Israel

The restorative impulse is not limited to biblical traditions. Ancient Middle Eastern legal codes, including the famous Code of Hammurabi, included provisions for restitution alongside their more famous retributive elements. While "an eye for an eye" is often cited as the epitome of retributive justice, these codes also required compensation for victims and established procedures for resolving disputes that aimed at restoration.

In ancient Greece, the Athenian legal system allowed citizens to play active roles in the administration of justice, with juries of ordinary citizens determining outcomes in ways that fostered community engagement with wrongdoing. The philosophical traditions of Greece, particularly Aristotelian virtue ethics, emphasized the development of moral character over mere rule-following—an orientation that resonates with restorative justice's focus on transformation.

Roman law, for all its emphasis on legal formalism, included provisions for restitution and compensation. The *Lex Aquilia*, governing damage to property, established principles of making victims whole that continue to influence legal thinking today. The Roman emphasis on *paterfamilias*—the father's role in maintaining household harmony—recognized the importance of resolving conflicts within the relational context in which they occurred.

Asian philosophical and religious traditions have also contributed to restorative thinking. Confucianism, with its emphasis on social harmony, filial piety, and the moral development of individuals within community, provides rich resources for understanding justice as relationship-maintenance rather than rule-enforcement. Buddhist teachings on compassion, non-attachment, and the interconnectedness of all beings offer profound insights into the nature of harm and healing. The Hindu emphasis on *dharma*—right living in accordance with cosmic order—understands wrongdoing as disruption of harmony that must be restored.

The Importance of Restorative Justice

As we stand at what many scholars call a "mass incarceration moment"—with the United States leading the world in imprisonment rates, with communities of color disproportionately affected by punitive policies, with prisons functioning more as warehouses than as sites of rehabilitation—the importance of restorative justice has never been clearer. The stakes extend far beyond criminal justice reform; they touch the very character of our society and our understanding of what it means to be human together.

Empowerment of Victims

Perhaps the most significant contribution of restorative justice is its capacity to empower those who have been harmed. In traditional justice systems, victims are often marginalized, treated as evidence rather than as persons with ongoing needs and legitimate interests in how their cases are resolved. They may never have opportunity to tell their stories fully, to ask the questions that haunt them, to receive acknowledgment of their suffering, or to participate in determining what would help them heal.

Restorative justice changes this entirely. Victims are not peripheral to the process but central. They have opportunity to speak—not only about what happened but about how it has affected them, about what they need to move forward, about what would constitute justice from their perspective. They can ask questions directly of the offender: Why me? What were you thinking? Do you understand what you've done? The answers to these questions, when offered sincerely, can be profoundly healing.

The psychological research supporting this is compelling. Victims who participate in restorative processes consistently report higher satisfaction than those whose cases proceed through conventional channels. They describe feeling heard, respected, and validated in ways that traditional justice rarely provides. They are less likely to experience ongoing symptoms of trauma and more likely to achieve genuine closure.

Rehabilitation of Offenders

Restorative justice also offers powerful pathways for offender rehabilitation. When offenders are simply punished—locked away, isolated from community, deprived of opportunity to understand the impact of their actions—they rarely emerge better than when they entered. Often, they emerge worse: more angry, more alienated, more deeply embedded in criminal subcultures.

Restorative justice takes a different approach. By requiring offenders to confront the human consequences of their actions, to hear directly from those they have harmed, to take active responsibility for making amends, it engages them in precisely the kind of moral reflection that leads to genuine change. This is not soft on crime; it is harder on crime than mere punishment, because it demands that offenders actually face what they have done and take steps to repair it.

The theological significance of this approach should not be missed. In the Christian tradition, repentance (*metanoia*) is not merely feeling sorry but turning around, changing direction, actively pursuing restoration. When offenders engage in restorative processes, they are given opportunity for precisely this kind of transformative repentance.

Strengthening Communities

Crime and conflict do not occur in a vacuum. They happen in communities, affect communities, and reveal vulnerabilities within communities. Restorative justice recognizes that communities are not merely bystanders to harm but stakeholders in its resolution and essential partners in prevention.

When communities are involved in restorative processes, they develop capacity to address their own problems rather than outsourcing them to distant authorities. They build relationships across lines that might otherwise divide them. They develop shared norms and collective efficacy—the sense that "we" can solve "our" problems together.

Research in community psychology consistently demonstrates that communities with strong social networks and high collective efficacy experience less crime and violence. Restorative justice builds precisely these community resources, creating the relational infrastructure that prevents harm before it occurs.

Reduction in Recidivism

The empirical evidence for restorative justice's effectiveness in reducing reoffending is increasingly robust. Multiple meta-analyses have found that restorative programs produce statistically significant reductions in recidivism compared to conventional processing. These effects are particularly strong for violent offenses—precisely the cases where one might expect restorative approaches to be least appropriate.

The reasons for this effectiveness are not mysterious. When offenders understand the impact of their actions, develop empathy for those they have harmed, and experience the support of community in making positive changes, they are fundamentally transformed. They are not merely deterred by fear of future punishment but internally motivated to live differently.

Holistic Approach

Finally, restorative justice offers a holistic approach that addresses the root causes of crime rather than merely responding to symptoms. By bringing all stakeholders together, by attending to the full range of needs created by harm, by seeking solutions that address underlying issues, restorative justice creates the possibility of genuine transformation rather than temporary containment.

This holistic orientation aligns with the best insights from multiple disciplines. Psychology teaches us that human behavior is shaped by complex interactions of individual, relational, and systemic factors. Sociology reveals how crime emerges from social conditions and community dynamics. Theology reminds us that human beings are more than their worst actions, that redemption is possible, that reconciliation is worth pursuing.

The Purpose of This Book

As we journey together through these pages, my goal is to provide you with a comprehensive understanding of restorative justice—its philosophical foundations, its practical applications, and its transformative potential. This book is designed to be both accessible to those new to these ideas and substantive enough to engage readers already familiar with restorative principles.

Philosophical Foundations

We will explore together the rich philosophical traditions that undergird restorative justice. These include:

Relational Ethics: The recognition that human beings are fundamentally interconnected, that our identities are formed in relationship, and that our moral obligations arise from these relationships. When harm occurs, it damages not only individuals but the relational fabric itself. Justice, therefore, must be concerned with repairing that fabric.

Communitarianism: The understanding that healthy communities require both individual rights and collective responsibility. Restorative justice operationalizes this insight by involving community in the justice process and by emphasizing the community's stake in restoration.

Virtue Ethics: Drawing on Aristotelian traditions, restorative justice focuses not merely on rules and consequences but on the formation of moral character. Through restorative processes, both victims and offenders can develop virtues—empathy, compassion, responsibility—that enable flourishing.

Restorative Ontology: The philosophical claim that restoration is not merely one option among many but is fundamental to human existence. We are beings who need restoration, who seek healing, who long for reconciliation. Justice that ignores this ontological reality will always be incomplete.

Psychological Dimensions

We will also examine the psychological insights that inform restorative practice. These include understandings of trauma and its healing, the role of empathy in moral development, the importance of procedural justice in shaping perceptions of fairness, and the conditions under which genuine behavioral change occurs.

Theological Resources

For readers interested in the theological dimensions of restorative justice, we will explore how restorative principles are woven through scripture and tradition. We will examine concepts of justice in the Hebrew Bible, the teaching and example of Jesus, Pauline understandings of reconciliation, and the resources various theological traditions offer for restorative practice.

Practical Applications

Perhaps most importantly, we will examine how restorative principles are applied in real-world contexts. Through case studies and examples, we will see restorative justice at work in criminal justice systems, schools, workplaces, and communities. We will learn from successes and failures, from programs that have thrived and those that have struggled.

The Structure of Our Journey

To guide us through this comprehensive exploration, the book is organized into ten chapters, each building on those that precede it while offering distinct contributions to our understanding.

Chapter 1: Historical Foundations will trace restorative justice from ancient practices through its modern resurgence, showing how wisdom from the past continues to inform present practice.

Chapter 2: Theoretical Frameworks will examine the philosophical and ethical foundations that give restorative justice its intellectual coherence and moral power.

Chapter 3: Core Principles and Values will explore in depth the essential elements that make restorative justice distinctive: accountability, reparation, community involvement, empathy, and healing.

Chapter 4: Restorative Practices and Models will provide detailed examination of specific approaches: victim-offender mediation, family group conferencing, circle processes, and community restorative boards.

Chapter 5: Case Studies and Real-World Applications will show restorative justice at work in criminal justice, education, workplaces, and communities, offering concrete examples of success and lessons learned.

Chapter 6: Benefits and Challenges will honestly examine both the positive outcomes associated with restorative justice and the obstacles to its implementation, including thoughtful engagement with criticisms.

Chapter 7: Restorative Justice and the Legal System will explore how restorative practices can complement and enhance traditional legal frameworks, examining legislative support and notable legal cases.

Chapter 8: International Contexts will provide global perspective, examining restorative practices across cultures and in transitional justice settings.

Chapter 9: Restorative Justice and Social Justice will explore intersections with issues of race, class, gender, and social equity, examining how restorative practices can promote fairness and community empowerment.

Chapter 10: The Future of Restorative Justice will look forward, exploring emerging trends, innovations, and the visionary potential of restorative approaches to transform society.

A Personal Word

Before we begin this journey together, I want to share something of why this topic matters so deeply to me. Over years of studying, practicing, and teaching restorative justice, I have witnessed its power to transform lives in ways that conventional approaches simply cannot match. I have seen victims find healing they thought impossible. I have seen offenders genuinely transformed, taking responsibility and making amends in ways that restored them to community. I have seen communities grow stronger, more cohesive, more capable of addressing their own challenges.

But I have also seen the obstacles—the resistance to change, the resource constraints, the skepticism of those invested in punitive approaches, the legitimate concerns about whether restorative justice can work for serious crimes or in complex situations. I have seen programs struggle and sometimes fail. I have wrestled with the hard questions: How do we ensure safety? How do we protect the vulnerable? How do we maintain standards while remaining flexible?

This book is my attempt to share both the promise and the complexity, to offer a vision that is hopeful without being naive, practical without being reductionist, grounded in evidence while open to mystery. My hope is that whether you come to this topic as a student, a practitioner, a policymaker, or simply someone who cares about justice, you will find here resources for understanding and tools for action.

As we proceed, I invite you to bring your own questions, your own experiences, your own hopes and concerns. The journey we are undertaking together is not merely academic; it is deeply personal and profoundly consequential. For how we understand justice shapes how we live together, how we respond to harm, how we create communities capable of both accountability and compassion.

Let us begin.

CHAPTER 01

HISTORICAL FOUNDATIONS OF RESTORATIVE JUSTICE

What Is Philosophy?

Before we can fully appreciate the historical foundations of restorative justice, we must first understand the philosophical lens through which we will examine this journey. Philosophy, dear reader, is not some abstract discipline confined to university classrooms and ancient texts. It is the most human of endeavors—the ongoing quest to understand ourselves, our world, and our place within it. Philosophy asks the questions that children ask and that the wisest among us never stop asking: What is real? How can we know? What is good? How should we live?

When we speak of philosophy, we are speaking of the love of wisdom—*philosophia* in the ancient Greek—and this love manifests in systematic reflection on the deepest matters of human existence. Philosophy examines the nature of reality itself (metaphysics), the foundations and limits of human knowledge (epistemology), the principles that should guide our conduct (ethics), the nature of beauty and artistic expression (aesthetics), the structures of valid reasoning (logic), and the proper organization of human society (political philosophy).

These branches of philosophy are not separate silos but interconnected ways of approaching the fundamental questions of human existence. When we ask about justice, we are engaging all of them. We are asking about the nature of reality—what does it mean to be human? We are asking about knowledge—how can we know what justice requires? We are asking about ethics—what principles should guide our responses to wrongdoing? We are asking about politics—how should we organize our common life?

Throughout this chapter, and indeed throughout this entire book, we will be engaged in philosophical reflection. But we will not be doing philosophy in the abstract, detached from the messiness of human experience. Rather, we will be exploring how philosophical wisdom has been embodied in the concrete practices of communities across time and around the world. We will see how the deepest questions about justice have been answered not merely in theory but in the lived experience of people seeking to respond to harm in ways that heal rather than wound.

Philosophy and Restorative Justice

The relationship between philosophy and restorative justice is not incidental but essential. Restorative justice is not merely a set of techniques or programs; it is a philosophy of justice—a way of understanding what justice means and what it requires. Every restorative practice embodies philosophical commitments about the nature of human beings, the meaning of community, the purpose of accountability, and the possibility of healing.

Let me invite you to consider these philosophical foundations with me, not as abstract propositions to be memorized but as living ideas that have shaped and continue to shape how communities respond to harm.

Relational Ethics

At the heart of restorative justice lies a philosophical insight so profound yet so simple that we might easily miss its significance: human beings are fundamentally relational creatures. We do not exist as isolated individuals, each pursuing our own private good. We exist in relationship—with family, with friends, with neighbors, with colleagues, with strangers, with the natural world, and, for those who share theistic faith, with the divine.

Relational ethics, as a philosophical tradition, takes this insight as its starting point. It asserts that our moral obligations arise not from abstract principles alone but from the concrete relationships in which we find ourselves. We owe things to one another not merely because we are all rational beings but because we are connected—because our lives are intertwined, because what affects one affects all, because we are, in the deepest sense, members one of another.

This philosophical perspective finds expression in diverse traditions. In African thought, it is captured in the concept of *Ubuntu*—"I am because we are." In Hebrew scripture, it is embodied in the covenant relationship between God and Israel, and among the people themselves. In Christian theology, it is expressed in Paul's image of the body, where each member belongs to and depends on all the others. In feminist ethics, it appears in the emphasis on care and connection rather than abstract rules.

For restorative justice, this relational understanding is foundational. When harm occurs, it is not merely a rule that has been broken but relationships that have been damaged. The victim has been harmed, certainly—but the harm ripples outward, affecting families, communities, and even the offender themselves. Justice, therefore, cannot be satisfied simply by punishing the offender. It must address the full web of relationships that has been torn.

Consider, for a moment, how different this is from the conventional understanding. In the traditional criminal justice system, a crime is primarily an offense against the state. The state prosecutes, the state punishes, and the state claims to have done justice. The victim is largely incidental—a witness, perhaps, but not a party to the proceedings. The community is entirely absent. The offender is a passive recipient of punishment.

Restorative justice, grounded in relational ethics, sees all of this differently. The crime is first and foremost an offense against persons and relationships. The state's interest is secondary. The victim must be central. The community must be involved. The offender must be an active participant in making things right. The goal is not to punish but to restore—to mend what has been torn, to heal what has been wounded, to rebuild what has been broken.

Communitarianism

Closely related to relational ethics is the philosophical tradition of communitarianism. While relational ethics emphasizes the interpersonal dimension of human existence, communitarianism focuses on the community as a whole—on the shared values, common purposes, and collective well-being that make human flourishing possible.

Communitarianism arose partly in response to the excesses of individualism that have characterized much modern Western thought. It does not deny the importance of individual rights and dignity, but it insists that individuals are formed in and through communities, that our identities are shaped by the traditions and practices into which we are born, and that a just society must attend to the health of communities, not merely the liberties of individuals.

This philosophical perspective has profound implications for justice. If individuals are constituted by their communities, then crime is not merely an individual act but a community wound. When one person harms another, the entire community is diminished. The bonds of trust that make community possible are weakened. The sense of shared identity and mutual responsibility is frayed.

Restorative justice embraces this communitarian insight. It insists that communities must be involved in responding to crime—not as spectators but as participants. Communities have a stake in what happens; they have resources to contribute; they have wisdom to offer. Moreover, communities themselves are changed by crime and by the response to crime. They can be weakened by punitive responses that alienate offenders and ignore victims, or they can be strengthened by restorative responses that bring people together, build relationships, and foster shared responsibility.

This is why restorative practices so often involve community members directly. In circle processes, community members sit alongside victims and offenders, sharing their perspectives, offering their support, participating in the search for resolution. In family group conferencing, extended family and community networks are central to the process. In community restorative boards, local volunteers take responsibility for addressing harm within their own neighborhoods.

The communitarian vision that animates these practices is not nostalgic or romantic. It recognizes that communities can be broken, divided, conflicted, and unjust. It does not idealize community but seeks to build the kind of community worth having—one where people know and care for one another, where differences are respected, where conflicts are addressed constructively, and where everyone has a place.

Virtue Ethics

From the ancient Greeks, particularly Aristotle, we inherit another philosophical tradition that deeply informs restorative justice: virtue ethics. Unlike ethical systems that focus primarily on rules (deontology) or consequences (utilitarianism), virtue ethics focuses on character—on the kind of people we become through our actions and habits.

For Aristotle, the goal of human life is *eudaimonia*—flourishing, well-being, living well. And we achieve this goal not by following rules or calculating consequences but by cultivating virtues: dispositions to act, feel, and think in ways that are excellent. Courage, temperance, justice, wisdom, friendship—these are not merely nice additions to life but essential components of human flourishing.

Virtue ethics asks not "What should I do?" but "What kind of person should I become?" It recognizes that our actions shape our character, and our character shapes our actions. We become just by doing just acts; we become courageous by acting courageously. Over time, these actions become habitual, woven into the fabric of who we are.

Restorative justice is deeply consonant with virtue ethics. It is not merely concerned with resolving specific incidents but with shaping the character of all involved. Victims are given opportunity to practice forgiveness, to move from anger and fear toward healing and hope. Offenders are given opportunity to practice accountability, to develop empathy, to take responsibility, to make amends. Communities are given opportunity to practice hospitality, to welcome back those who have caused harm, to support both victims and offenders in their healing journeys.

This focus on character formation is not incidental to restorative justice but central to it. Restorative processes are designed not merely to produce agreements but to transform people. When victims and offenders sit together, speak truth to one another, listen with open hearts, and work together to find a way forward, they are engaged in moral formation. They are becoming different kinds of people—people capable of empathy, accountability, forgiveness, and reconciliation.

The theological dimensions of this are profound. In the Christian tradition, the virtues are understood as gifts of grace that are also cultivated through practice. We are saved by grace, but we also work out our salvation with fear and trembling. The Holy Spirit produces fruit in our lives—love, joy, peace, patience, kindness, goodness, faithfulness, gentleness, self-control—but we also cooperate with that grace, practicing these virtues until they become second nature.

Restorative justice, understood in this light, is not merely a technique for resolving conflicts but a school of virtue—a place where people can learn and practice the habits of heart and life that make for human flourishing.

Restorative Ontology

Perhaps the most profound philosophical foundation of restorative justice is what we might call restorative ontology—the claim that restoration is not merely one option among many but is woven into the very fabric of reality. This is a bold claim, and it deserves careful consideration.

Ontology is the branch of philosophy that studies the nature of being, existence, and reality. When we speak of restorative ontology, we are suggesting that reality itself has a restorative character—that the universe is oriented toward healing, that wholeness is more fundamental than brokenness, that reconciliation is the deepest truth about things.

This is not a claim that can be proven empirically, though evidence can certainly be marshaled in its support. It is, rather, a philosophical and theological claim about the ultimate nature of things. In the Judeo-Christian tradition, it finds expression in the doctrine of creation: God made all things good, and though that goodness has been marred by sin, it has not been destroyed. The creation groans, as Paul puts it, waiting for redemption—but it groans in hope, not despair.

It finds expression, too, in the doctrine of the incarnation and atonement. In Christ, God enters into broken humanity to heal it from within. The cross and resurrection are not merely events in the past but cosmic signs of God's determination to restore all things. In Christ, God was reconciling the world to himself—

not counting trespasses but making peace through the blood of the cross.

For restorative justice, this ontological claim has practical implications. If restoration is built into the nature of things, then restorative justice is not imposing something foreign on human conflict but cooperating with the deepest grain of the universe. When we seek to heal harm rather than merely punish offenders, we are aligning ourselves with the way things are supposed to be. When we work for reconciliation, we are participating in God's own work in the world.

This does not mean that restoration is easy or automatic. The brokenness of the world is real, and the resistance to healing is powerful. But restorative ontology gives us hope that our efforts are not futile—that we are not swimming against the current but with it, not fighting reality but cooperating with its deepest tendencies.

Ethical Responsibility

Finally, restorative justice is grounded in the philosophical principle of ethical responsibility—the conviction that we are accountable for our actions and obligated to address the harm we cause. This principle is so fundamental that we might take it for granted, but it deserves careful examination.

Ethical responsibility has both individual and collective dimensions. Individually, each of us is accountable for our choices and actions. We cannot simply blame our circumstances, our upbringing, our genes, or our environment. However much these factors may influence us, we remain moral agents capable of choice and therefore responsible for what we choose.

Collectively, we share responsibility for the communities in which we live. We are not merely isolated individuals but members of families, neighborhoods, organizations, and societies. When harm occurs in our midst, we have some responsibility to respond—not because we caused the harm but because we are part of the community that has been harmed and that must find a way forward.

Restorative justice honors both dimensions of ethical responsibility. It holds offenders accountable for their actions—not by imposing punishment from without but by creating conditions in which they can take responsibility from within. It also engages the community in its collective responsibility to support victims, to hold offenders accountable, and to work for healing and prevention.

This understanding of responsibility is deeply rooted in biblical teaching. The prophets of Israel consistently called the people to account for their failures—not merely as individuals but as a community. Jesus taught that we will give account for every idle word, but he also taught that we are our brother's keeper. Paul insisted that we are members one of another, so that when one suffers, all suffer.

Ethical responsibility, understood in this way, is not a burden to be avoided but a dignity to be embraced. To be responsible is to be a moral agent, capable of choice, accountable for actions, able to make things right. When restorative justice invites offenders to take responsibility, it is honoring their dignity as moral beings. When it engages community in collective responsibility, it is honoring the dignity of community as a moral agent.

Historical Foundations of Restorative Justice

With these philosophical foundations in mind, we are now prepared to explore the historical roots of restorative justice. And here, dear reader, we encounter something remarkable: restorative justice is not a modern invention but an ancient wisdom, rediscovered and renewed in our time but deeply rooted in the practices of our ancestors.

The story I am about to tell you is not a story of linear progress—from primitive to advanced, from simple to complex. It is, rather, a story of loss and recovery, of forgetting and remembering, of wisdom obscured and wisdom regained. For much of human history, communities understood instinctively what we have had to learn again through painful experience: that justice is about healing, not merely punishment; that relationships matter more than rules; that community is essential to human flourishing.

Ancient Practices

Let us begin our journey in the ancient world, among peoples whose wisdom still has much to teach us.

Indigenous Traditions of North America

Imagine yourself sitting in a circle with your community. In the center, a fire burns, its light flickering on the faces of those gathered. An elder speaks, her voice calm and measured, inviting each person to share what is in their heart. A young man who has caused harm hangs his head, but as he hears the stories of those he has hurt—not accusations but honest accounts of pain—something shifts within him. He begins to understand what he has done, not as an abstract wrong but as a wound to real people he knows and loves. When it is his turn to speak, he does not make excuses. He acknowledges his actions, expresses his sorrow, and asks what he can do to make things right.

This scene, or something like it, played out countless times among Native American tribes across the continent. The peacemaking circle—also known as the talking circle—was not merely a way of resolving disputes but a way of being community. It embodied deep wisdom about human nature and the dynamics of healing.

Several aspects of these practices are worth noting. First, the circle itself was significant. In a circle, no one is at the head; all are equal. The arrangement of bodies embodied the philosophical principle of equality and mutual respect. Second, the use of a talking piece—an object passed from person to person, indicating who has the right to speak—ensured that every voice could be heard. No one could dominate; no one could be silenced. Third, the involvement of elders brought wisdom and authority to the process. Elders were not judges imposing sentences but guides facilitating healing.

The focus was consistently on restoration rather than retribution. The goal was not to make the offender suffer but to restore harmony within the community. This required the offender to understand the impact of their actions, to make amends where possible, and to be reintegrated into community life. It required the victim to be heard, to receive acknowledgment, and to participate in determining what would constitute justice. It required the community to support both victim and offender and to take responsibility for creating conditions in which harm would be less likely to recur.

African Justice Systems and Ubuntu

Travel with me now across the Atlantic to the African continent, where similar wisdom developed in diverse cultural contexts. Across Africa, traditional justice systems were characterized by a profound commitment to reconciliation and community healing.

The Gacaca courts of Rwanda, though revitalized in the aftermath of the 1994 genocide, drew on ancient practices that long predated colonial intervention. In traditional Rwandan communities, when conflicts arose, the community would gather under the leadership of elders—the *inyangamugayo*, or "people of integrity"—to hear the matter and work toward resolution. The emphasis was on truth-telling, accountability, and restoration rather than punishment.

After the genocide, when the conventional justice system was overwhelmed by hundreds of thousands of cases, Rwanda turned to this traditional wisdom. The Gacaca courts that were established across the country brought communities together to hear the truth about what had happened, to hold perpetrators accountable, and to begin the long work of healing and reconciliation. Perpetrators who confessed their crimes, expressed remorse, and sought forgiveness could receive reduced sentences and, more importantly, could be reintegrated into their communities.

The philosophical foundation of these practices is captured in the concept of *Ubuntu*—a Nguni Bantu term that has been translated as "humanity toward others" but that carries deeper meaning. Archbishop Desmond Tutu, who chaired South Africa's Truth and Reconciliation Commission, explained it this way: "Ubuntu speaks particularly about the fact that you can't exist as a human being in isolation. It speaks about our interconnectedness. You can't be human all by yourself, and when you have this quality—Ubuntu—you are known for your generosity."

In the context of justice, Ubuntu means that crime is not merely an individual act but a breach in the fabric of community. The offender has not only broken a rule but has damaged relationships. Justice, therefore, requires more than punishment; it requires healing those relationships, restoring the offender to community, and strengthening the communal bonds that prevent future harm.

This understanding resonates deeply with biblical teaching. When Paul writes that we are members one of another, he is expressing something very like Ubuntu. When Jesus teaches that we must be reconciled to our brother before offering our gift at the altar, he is prioritizing relationship over ritual. The African concept of Ubuntu, though developed independently, captures truths that are universal.

Maori Practices in New Zealand

Our journey now takes us to the islands of New Zealand, where the Maori people developed restorative practices that would eventually shape the justice system of an entire nation.

Maori culture is built on principles of collective responsibility, reciprocity, and restoration. When harm occurred, the response was not to isolate and punish the wrongdoer but to bring together the extended family groups—the *whānau* and *hapū*—to address the harm and find a way forward. These gatherings, called *hui*, were characterized by extensive discussion, the airing of grievances, the expression of remorse, and the search for consensus.

The Family Group Conference, which has become a cornerstone of New Zealand's juvenile justice system and has been adopted in various forms around the world, is a direct descendant of these Maori practices. When a young person offends, their family, the victim and their family, and relevant community members come together with a facilitator to discuss what happened and to develop a plan for making things right. The family is given private time to develop their proposals, which are then presented to the larger group for discussion and agreement.

This process embodies deep respect for family and community as the primary contexts in which young people develop and in which accountability and restoration must occur. It recognizes that the state, however well-intentioned, cannot replace the relationships and responsibilities of family and community. And it gives victims a genuine voice and role in determining what justice requires.

The Maori concept of *tikanga*—customary law, or more literally, "the right way of doing things"—provides the framework for these practices. Tikanga is not a fixed code of rules but a living tradition that guides behavior and resolves disputes in ways that maintain balance and harmony. It emphasizes restoration over punishment, collective responsibility over individual blame, and the ongoing health of relationships over the finality of judgment.

Biblical Foundations

Before we leave the ancient world, we must attend to another tradition that has profoundly shaped Western understanding of justice: the biblical tradition of ancient Israel and the early

Christian community. This tradition, which I have touched on already, deserves fuller exploration.

The Hebrew scriptures present a God who is characterized by justice and mercy—*mishpat* and *tzedekah*. These terms, often translated simply as "justice" and "righteousness," carry richer meanings. *Mishpat* refers to the proper ordering of community, the protection of the vulnerable, the fair treatment of all. *Tzedekah* refers to right relationship, both with God and with neighbor. Together, they describe a society in which everyone has what they need, where relationships are healthy, where the vulnerable are protected, and where God's presence is known.

When the prophets call for justice, they are not primarily calling for punishment of wrongdoers but for the restoration of right relationship. Amos's famous demand that "justice roll down like waters" (Amos 5:24) comes in a context of condemning religious observance divorced from ethical practice. What God desires, the prophet makes clear, is not sacrifice but justice—not ritual but right relationship.

The Torah itself contains numerous provisions that embody restorative principles. Consider the laws of restitution in Exodus 22: when someone steals an ox or a sheep, they must repay—five oxen for an ox, four sheep for a sheep. The emphasis is on making the victim whole, not merely punishing the offender. Consider the cities of refuge established in Numbers 35, where someone who caused accidental death could flee from the avenger of blood and receive fair hearing. The law distinguished between intent and accident, recognizing that justice requires attention to context and motive.

Consider, too, the institution of the Jubilee year in Leviticus 25, when debts were forgiven, slaves were freed, and land was returned to its original families. Every fifty years, the community was to hit the reset button, restoring relationships that had become distorted by economic inequality and debt. This was restoration on a societal scale—a recognition that justice requires periodic restoration of right relationship.

In the New Testament, Jesus embodies and teaches restorative principles. His parable of the prodigal son (Luke 15) is a masterful depiction of restorative justice: the son who has caused harm returns home, confesses his wrongdoing, and is welcomed not with punishment but with celebration. The father's response is not retributive but restorative—he restores the son to relationship, to family, to community.

Jesus's teaching on conflict resolution in Matthew 18 outlines a process that bears remarkable similarity to modern restorative practices: go directly to the person who has wronged you; if that fails, take one or two others; if that fails, tell it to the church. The goal throughout is not to condemn but to "win your brother"—to restore relationship.

The apostle Paul develops these themes theologically, particularly in his letters to the Corinthians and the Colossians. In Christ, Paul writes, God was reconciling the world to himself—not counting trespasses but making peace through the blood of the cross. This reconciliation is not merely individual but cosmic: "For in him all the fullness of God was pleased to dwell, and through him to reconcile to himself all things, whether on earth or in heaven, making peace by the blood of his cross" (Colossians 1:19-20).

The early Christian community sought to embody this reconciliation in their common life. They shared possessions, cared for the vulnerable, and resolved disputes within the community rather than taking them to secular courts (1 Corinthians 6). They understood themselves as a new creation, a community in which old divisions—Jew and Greek, slave and free, male and female—were being overcome.

Ancient Middle Eastern Practices

Beyond the biblical tradition, other ancient Middle Eastern societies developed practices that balanced retributive and restorative elements. The Code of Hammurabi, dating to around 1750 BCE, is often cited for its retributive "eye for an eye" provisions. But it also included extensive provisions for restitution. For example, if a builder constructed a house that collapsed and killed the owner's son, the builder's son would be put to death—a troubling provision by modern standards but one that reflects the principle of proportional response. More positively, the code required compensation for various forms of property damage and personal injury, aiming to make victims whole.

These provisions reflect an understanding that justice requires attention to the needs of victims, not merely the punishment of offenders. While the retributive elements are what most remember, the restorative elements were equally important in practice.

Ancient Greek Practices

In ancient Greece, we find another tradition that has shaped Western thinking about justice. The Athenian legal system, particularly in the democratic period, emphasized citizen participation in the administration of justice. Large juries, sometimes numbering in the hundreds, decided cases by majority vote. This participatory approach fostered a sense of collective responsibility for justice.

The philosophical traditions of Greece also contributed to restorative thinking. Aristotle's virtue ethics, which we have already discussed, emphasized the formation of character through practice. Plato's dialogues explore the nature of justice, with Socrates insisting that it is better to suffer injustice than to commit it—a claim that challenges purely retributive understandings.

The Amphictyonic League, a religious association of Greek tribes, administered justice through councils that sought to resolve conflicts and restore peace among member states. This intertribal approach recognized that justice must sometimes transcend local boundaries and that reconciliation is essential to lasting peace.

Ancient Roman Practices

Roman law, which has so deeply influenced Western legal systems, also contained restorative elements. The Twelve Tables, Rome's earliest code of law, included provisions for restitution and compensation. For property crimes, offenders were often required to pay double or triple the value of what they had stolen—a form of restitution that went beyond mere compensation to include a punitive element but that still focused on making victims whole.

The *Lex Aquilia*, a later law governing damage to property, established the principle that offenders should compensate victims for their losses. This principle of compensation—making the victim whole—is fundamentally restorative, even when embedded in a largely retributive system.

In cases of familial disputes, the head of the household—the *paterfamilias*—often acted as mediator, seeking to resolve conflicts within the family and restore harmony. This domestic jurisdiction recognized that some conflicts are best resolved within the relationships where they occur, rather than through formal legal processes.

Ancient Asian Practices

Our journey through ancient restorative practices would be incomplete without considering the rich traditions of Asia. In China, Confucian philosophy profoundly shaped approaches to justice. Confucius emphasized the importance of social harmony, filial piety, and moral cultivation. For Confucius, the goal of governance was not merely to enforce laws but to cultivate virtue—to create conditions in which people would naturally do what is right.

This emphasis on harmony and virtue led to practices that prioritized mediation and reconciliation over punishment. Local magistrates often served as mediators, seeking to resolve disputes through dialogue and mutual agreement rather than through adversarial proceedings. The goal was to restore harmony within the community, not merely to assign blame and impose punishment.

In India, Hindu and Buddhist traditions shaped justice practices in distinctive ways. The concept of *dharma*—right living in accordance with cosmic order—provided a framework for understanding wrongdoing as disruption of harmony that must be restored. The Panchayat system, a traditional village council, played a crucial role in resolving disputes through consensus and mediation. These councils, composed of respected community members, sought solutions that would restore harmony and satisfy all parties.

Buddhist teachings on compassion, non-violence, and the interconnectedness of all beings further reinforced restorative approaches. The Buddha's emphasis on understanding the causes of suffering and finding paths to its cessation provided a framework for addressing harm that focused on healing rather than punishment. Monastic communities often served as mediators in disputes, using their moral authority to guide parties toward peaceful resolution.

Medieval and Early Modern Periods

As we move from the ancient world into the medieval and early modern periods, we encounter significant changes in the organization of justice. The story here is complex—one of both loss and persistence, of centralization and resistance, of formalization and informal wisdom.

Community-Based Justice in the Medieval Period

In medieval Europe, justice was predominantly local. Manorial courts, presided over by local lords, handled disputes within the manor—land conflicts, breaches of contract, minor criminal offenses. These courts were not professionalized in the modern sense; they drew on local custom and the lord's judgment, but they also reflected community norms and values.

The focus in these courts was often on restoring relationships and ensuring the smooth functioning of the community. When neighbors quarreled, the goal was not merely to determine who was right but to find a way for them to live together peaceably. When someone caused harm, the response might include restitution, apology, and reconciliation—not merely punishment.

The tithing and frankpledge systems, which required groups of households to take collective responsibility for each other's behavior, embodied the principle of communal accountability. If one member of the group committed a crime, the entire group was responsible for ensuring that justice was done. This system recognized what modern research has confirmed: that informal social control—the watchful eyes and caring concern of neighbors—is often more effective than formal law enforcement in preventing crime and maintaining order.

Church courts, or ecclesiastical courts, handled matters of moral and religious conduct—marriage disputes, wills, breaches of faith. These courts emphasized penance, reconciliation, and the restoration of spiritual harmony. The penitential system, though sometimes distorted in practice, was fundamentally restorative: the sinner confessed, performed acts of penance, and was reconciled to the church and to God.

Restorative Elements in Medieval Practice

Despite the harshness of much medieval justice, restorative elements persisted. The Germanic concept of *wergild*—"man price"—required offenders to compensate victims or their families for harm caused. This practice aimed to prevent blood feuds by providing a structured alternative to vengeance. By requiring material compensation, it acknowledged the harm done and provided a means of making amends.

Public apology and acts of penance were common in resolving disputes and offenses. These acts, often performed before the assembled community, served multiple purposes: they acknowledged wrongdoing, expressed remorse, sought forgiveness, and demonstrated commitment to changed behavior. The public nature of these acts was important; it engaged the community in the process of reconciliation and gave the community confidence that the offender was genuinely penitent.

Even practices that seem strange to us today, such as trial by ordeal or compurgation, often involved community participation and sought resolution through methods perceived as fair. Compurgation, for example, required the accused to bring a certain number of "oath-helpers"—community members willing to swear to their character and truthfulness. This practice recognized that a person's standing in the community was relevant to determining truth and resolving disputes.

The Shift Toward Centralization

The early modern period brought significant changes. The rise of nation-states led to the centralization of legal systems. Monarchs and central governments established courts and legal codes that applied across their realms, reducing local variation and local control. This centralization had benefits—more consistent application of law, reduction of arbitrary local power—but it also meant the loss of community involvement and local wisdom.

The professionalization of the judiciary created a class of trained judges and lawyers who administered justice according to formal rules rather than local custom. This development brought expertise and consistency but also distance—justice was increasingly something done *to* communities by outsiders rather than something done *within* communities by members.

The codification of laws, exemplified by the Napoleonic Code in France, created comprehensive legal frameworks that left little room for local variation or restorative alternatives. Law became a matter of applying rules to facts, not of restoring relationships or healing communities.

Yet restorative practices did not disappear entirely. Community mediation and arbitration continued, especially in rural areas and for minor disputes. Local leaders and respected individuals still played roles in resolving conflicts and maintaining peace. Restitution and compensation remained important, even within formal legal systems. Reconciliation rituals—public apologies, acts of contrition, ceremonies of forgiveness—persisted as ways of addressing harm and restoring relationships.

The Influence of Enlightenment Thought

The Enlightenment of the 17th and 18th centuries brought new perspectives on justice that both challenged and reinforced restorative principles. Thinkers like John Locke emphasized individual rights and the social contract—the idea that legitimate government rests on the consent of the governed and exists to protect rights. This emphasis on rights would eventually support victim-centered approaches, as victims' rights gained recognition alongside offenders' rights.

Jean-Jacques Rousseau's concept of the general will—the common good that transcends individual interests—resonates with communitarian themes. If justice is about the common good, then responses to crime must consider the health of the whole community, not merely the fate of individual offenders.

Perhaps most significantly, Cesare Beccaria's *On Crimes and Punishments* (1764) argued for rational and proportional punishment. Beccaria challenged the arbitrary and excessive punishments of the ancien régime, arguing that penalties should be designed to prevent future crimes and promote societal well-being, not merely to inflict suffering. This utilitarian approach opened space for considering what actually works to reduce crime and promote safety—an empirical question that restorative justice would later address with encouraging results.

The Enlightenment also saw the emergence of human rights discourse—the idea that all persons possess inherent dignity and rights that governments must respect. This discourse would eventually support restorative justice by emphasizing the dignity of victims, the humanity of offenders, and the importance of treating all persons with respect.

The Modern Resurgence

After centuries dominated by retributive approaches, the 20th and 21st centuries have witnessed a remarkable resurgence of restorative justice. This resurgence is not an accident but the result of multiple converging factors—dissatisfaction with existing systems, emerging research, influential figures and movements, and growing recognition of restorative justice's transformative potential.

Dissatisfaction with Retributive Justice

The modern resurgence of restorative justice began with dissatisfaction—a growing sense that traditional punitive systems were failing in fundamental ways.

First, there was the problem of recidivism. Prisons were filled with repeat offenders, suggesting that punishment alone was not changing behavior. People were being punished, often severely, and then returning to crime upon release. Something was not working.

Second, there was victim dissatisfaction. Victims of crime frequently felt neglected by a system that focused on the state versus the offender, leaving them on the sidelines. They wanted to be heard, to have their suffering acknowledged, to receive answers to their questions, to have a say in what justice required. The conventional system gave them none of this.

Third, there was community disengagement. Communities affected by crime felt left out of the justice process, powerless to address problems in their midst. The system took conflicts out of communities and processed them in distant courts, returning offenders to the same communities with no investment in their successful reintegration.

These failures created space for alternative approaches. If punishment alone was not working, perhaps something else was needed. If victims were dissatisfied, perhaps they should have a larger role. If communities were disengaged, perhaps they should be re-engaged.

Emerging Theoretical and Empirical Support

As dissatisfaction grew, so did theoretical and empirical support for restorative alternatives.

Criminological research increasingly highlighted the limitations of punitive approaches. Studies showed that harsh punishment, by itself, does little to reduce recidivism and may actually increase it by reinforcing criminal identities and切断 ties to conventional society. At the same time, research on what does work—programs that address underlying causes, build skills, strengthen relationships—pointed toward restorative approaches.

Psychological research underscored the importance of addressing emotional and relational aspects of crime. Trauma-informed approaches recognized that both victims and offenders often carry deep wounds that must be healed if lasting change is to occur. Research on empathy showed its crucial role in moral development and behavioral change—and restorative practices, by bringing victims and offenders into direct dialogue, create powerful opportunities for empathy to develop.

Human rights advocacy contributed as well. The global human rights movement insisted that justice systems must respect the dignity and rights of all persons—including offenders. This emphasis on dignity supported restorative approaches that treat offenders as moral agents capable of responsibility rather than as objects to be managed.

Influential Social Movements

The civil rights movements of the mid-20th century challenged systemic injustices and advocated for more equitable approaches to justice. The movement's emphasis on dignity, equality, and inclusion resonated with restorative principles.

Post-conflict reconciliation efforts provided powerful demonstrations of restorative potential. South Africa's Truth and Reconciliation Commission, established after the end of apartheid, showed how restorative approaches could address massive human rights violations and promote national healing. The TRC's emphasis on truth-telling, accountability, and reconciliation—rather than purely punitive responses—captured global attention and inspired similar efforts elsewhere.

Indigenous rights movements also contributed, as indigenous peoples around the world asserted the validity of their traditional justice practices and demanded recognition within dominant legal systems. These movements helped restore visibility to restorative approaches that had long been marginalized.

Key Figures and Movements

Several key figures and movements have been instrumental in the modern resurgence of restorative justice.

Howard Zehr, often called the "grandfather of restorative justice," articulated the philosophy and principles that have guided the movement. His book *Changing Lenses*, published in 1990, offered a comprehensive vision of restorative justice as an alternative to retributive approaches. Zehr's framing—the three core questions of restorative justice (who has been harmed, what are their needs, whose obligations have arisen)—provided a clear and accessible framework that has been widely adopted.

The Victim-Offender Reconciliation Program (VORP), begun in Kitchener, Ontario, in the 1970s, demonstrated the practical feasibility of restorative approaches. By facilitating direct meetings between victims and offenders, VORP showed that such encounters could be safe, constructive, and healing. The success of this program led to replication across North America and beyond.

Truth and Reconciliation Commissions, beginning with South Africa's, showed the power of restorative approaches at societal scale. These commissions, despite their limitations and challenges, demonstrated that truth-telling, accountability, and reconciliation are possible even in the aftermath of massive human rights violations.

Adoption Across Sectors

The resurgence of restorative justice has not been limited to criminal justice. Its principles and practices have been adopted across multiple sectors.

In criminal justice, restorative programs now operate at every stage—as diversion from prosecution, as part of sentencing, within prisons, and as part of reentry. Research consistently shows that these programs reduce recidivism, increase victim satisfaction, and cost less than traditional processing.

In education, schools have embraced restorative practices as alternatives to punitive discipline. Restorative circles, peer mediation, and restorative conferences address conflicts, build community, and create positive school climates. Schools that implement restorative practices report reduced suspensions and expulsions, improved student behavior, and stronger relationships among students and staff.

In workplaces, restorative approaches resolve conflicts, improve communication, and build positive organizational cultures. Mediation, facilitated dialogue, and restorative circles help address grievances, repair relationships, and create environments where people can do their best work.

In communities, restorative programs address neighborhood disputes, support victims, hold offenders accountable, and build social cohesion. Some cities have embraced restorative principles at the municipal level, integrating restorative practices into governance, policing, and community services.

The Impact of Restorative Justice

The impact of restorative justice on victims, offenders, and communities has been profound.

For victims, restorative justice offers empowerment, voice, and healing. Research consistently finds that victims who participate in restorative processes report higher satisfaction than those whose cases go through conventional channels. They appreciate the opportunity to tell their stories, to ask questions, to receive acknowledgment, and to have a say in outcomes. They often experience healing that conventional justice cannot provide.

For offenders, restorative justice offers genuine accountability and opportunity for change. When offenders face those they have harmed, hear their stories, and work to make amends, they often experience moral transformation. They develop empathy, take responsibility, and commit to changed behavior. Recidivism studies show that restorative approaches reduce reoffending—sometimes dramatically.

For communities, restorative justice strengthens social bonds, builds trust, and creates capacity to address conflicts constructively. When communities are involved in restorative processes, they develop relationships and skills that serve them well beyond any particular case. They become more resilient, more cohesive, more capable of solving their own problems.

As we look to the future, the potential of restorative justice continues to grow. Policymakers, practitioners, and advocates are working to embed restorative practices within legal frameworks, educational policies, and community programs. Researchers are studying long-term outcomes, developing new models, and exploring restorative justice in diverse cultural contexts. International networks are sharing knowledge and building a global movement.

The journey we have taken in this chapter—from ancient indigenous practices through medieval communities to modern innovations—reveals something important: restorative justice is not a passing fad or a marginal experiment. It is a return to wisdom that humans have possessed for millennia, wisdom that was obscured but never entirely lost. It is a recovery of insights about human nature, community, and justice that are as relevant today as they were thousands of years ago.

As we move forward into the chapters that follow, we will build on this historical foundation. We will explore the theoretical frameworks that give restorative justice its intellectual coherence. We will examine the core principles and values that guide restorative practice. We will study the various models and practices through which restorative justice is implemented. We will consider case studies and real-world applications. We will wrestle with benefits and challenges. We will explore the relationship between restorative justice and legal systems, international contexts, and social justice. And we will look to the future, imagining how restorative justice might continue to transform our world.

The story of restorative justice is still being written. And you, dear reader, are part of that story. Whether you come to this topic as a student, a practitioner, a policymaker, or simply someone who cares about justice, you have a role to play. The wisdom of the ages is now in your hands. The question is what you will do with it.

CHAPTER 02

THEORETICAL FRAMEWORKS

Philosophical Underpinnings: Key Philosophical Theories that Support Restorative Justice

Every great movement, every profound transformation of human society, rests upon foundations that are deeper than the practices themselves. Before there can be restorative practices, there must be restorative thinking—a way of understanding the world, human nature, and justice that makes restorative approaches not merely possible but necessary. In this chapter, dear reader, we will explore together the philosophical foundations upon which the entire edifice of restorative justice is built.

As we journey through these theoretical frameworks, I invite you to hold them not as abstract concepts to be memorized but as living ideas—ways of seeing that can transform how you understand every conflict, every harm, every opportunity for healing that you encounter. For these philosophies are not merely academic; they are lenses through which we can perceive more clearly what justice truly requires.

Relational Ethics

Let us begin with what may be the most fundamental insight of restorative justice: that human beings are not isolated atoms, bouncing through life without connection to one another, but relational creatures whose very identities are formed in and through relationship. This insight, simple though it may seem, has profound implications for how we understand morality, justice, and the good life.

The Interconnectedness of Individuals

Relational ethics, as a philosophical tradition, takes as its starting point the recognition that we are, in the deepest sense, beings-in-relationship. Our identities are not self-contained; they are formed through interaction with parents, siblings, friends, teachers, neighbors, and countless others who shape who we become. Our actions ripple outward, affecting not only ourselves but all those connected to us. Our well-being is intertwined with the well-being of others; we cannot flourish alone.

This understanding is not new, though modern Western thought has often obscured it. The African concept of *Ubuntu*, which we encountered in the previous chapter, captures it beautifully: "A person is a person through other persons." We become human only in and through community. The Hebrew scriptures express it in the covenant relationship between God and Israel, and among the people themselves: "I will be your God, and you shall be my people" (Leviticus 26:12). The people are constituted as a people through their relationship with God and with one another.

The Christian tradition develops this theme further. Paul's image of the body in 1 Corinthians 12 is a powerful expression of relational ethics: "For just as the body is one and has many members, and all the members of the body, though many, are one body, so it is with Christ." When one member suffers, all suffer together; when one member is honored, all rejoice together. We are not independent units but interdependent members of one another.

Modern psychology has confirmed what these ancient traditions always knew. Attachment theory, developed by John Bowlby and Mary Ainsworth, demonstrates that secure relationships in early childhood are essential for healthy development throughout life. Object relations theory shows how our internal world is populated by representations of significant others who continue to shape us. Social psychology reveals how profoundly our behavior is influenced by the presence and expectations of others. We are, as the research consistently shows, relational to our core.

From this relational understanding flow moral obligations. If we are interconnected, then what affects one affects all. If our identities are formed in relationship, then we have responsibilities to those who have formed us and to those we are forming. If our actions ripple outward, then we must consider those ripples. Morality is not merely about abstract rules or individual choices; it is about the quality of our relationships and the health of our communities.

Restorative Justice Application

How does this relational understanding shape restorative justice? In the most fundamental way possible: it defines the very nature of the problem to be solved and the goal to be achieved.

When crime occurs, relational ethics teaches us to see it not merely as a rule broken but as a relationship damaged. The victim has been harmed, certainly—physically, emotionally, materially. But the harm does not stop there. The offender has been harmed as well, alienated from community, cut off from the relationships that could support their flourishing. The community has been harmed, its bonds of trust weakened, its sense of safety diminished, its fabric torn.

Justice, therefore, cannot be satisfied simply by punishing the offender. Punishment may express society's condemnation, may provide a measure of retribution, may even deter some future offenses. But it does nothing directly to heal the relationships that have been damaged. It may, in fact, make things worse, further alienating the offender and leaving the victim's needs unaddressed.

Restorative justice, grounded in relational ethics, takes a different approach. It seeks to repair the harm by restoring relationships. This means bringing together those who have been affected—victim, offender, community—in processes that allow for truth-telling, accountability, and healing. It means acknowledging the interconnectedness that crime has disrupted and working to mend the web of relationships that has been torn.

This is why community involvement is not optional but essential in restorative justice. If we are interconnected, then the community is not merely a bystander to crime but a stakeholder in its resolution. The community has been harmed; the community must be involved in healing. The community has relationships with both victim and offender; those relationships must be engaged if genuine restoration is to occur.

Communitarianism

Closely related to relational ethics, but with its own distinctive emphasis, is the philosophical tradition of communitarianism. While relational ethics focuses on the interpersonal bonds between individuals, communitarianism attends to the community as a whole—its shared values, common purposes, and collective well-being.

Community Values and the Common Good

Communitarianism arose, in large part, as a response to the excesses of liberal individualism that have characterized much modern Western thought. Liberalism, in its classical form, emphasizes individual rights, autonomy, and choice. It tends to see the individual as prior to society, and society as a contract among individuals for mutual benefit. Communitarians do not deny the importance of individual rights, but they insist that individuals are formed in and through communities, that our values and identities are shaped by the traditions into which we are born, and that a just society must attend to the health of communities, not merely the liberties of individuals.

The communitarian view sees society as a complex web of relationships, a fabric of mutual obligations and shared meanings. The well-being of individuals is intertwined with the health of the whole. When communities are strong—when people know and care for one another, when shared values are widely held, when institutions are trustworthy—individuals flourish. When communities are weak—when relationships are fractured, when values are contested, when institutions are distrusted—individuals suffer.

From this understanding flows the principle of collective responsibility. If we are members of communities, then we share responsibility for what happens in those communities. We cannot simply say, "That's not my problem," when our neighbors are in need, when conflicts arise, when harm occurs. We are implicated in one another's lives, and we have obligations to one another that arise from our shared membership in community.

This principle has deep roots in biblical tradition. The prophets of Israel consistently held the entire nation accountable for its failures, not merely individuals. When Amos thunders against injustice, he addresses the whole people: "They sell the righteous for silver, and the needy for a pair of sandals" (Amos 2:6). The "they" is the nation, the community, not merely isolated individuals. When Jesus teaches about the final judgment in Matthew 25, he speaks to all nations, and the basis of judgment is how they have treated "the least of these"—a collective responsibility for the vulnerable.

Restorative Justice Application

Communitarianism provides a philosophical foundation for several key features of restorative justice.

First, it explains why restorative justice prioritizes the restoration of community harmony. If communities are essential to human flourishing, then harm that disrupts community harmony must be addressed not merely for the sake of the individuals directly involved but for the sake of the community as a whole.

Restorative justice seeks not only to heal individual victims and offenders but to restore the community to health.

Second, it justifies the involvement of the community in the justice process. If communities have a stake in what happens, then communities should have a voice. If communities are affected by crime, then communities should participate in responding to crime. This is not merely a matter of practicality—though involving community can certainly improve outcomes—but of principle. Communities have a right to be involved in matters that affect them, and they have responsibilities that cannot be delegated entirely to the state.

Third, it supports collective decision-making in restorative processes. When victims, offenders, and community members come together to find solutions, they are not merely negotiating individual interests but discerning together what will serve the common good. The goal is not simply to satisfy each party's private preferences but to find outcomes that promote the health of the whole community. This requires dialogue, deliberation, and consensus-building—processes that communitarianism values highly.

Virtue Ethics

From the ancient Greeks, particularly Aristotle, we inherit a third philosophical tradition that deeply informs restorative justice: virtue ethics. Unlike ethical systems that focus primarily on rules (deontology) or consequences (utilitarianism), virtue ethics focuses on character—on the kind of people we become through our actions and habits.

Moral Character and Virtues

For Aristotle, the goal of human life is *eudaimonia*—flourishing, well-being, living well. And we achieve this goal not primarily by following rules or calculating consequences but by cultivating virtues: dispositions to act, feel, and think in ways that are excellent. Courage, temperance, justice, wisdom, friendship—these are not merely nice additions to life but essential components of human flourishing.

Virtues are not innate; they are developed through practice. We become just by doing just acts; we become courageous by acting courageously. Over time, these actions become habitual, woven into the fabric of who we are. The virtuous person does not have to struggle to do the right thing; they do it naturally, because it has become part of their character.

The development of virtues requires community. We learn what courage looks like by observing courageous people. We practice justice in the context of relationships that call us to be fair. We are shaped by the expectations, examples, and encouragement of those around us. Virtue ethics, like communitarianism, recognizes that individuals are formed in and through communities.

This philosophical tradition has deep resonances with biblical teaching. The Beatitudes (Matthew 5:3-12) describe the characteristics of those who belong to the kingdom of God—the poor in spirit, the meek, the merciful, the pure in heart, the peacemakers. These are not merely rules to follow but virtues to embody, dispositions that shape how one lives in every situation. The fruit of the Spirit that Paul describes in Galatians 5—love, joy, peace, patience, kindness, goodness, faithfulness, gentleness, self-control—are virtues cultivated through the work of the Holy Spirit in the life of the believer.

Restorative Justice Application

Virtue ethics illuminates restorative justice in several important ways.

First, restorative justice practices are designed to foster specific virtues. Through dialogue with victims, offenders are invited to develop empathy—to understand and feel the impact of their actions on others. Through taking responsibility and making amends, they practice accountability and develop the virtue of justice. Through participation in restorative processes, both victims and offenders have opportunities to practice forgiveness, compassion, and hope.

Second, restorative justice is concerned with moral formation, not merely conflict resolution. The goal is not simply to resolve the immediate incident but to transform the people involved—to help victims heal, to help offenders change, to help communities grow stronger. This is why restorative processes emphasize dialogue, understanding, and personal engagement rather than impersonal procedures and imposed outcomes.

Third, restorative justice recognizes the role of community in moral formation. Virtues are cultivated in relationship, through the example and encouragement of others. When communities are involved in restorative processes, they provide the relational context in which moral growth can occur. Offenders are surrounded by people who model accountability and care. Victims are supported by people who validate their experience and encourage their healing.

Restorative Ontology

We come now to perhaps the most profound philosophical foundation of restorative justice—one that moves beyond ethics into the nature of reality itself. Restorative ontology is the claim that restoration is not merely one option among many but is woven into the very fabric of existence.

The Need for Restoration

Ontology is the branch of philosophy that studies the nature of being, existence, and reality. When we speak of restorative ontology, we are making a claim about the fundamental character of reality: that it is oriented toward restoration, that healing is more fundamental than brokenness, that reconciliation is the deepest truth about things.

This claim has several dimensions. First, it recognizes that harm is real—that wrongdoing genuinely damages individuals, relationships, and communities. This is not a naive optimism that pretends harm doesn't matter. Harm matters enormously. It wounds, it breaks, it destroys.

But second, it recognizes that harm is not the final word. The damage caused by wrongdoing can be repaired. Relationships can be healed. Communities can be restored. This is not guaranteed in every case—some harms may be irreparable, some relationships may never be reconciled—but the possibility of restoration is real.

Third, it recognizes that the impulse toward restoration is deep in human nature and in the nature of reality itself. When harm occurs, something in us cries out for healing. When relationships are broken, something in us longs for reconciliation. These are not merely cultural constructions but expressions of our deepest nature as beings created for relationship.

In the Judeo-Christian tradition, this restorative ontology finds expression in the doctrine of creation. God made all things good, and though that goodness has been marred by sin, it has not been destroyed. The creation groans, as Paul puts it in Romans 8, waiting for redemption—but it groans in hope, not despair. The goodness of creation is the ground of the possibility of restoration.

It finds expression, too, in the doctrine of the atonement. In Christ, God enters into broken humanity to heal it from within. The cross and resurrection are not merely events in the past but cosmic signs of God's determination to restore all things. "For in him all the fullness of God was pleased to dwell, and through him to reconcile to himself all things, whether on earth or in heaven, making peace by the blood of his cross" (Colossians 1:19-20). The reconciliation of all things is God's ultimate purpose.

Restorative Justice Application

Restorative ontology has profound implications for restorative justice.

First, it means that restorative justice is not imposing something foreign on human conflict but cooperating with the deepest grain of the universe. When we seek to heal harm rather than merely punish offenders, we are aligning ourselves with the way things are supposed to be. When we work for reconciliation, we are participating in God's own work in the world.

Second, it gives us hope even in difficult cases. Not every restorative process succeeds; not every harm can be fully healed; not every relationship can be restored. But restorative ontology reminds us that failure is not the final word. The possibility of restoration remains, and our efforts, however imperfect, are not wasted.

Third, it calls us to persistence. If restoration is woven into the fabric of reality, then we are not chasing an illusion when we pursue it. The difficulties we encounter are real, but they are not ultimate. The resistance to healing is powerful, but it is not the deepest truth about things.

Ethical Responsibility

The fifth philosophical foundation of restorative justice is the principle of ethical responsibility—the conviction that we are accountable for our actions and obligated to address the harm we cause.

Moral Duty and Accountability

Ethical responsibility has both individual and collective dimensions. Individually, each of us is accountable for our choices and actions. However much we may be influenced by circumstances, upbringing, genetics, or environment, we remain moral agents capable of choice and therefore responsible for what we choose. This is not to deny the reality of mitigating factors; it is to affirm that, in the end, we are not merely passive victims of forces beyond our control but active agents who make real choices with real consequences.

Collectively, we share responsibility for the communities in which we live. We are members of families, neighborhoods, organizations, and societies. When harm occurs in our midst, we have some responsibility to respond—not because we caused the harm but because we are part of the community that has been harmed and that must find a way forward. This collective responsibility does not replace individual responsibility but supplements it.

This understanding of responsibility is deeply rooted in biblical teaching. The prophets consistently called Israel to account for its failures—not merely as individuals but as a nation. Jesus taught that we will give account for every idle word (Matthew 12:36), but he also taught that we are our brother's keeper. Paul insisted that we are members one of another, so that when one suffers, all suffer (1 Corinthians 12:26).

Restorative Justice Application

Restorative justice honors both dimensions of ethical responsibility.

It holds offenders accountable for their actions—not by imposing punishment from without but by creating conditions in which they can take responsibility from within. In restorative processes, offenders are not passive recipients of sanctions but active participants in making things right. They are invited to acknowledge their wrongdoing, to understand its impact, and to contribute to repairing the harm.

It also engages the community in its collective responsibility. Community members are not mere spectators but participants in the justice process. They support victims, hold offenders accountable, and work to create conditions that prevent future harm. This collective engagement strengthens community bonds and builds the social capital that makes communities more resilient.

The psychological dimension of this is crucial. Research in moral development consistently shows that genuine behavioral change requires more than external sanctions; it requires internalization of moral norms and development of empathy. When offenders are given opportunity to take genuine responsibility—to understand the harm they have caused, to make amends, to be restored to community—they are far more likely to change than when they are simply punished and released.

Dialogical Ethics

The final philosophical foundation we will explore is dialogical ethics—the understanding that ethical truth and mutual respect arise through genuine dialogue between persons.

The Ethics of Dialogue

Dialogical ethics draws on the work of philosophers such as Martin Buber and Jürgen Habermas. Buber distinguished between two fundamental ways of relating to others: the I-It relationship, in which we treat others as objects to be used or manipulated, and the I-Thou relationship, in which we encounter others as whole persons, as subjects with their own dignity and agency. Genuine ethics, for Buber, arises from I-Thou encounters—moments of genuine meeting in which we see the other as a person, not a thing.

Habermas developed the concept of communicative action—the idea that rational dialogue, free from coercion and distortion, is the foundation of legitimate social norms. When we engage in open, inclusive, reasoned communication, we can reach genuine understanding and consensus about how we should live together. Ethical norms are not imposed from above but emerge from dialogue among free and equal persons.

These philosophical insights have deep resonances with biblical themes. The God of the Bible is a God who speaks, who enters into dialogue with human beings, who calls them into relationship. The covenant is not a unilateral imposition but a relationship entered through dialogue and mutual commitment. Jesus's ministry is characterized by conversation—with disciples, with sinners, with religious leaders, with outsiders. He meets people where they are, engages them in dialogue, and calls them to transformation.

Restorative Justice Application

Dialogical ethics provides a philosophical foundation for the central role of dialogue in restorative justice.

Restorative practices—victim-offender mediation, restorative circles, family group conferences—are fundamentally dialogical. They create spaces in which people can meet as persons, not as categories. Victims are not merely "the victim" but whole persons with stories, feelings, needs. Offenders are not merely "the offender" but whole persons capable of change. Community members are not merely "the community" but particular people with their own perspectives and contributions.

In these dialogical encounters, genuine understanding becomes possible. Victims can tell their stories and be heard. Offenders can explain their actions and express remorse. Community members can share their concerns and offer support. Through dialogue, parties can come to see one another differently—not as enemies or stereotypes but as fellow human beings.

From this dialogue, consensus can emerge. Not imposed solutions but mutually agreed outcomes. Not decisions made by authorities and imposed on others but agreements reached through genuine communication. When people have truly heard one another, when they have come to understand one another's needs and perspectives, they can often find solutions that no outsider could have imposed.

This is why restorative justice emphasizes voluntary participation. Coerced dialogue is not genuine dialogue. When people are forced to participate, the I-Thou encounter becomes impossible. The goal is not to manipulate people into agreement but to create conditions in which genuine meeting can occur and authentic agreement can emerge.

The Theological Dimensions of Restorative Justice

Having explored the philosophical foundations of restorative justice, we must now attend to the theological dimensions that give these philosophies their deepest meaning and most powerful motivation. For many of us, restorative justice is not merely a philosophical commitment but a theological one—a response to God's own restorative work in the world.

Creation and the Image of God

The biblical account of creation provides a foundation for restorative justice in its declaration that human beings are made in the image of God (Genesis 1:26-27). This affirmation has profound implications. It means that every human being—victim, offender, community member—possesses inherent dignity and worth. This dignity is not earned or achieved; it is given. It cannot be forfeited by wrongdoing. Even the worst offender remains a bearer of God's image.

This theological foundation grounds the restorative commitment to treat all persons with respect. Victims must be treated with dignity, not used as evidence in a case against the offender. Offenders must be treated with dignity, not reduced to their worst actions. Community members must be treated with dignity, not ignored in processes that affect their lives.

It also grounds the possibility of restoration. If human beings are made in God's image, then even the most broken among us retain the capacity for healing and wholeness. The image may be marred, but it is not destroyed. Restoration is possible because the original goodness remains.

The Fall and the Reality of Harm

The biblical account of the Fall (Genesis 3) acknowledges the reality of sin and its consequences. Harm is real; relationships are broken; the world is not as it should be. This is not naive optimism that pretends away the reality of evil. It is honest about the depth of human brokenness.

But the Fall is not the final word. The same scriptures that narrate the Fall also narrate God's response to it—a response of judgment, certainly, but also of mercy, of promise, of ongoing relationship. God does not abandon the fallen creation but begins the long work of redemption.

This theological framework helps restorative justice hold two truths together: the reality of harm and the possibility of healing. We do not minimize the harm that victims have suffered. We do not pretend that wrongdoing doesn't matter. But we also do not give up on the possibility of restoration. We work for healing, trusting that it is possible even when it seems impossible.

The Covenant and Community

The covenant relationship between God and Israel, and the new covenant in Christ, establishes community as the context of salvation. God does not save isolated individuals but calls a people, forms a community, creates a body. Salvation is not merely individual but corporate.

This covenantal framework grounds the restorative emphasis on community. Justice is not merely about individuals getting what they deserve but about communities being restored to health. When harm occurs, it is not only individuals who are affected but the whole community. When healing occurs, it is not only individuals who are restored but the whole community.

The covenant also establishes the principle of mutual responsibility. In covenant, we are bound to one another. We are accountable not only to God but to one another. We are responsible not only for ourselves but for our neighbors. This covenantal responsibility is the theological ground of restorative accountability.

The Incarnation and Encounter

The incarnation—God's becoming human in Jesus Christ—reveals the depth of God's commitment to encounter. God does not remain distant, issuing commands from afar, but enters into human life, shares human experience, meets us where we are. The Word becomes flesh and dwells among us (John 1:14).

This incarnational theology grounds the restorative emphasis on encounter. Justice is not achieved through distant procedures but through personal meeting. Victims and offenders must encounter one another, must see one another as persons, must hear one another's stories. This encounter is not easy; it can be painful and frightening. But it is essential if genuine healing is to occur.

The incarnation also reveals that God is present in these encounters. When victims and offenders meet, when they speak truth to one another, when they work toward reconciliation, God is there. The Spirit who empowers healing and reconciliation is present in the midst of the circle, the conference, the mediation.

The Cross and Atonement

The cross of Christ is the ultimate demonstration of God's restorative justice. On the cross, God in Christ absorbs the worst that human sin can do and refuses to return evil for evil. Jesus prays, "Father, forgive them, for they know not what they do" (Luke 23:34). He does not retaliate; he does not condemn; he forgives.

This is not to say that the cross is merely an example of non-retaliation, though it is certainly that. In Christian theology, the cross is also the means of atonement—the place where sin is dealt with, where reconciliation is accomplished, where the broken relationship between God and humanity is healed. "God was in Christ reconciling the world to himself, not counting their trespasses against them" (2 Corinthians 5:19).

This atoning work provides a model for restorative justice. It shows that justice and mercy are not opposed but integrated. It demonstrates that accountability and forgiveness can coexist. It reveals that the deepest justice is not retributive but restorative.

The Resurrection and Hope

The resurrection of Jesus Christ is the ultimate ground of hope for restorative justice. The resurrection declares that death does not have the final word, that brokenness can be healed, that new life is possible. The same power that raised Jesus from the dead is at work in the world, bringing life out of death, hope out of despair, reconciliation out of alienation.

This resurrection hope sustains restorative work even when it seems futile. Not every restorative process succeeds. Not every harm can be fully healed in this life. Not every relationship can be restored. But the resurrection assures us that these failures are not the final word. The God who raised Jesus from the dead is at work bringing restoration, and that work will ultimately triumph.

The Spirit and Transformation

The Holy Spirit, in Christian theology, is the agent of transformation—the one who works in human hearts to produce the fruit of love, joy, peace, patience, kindness, goodness, faithfulness, gentleness, and self-control (Galatians 5:22-23). The Spirit empowers the moral formation that restorative justice seeks.

This pneumatological dimension reminds us that restorative transformation is not merely a human achievement. It is a work of grace. When victims find healing, when offenders experience genuine change, when communities are restored, the Spirit is at work. Our restorative practices are not techniques for producing these outcomes but ways of cooperating with the Spirit's work.

Ethical Considerations: Morality, Ethics, and the Philosophy of Punishment

Having explored the philosophical and theological foundations of restorative justice, we must now consider the ethical dimensions more directly. What are the moral principles that guide restorative practice? How does restorative justice relate to traditional theories of punishment? What ethical challenges arise in its implementation?

Morality and Ethics

Let us begin by clarifying terms. Morality and ethics are closely related but distinct concepts. Morality refers to the principles and values that individuals and societies hold regarding right and wrong, good and bad. These principles guide behavior and form the basis for moral judgments. Morality can be derived from various sources—religious beliefs, cultural norms, personal values, philosophical reasoning.

Ethics is the systematic study of moral principles. It examines how moral principles apply to specific situations and guides decision-making processes. Ethics involves critical reflection on what constitutes right action and the justification for moral choices. It is divided into several branches: normative ethics (exploring moral standards and principles), applied ethics (addressing specific ethical issues), and meta-ethics (examining the nature and meaning of ethical terms and concepts).

In restorative justice, both morality and ethics are important. The moral commitments that animate restorative practice—to healing, accountability, community—arise from deeply held values about human dignity and the good society. The ethical reflection that guides restorative practice—ensuring fairness, protecting rights, addressing power imbalances—applies these values to concrete situations.

The Philosophy of Punishment

The philosophy of punishment addresses the reasons and justifications for imposing penalties on those who commit wrongdoing. Three major theories have dominated Western thinking about punishment: retributivism, utilitarianism, and restorative justice.

Retributive Justice

Retributive justice is based on the principle of "just deserts"—the idea that offenders should be punished in proportion to the severity of their offenses. This is a backward-looking approach: it focuses on the past act and seeks to impose a penalty that matches its seriousness.

The ethical basis of retributivism is the belief that wrongdoing deserves punishment. Justice requires that the scales be balanced, that the offender suffer in proportion to the harm they have caused. This is not merely about deterrence or rehabilitation but about moral accountability. The offender has done wrong; they must pay for it.

There are several critiques of retributivism. First, it can be overly punitive, justifying harsh punishments that do more harm than good. Second, it fails to address the needs of victims, focusing instead on the offender and the state. Third, it may not contribute to rehabilitation or restoration, leaving offenders unchanged and communities unhealed. Fourth, it struggles with questions of proportionality: how much punishment does a given offense deserve? There is no objective way to measure this.

Utilitarianism

Utilitarianism is a consequentialist theory that evaluates actions based on their outcomes. In the context of punishment, it seeks to impose penalties that maximize overall happiness and minimize suffering. This is a forward-looking approach: it focuses on the future consequences of punishment.

Utilitarian theories emphasize deterrence (preventing future crimes by making an example of the offender) and rehabilitation (reforming the offender to prevent future wrongdoing). Punishment is justified not because it is deserved but because it produces good consequences—less crime, safer communities, reformed offenders.

Critiques of utilitarianism include the following. First, it can justify excessively harsh punishments if they are believed to deter crime effectively. Second, it may overlook the moral responsibility of the offender, treating them as a means to social ends rather than as an end in themselves. Third, it may not adequately address the needs of victims, focusing instead on the future good of society.

Restorative Justice

Restorative justice offers a third approach to punishment—one that focuses on repairing harm, involving stakeholders, and promoting healing. It is both backward-looking (addressing the harm that has occurred) and forward-looking (seeking to prevent future harm).

The ethical basis of restorative justice is grounded in the philosophical traditions we have explored: relational ethics, communitarianism, virtue ethics, restorative ontology, ethical responsibility, and dialogical ethics. It seeks to restore relationships, promote accountability, and address the needs of victims, offenders, and communities.

Critiques of restorative justice include concerns that it may be too lenient on offenders, that it may not be appropriate for serious crimes, that it may pressure victims to forgive, and that it may produce inconsistent outcomes. Proponents respond that restorative justice, properly implemented, holds offenders genuinely accountable, can be adapted for serious cases, respects victims' autonomy, and produces outcomes that are fair and satisfying to all parties.

Ethical Principles in Restorative Justice

Restorative justice is guided by several key ethical principles that shape its practices and objectives.

Accountability

In restorative justice, accountability means more than accepting punishment. It means taking moral responsibility for one's actions—acknowledging the harm caused, understanding its impact, and actively participating in making amends. This kind of accountability is not imposed from without but developed from within, through dialogue and reflection.

Psychological research supports this approach. Studies of moral development show that genuine behavioral change requires internalization of moral norms, not merely fear of punishment. When offenders understand the harm they have caused and choose to make amends, they are far more likely to change than when they simply serve time and are released.

Theologically, this understanding of accountability reflects the biblical concept of repentance (*metanoia*)—a turning around, a change of heart and life, not merely feeling sorry but actively changing direction. Genuine repentance involves confession, restitution, and changed behavior.

Reparation

Reparation is the principle that harm should be repaired. This involves addressing the needs of victims—material, emotional, relational—and taking concrete actions to make things right. Reparation may include restitution (returning what was taken or compensating for loss), community service (giving back to the community), or symbolic acts (apologies, ceremonies of reconciliation).

The ethical basis of reparation is the recognition that victims have been harmed and deserve to have that harm addressed. Justice is not merely about what happens to the offender but about what happens for the victim. Victims should not be left to suffer while the state focuses on punishing the offender.

Biblical support for reparation is abundant. The law of Moses required restitution for theft and damage (Exodus 22). Zacchaeus, after his encounter with Jesus, promised to restore fourfold what he had taken (Luke 19). Reparation is a sign of genuine repentance and a step toward restoration.

Empathy and Compassion

Restorative justice seeks to foster empathy and compassion among all parties. Victims are invited to understand the offender's situation—not to excuse their actions but to see them as whole persons, not merely as wrongdoers. Offenders are invited to understand the impact of their actions on victims—to feel what they have caused, to develop genuine remorse.

The cultivation of empathy is supported by psychological research. Empathy is associated with pro-social behavior, reduced aggression, and better relationships. It can be developed through practice, and restorative processes provide structured opportunities for empathy to grow.

Theologically, empathy and compassion reflect the character of God, who is "gracious and merciful, slow to anger and abounding in steadfast love" (Psalm 145:8). Jesus's ministry was characterized by compassion for the suffering and by calls to love one another as he has loved us (John 13:34).

Community Involvement

Restorative justice recognizes that communities are affected by crime and must be involved in responding to it. Community members support victims, hold offenders accountable, and work to create conditions that prevent future harm. This involvement strengthens community bonds and builds social capital.

The ethical basis of community involvement is the principle of subsidiarity—that matters should be handled at the most local level possible. Communities have knowledge, relationships, and resources that distant authorities lack. They also have a stake in outcomes that outsiders do not share.

Biblical support for community involvement is found throughout scripture. The people of Israel were repeatedly addressed as a community, called to collective responsibility. The early church shared possessions, cared for the vulnerable, and resolved disputes within the community (Acts 2, 1 Corinthians 6).

Proportionality and Fairness

Restorative justice seeks to ensure that responses to wrongdoing are proportional and fair. This means considering the severity of the offense, the needs of the victim, the circumstances of the offender, and the impact on the community. Outcomes should be neither too lenient nor too harsh but appropriate to the situation.

This principle guards against the potential for restorative justice to be applied inconsistently or unfairly. While restorative processes are flexible and responsive to individual circumstances, they must also be guided by standards of proportionality that ensure similar cases receive similar treatment.

The biblical call to "do justice" (*mishpat*) includes the requirement of fairness. The law of Moses prohibited partiality—favoring the rich or the poor, the powerful or the weak (Leviticus 19:15). Justice must be blind to status but attentive to need.

Ethical Challenges and Considerations

While restorative justice offers a compelling ethical framework, it also faces several challenges that must be addressed.

Balancing Accountability and Compassion

Finding the right balance between holding offenders accountable and showing compassion can be difficult. Too much emphasis on accountability can become punitive, undermining the restorative goal. Too much emphasis on compassion can appear lenient, failing to take harm seriously.

This balance requires wisdom—the practical wisdom that Aristotle called *phronesis*. It cannot be reduced to rules but must be discerned in each situation. Facilitators must be trained to recognize when accountability is being avoided and when compassion is being withheld, and to guide processes toward the appropriate balance.

Ensuring Voluntary Participation

Restorative justice relies on the voluntary participation of victims, offenders, and community members. Coercion or pressure to participate undermines the authenticity of the process and the legitimacy of outcomes. Victims should not feel pressured to meet with offenders; offenders should not feel forced to participate to avoid harsher consequences.

Ensuring genuine voluntariness requires clear information about the process and its potential outcomes, opportunities to ask questions and raise concerns, and the freedom to withdraw at any time. It also requires that alternatives to restorative justice be genuinely available, so that participation is truly a choice.

Addressing Power Imbalances

Power imbalances between victims and offenders, or within the community, can affect the fairness and effectiveness of restorative processes. An offender who is more articulate, more confident, or more socially powerful may dominate the conversation. A victim who is traumatized, marginalized, or intimidated may be unable to speak freely.

Facilitators must be trained to recognize and address power imbalances. This may involve meeting separately with parties beforehand, providing support persons during the process, ensuring that all voices are heard, and intervening when necessary to maintain balance. Creating a safe and equitable environment is essential for genuine dialogue.

Cultural Sensitivity

Restorative justice practices must be culturally sensitive and appropriate for the communities in which they are implemented. A practice that works well in one cultural context may be ineffective or even harmful in another. Assumptions about communication, relationship, and justice that are taken for granted in one culture may not apply in another.

Engaging community leaders and members in the design and implementation of restorative programs is essential for cultural sensitivity. Local knowledge and wisdom must inform how restorative principles are applied. Practices should be adapted to fit local contexts while maintaining fidelity to restorative values.

Restorative vs. Retributive Justice: A Comparative Analysis

Having explored the philosophical and ethical foundations of restorative justice, we are now prepared to compare it systematically with the retributive model that has dominated Western justice systems for centuries. This comparison will illuminate the distinctive features of each approach and the strengths and limitations of both.

Principles Compared

Retributive Justice

Retributive justice is founded on several key principles. The principle of just deserts holds that offenders should receive punishment proportional to the severity of their offenses. This is rooted in the belief that wrongdoing deserves punishment and that justice requires balancing the scales.

The principle of deterrence aims to prevent future crimes by making an example of the offender. The threat of punishment is intended to discourage both the individual offender and others from committing similar acts. Deterrence can be specific (targeting the individual offender) or general (targeting the broader public).

The principle of retribution views punishment as a necessary response to wrongdoing. It emphasizes the need for offenders to suffer consequences for their actions. The focus is on the offender and ensuring that they receive their just deserts.

Restorative Justice

Restorative justice is founded on a different set of principles. The principle of repairing harm focuses on addressing the impact of the offense on victims, offenders, and communities. Rather than simply punishing the offender, restorative justice seeks to make things right.

The principle of accountability in restorative justice means taking responsibility for one's actions and actively participating in making amends. This is not passive acceptance of punishment but active engagement in restoration.

The principle of community involvement recognizes that crime affects not only individuals but the broader community. Communities have a stake in justice and a role to play in achieving it. They must be involved in processes and outcomes.

Processes Compared

Retributive Processes

Retributive justice typically follows a formal, adversarial process within the legal system. The adversarial system pits prosecution against defense, each presenting its case to a judge or jury. The focus is on determining guilt and imposing punishment. The state acts as the primary party, with the victim playing a secondary role, if any role at all.

The process is focused on guilt and punishment. Evidence is presented, arguments are made, and a determination of guilt is reached. Once guilt is established, a penalty is imposed—imprisonment, fines, probation, or other sanctions.

Victim involvement is limited. Victims may testify as witnesses, but they have no formal role in determining outcomes. Their needs and perspectives are secondary to the focus on punishment. This can leave victims feeling marginalized and unsatisfied.

Restorative Processes

Restorative justice involves a collaborative, inclusive process that engages all stakeholders. Facilitated meetings—victim-offender mediation, restorative circles, family group conferences—bring together those affected by the harm. The goal is open communication, mutual understanding, and collaborative problem-solving.

The focus is on healing and reparation. The process addresses the needs of all stakeholders—emotional healing for victims, accountability for offenders, restoration of community harmony. Offenders are encouraged to take concrete actions to make amends.

Victim and community involvement is central. Victims have a voice in the process and a role in determining outcomes. Community members support victims, hold offenders accountable, and help find solutions that benefit everyone.

Outcomes Compared

Retributive Outcomes

Retributive justice produces outcomes focused on punishment and deterrence. The offender receives a penalty proportional to the offense—imprisonment, fines, or other sanctions. There may be moral satisfaction in seeing the offender punished, reinforcing social norms and the rule of law.

The punishment serves to deter the individual offender and others from future crimes. The emphasis is on consequences for the offender rather than addressing underlying causes of behavior.

Potential negative outcomes include high recidivism rates (since root causes are not addressed) and victim dissatisfaction (since victims' needs are not met). The system may process cases efficiently but fail to achieve genuine justice.

Restorative Outcomes

Restorative justice produces outcomes focused on healing and reparation. The primary focus is addressing the harm caused by the offense, providing restitution to victims, and promoting emotional healing. Trust and relationships are rebuilt within the community.

Accountability and rehabilitation are achieved as offenders take responsibility, understand the impact of their behavior, and make amends. Personal growth reduces the likelihood of reoffending and supports reintegration.

Positive community impacts include strengthened social bonds, increased collective responsibility, and greater trust between community members and the justice system. Communities become more resilient and better equipped to address conflicts and prevent crime.

The Question of Integration

Having compared restorative and retributive justice, we must ask whether these models are mutually exclusive or whether they can be integrated. The answer, I believe, is that they can and should be integrated—not by blending them into a single approach that loses the distinctiveness of each, but by creating systems that draw on both as appropriate.

Some cases may be most appropriately handled through restorative processes. Minor offenses, first-time offenders, cases where victims desire restorative encounter—these are natural candidates for restorative justice. Other cases may require retributive response. Serious violent offenses, offenders who pose continuing danger, cases where victims are unwilling or unable to participate—these may need the formal processes and coercive power of the retributive system.

But even in cases where retributive response is necessary, restorative principles can inform how punishment is implemented. Prisons can incorporate restorative programs. Probation can include restorative elements. Reentry can be supported by restorative community engagement. The goal is not to replace retributive justice entirely but to infuse it with restorative values wherever possible.

The Psychological Foundations of Restorative Justice

Having explored the philosophical and theological dimensions of restorative justice, we must now attend to the psychological insights that inform and support restorative practice. For restorative justice is not merely a philosophical commitment or a theological vision; it is a set of practices that must work with the grain of human psychology if they are to be effective.

Trauma and Healing

Many victims of crime experience trauma—psychological wounds that persist long after the physical injuries have healed. Trauma affects how people think, feel, and relate to others. It can produce anxiety, depression, hypervigilance, and avoidance. It can shatter assumptions about safety, trust, and meaning.

Restorative justice, informed by trauma research, seeks to create conditions that support healing. The opportunity to tell one's story in a safe environment, to have that story heard and validated, to receive answers to questions that haunt—these can be profoundly healing for trauma survivors. The acknowledgment of harm by the offender, the expression of remorse, the commitment to making amends—these can help restore a sense of safety and control.

Research on trauma-informed practice emphasizes the importance of safety, choice, collaboration, trustworthiness, and empowerment. Restorative processes, when properly facilitated, embody these principles. Participants are not forced into encounters but choose to participate. They have control over what they share and how. They are supported by facilitators and community members. The process is transparent and predictable. They are empowered to contribute to outcomes.

Empathy and Moral Development

Research on empathy and moral development provides further support for restorative approaches. Empathy—the ability to understand and share the feelings of others—is associated with pro-social behavior, reduced aggression, and better relationships. It can be cultivated through experience and practice.

Restorative processes create powerful opportunities for empathy development. When offenders hear directly from victims about the impact of their actions, they cannot remain abstractly detached. They are confronted with the human consequences of their behavior. This confrontation, when facilitated skillfully, can evoke genuine empathy and remorse.

Studies of moral development, following the work of Lawrence Kohlberg and others, show that moral reasoning develops through stages. Higher stages involve greater capacity for perspective-taking, consideration of multiple viewpoints, and commitment to universal principles. Restorative dialogue, which requires participants to consider multiple perspectives and to reason together about just outcomes, may support movement toward higher stages of moral reasoning.

Procedural Justice

Research on procedural justice—the fairness of processes rather than outcomes—has important implications for restorative justice. Studies consistently show that people's satisfaction with legal processes depends not only on outcomes but on how those outcomes are reached. When people perceive that they have been treated fairly—with respect, with voice, with neutrality, with trustworthiness—they are more satisfied even with unfavorable outcomes.

Restorative processes excel on procedural justice dimensions. Participants have voice; they can tell their stories and express their views. They are treated with respect by facilitators and other participants. The process is neutral and transparent. Facilitators act with trustworthiness, honoring commitments and maintaining confidentiality.

This procedural justice contributes to the legitimacy of restorative outcomes. Even when participants do not get everything they want, they are more likely to accept and support outcomes reached through fair processes. This legitimacy, in turn, supports compliance and reduces future conflict.

Shame and Reintegration

The work of criminologist John Braithwaite on shame and reintegration has been particularly influential in restorative justice theory. Braithwaite distinguishes between two kinds of shame: stigmatizing shame, which labels the offender as a bad person and excludes them from community, and reintegrative shame, which condemns the wrongdoing while affirming the worth of the offender and offering a path back into community.

Stigmatizing shame tends to push offenders toward criminal subcultures where their deviance is accepted. Reintegrative shame, by contrast, pulls offenders back toward conventional society by maintaining bonds of respect and care even while condemning wrongdoing.

Restorative practices are designed to produce reintegrative shame. The offender's actions are condemned—victims and community members express their disapproval and hurt. But the offender is not condemned. They are addressed as a person of worth, capable of change, welcome to return to community when they have made amends. This combination of condemnation of the act and affirmation of the actor is precisely what reintegrative shame requires.

The Legal Dimensions of Restorative Justice

Finally, we must consider the legal dimensions of restorative justice—how restorative principles relate to legal systems, how they are embodied in legislation, and how courts have interpreted and applied them.

Restorative Justice and Legal Theory

Restorative justice challenges some fundamental assumptions of Western legal systems. The traditional model assumes that crime is an offense against the state, that the state is the proper party to prosecute, and that punishment is the appropriate response. Restorative justice sees crime as harm to persons and relationships, sees victims and communities as proper parties to the process, and sees repair as the appropriate goal.

This challenge has prompted theoretical reflection on the relationship between restorative and legal justice. Some scholars argue for restorative justice as a complete alternative to legal processing, at least for many cases. Others argue for integration, with restorative processes operating alongside or within legal frameworks. Still others see restorative justice as a supplement to legal justice, addressing needs that the legal system cannot meet.

The legal system's response to restorative justice has been varied. Some jurisdictions have embraced restorative approaches, enacting legislation that authorizes and funds restorative programs. Others have been more cautious, limiting restorative justice to minor offenses or juvenile cases. Still others have resisted restorative justice altogether, viewing it as incompatible with legal principles.

Legislative Frameworks

Several countries have enacted legislation supporting restorative justice. New Zealand's Children, Young Persons, and Their Families Act 1989 made Family Group Conferencing mandatory for most youth offenses. Canada's Youth Criminal Justice Act 2003 encourages the use of restorative justice for young offenders. The European Union has issued directives encouraging member states to implement restorative justice programs.

These legislative frameworks typically address several key issues: the types of cases eligible for restorative processes, the stages at which restorative justice may be used (pre-charge, post-charge but pre-sentence, post-sentence), the qualifications and training of facilitators, the rights of participants, and the relationship between restorative agreements and legal outcomes.

Effective legislation balances several considerations. It must provide sufficient structure to ensure consistency and fairness while allowing flexibility for restorative processes to respond to individual circumstances. It must protect the rights of participants while encouraging voluntary participation. It must integrate restorative justice with legal systems without allowing legal requirements to overwhelm restorative values.

Case Law and Precedents

Courts in various jurisdictions have addressed restorative justice in their decisions. Some cases have affirmed the importance of restorative principles, encouraging their use in appropriate cases. Others have raised concerns about consistency, fairness, and the rights of participants.

In Canada, the Supreme Court's decision in *R v. Gladue* (1999) required judges to consider the unique circumstances of Indigenous offenders and to prioritize restorative justice principles in sentencing. This decision has led to increased use of restorative approaches for Indigenous offenders and has influenced sentencing practices more broadly.

In New Zealand, courts have generally supported Family Group Conferencing, recognizing its benefits for young offenders and their families. Judicial decisions have addressed issues such as the confidentiality of conference proceedings, the enforceability of conference agreements, and the relationship between conference outcomes and court dispositions.

In the United States, restorative justice has been addressed in various contexts—juvenile justice, school discipline, community courts. While there is no single national approach, state courts and legislatures have developed diverse frameworks for implementing restorative practices.

Conclusion: The Theoretical Foundations of a Restorative Society

As we conclude this exploration of the theoretical frameworks that support restorative justice, we see a rich tapestry of philosophical, theological, psychological, and legal insights converging on a common vision: a society in which justice is not about punishment but about healing, not about exclusion but about restoration, not about winning and losing but about finding ways forward together.

The philosophical traditions we have explored—relational ethics, communitarianism, virtue ethics, restorative ontology, ethical responsibility, dialogical ethics—provide intellectual foundations for this vision. They show us why restorative justice makes sense, why it is not merely a collection of practices but a coherent way of understanding justice and human flourishing.

The theological dimensions we have examined—creation and the image of God, the fall and the reality of harm, covenant and community, incarnation and encounter, cross and atonement, resurrection and hope, Spirit and transformation—provide deeper grounding for those who see restorative justice as participating in God's own work in the world. They show us that restorative justice is not merely a human invention but a response to divine initiative.

The psychological insights we have considered—trauma and healing, empathy and moral development, procedural justice, shame and reintegration—provide empirical support for restorative practices. They show us that restorative justice works with the grain of human nature, addressing deep needs and supporting genuine change.

The legal dimensions we have surveyed—legislative frameworks, case law and precedents—show us that restorative justice can be integrated with existing legal systems, that it can be embodied in law without losing its distinctive character, that it can influence legal practice while respecting legal principles.

As we move forward into the remaining chapters, we will build on these theoretical foundations. We will explore the core principles and values that guide restorative practice. We will examine the various models and practices through which restorative justice is implemented. We will consider case studies and real-world applications. We will wrestle with benefits and challenges. We will explore restorative justice in legal systems, international contexts, and social justice movements. And we will look to the future, imagining how restorative justice might continue to transform our world.

The theoretical frameworks we have explored in this chapter are not merely academic abstractions. They are lenses through which we can see more clearly what justice requires. They are tools we can use to design better practices and evaluate existing ones. They are resources we can draw on when we face difficult questions and challenging situations. And they are foundations on which we can build a more just and compassionate society—a restorative society, where healing justice transforms our world.

CHAPTER 03

CORE PRINCIPLES AND VALUES

As we journey deeper into the heart of restorative justice, we arrive at its very core—the principles and values that give it shape, substance, and soul. Principles are not merely abstract ideas to be admired from a distance; they are the living convictions that guide practice, shape decisions, and animate the entire restorative endeavor. Values are not optional additions to be adopted or discarded as convenience dictates; they are the moral commitments that define what restorative justice is and what it seeks to accomplish.

In this chapter, dear reader, we will explore together the foundational principles that make restorative justice what it is: accountability, reparation, community involvement, empathy, and healing. We will examine each of these principles in depth, considering their philosophical grounding, their psychological dimensions, their theological significance, and their practical implications. We will see how they interrelate, how they support one another, and how together they create a coherent vision of justice that heals rather than harms.

Accountability: The Role of Taking Responsibility in Restorative Justice

Let us begin with accountability—a word that appears in discussions of justice perhaps more than any other, but a word whose meaning in restorative contexts differs profoundly from its meaning in conventional discourse. In retributive justice, accountability means being punished. In restorative justice, accountability means taking responsibility—actively, willingly, and with understanding.

Understanding Accountability in Restorative Justice

When we speak of accountability in restorative justice, we are speaking of something far richer and more demanding than simply accepting punishment. We are speaking of a process in which offenders come to genuinely understand the harm they have caused, to feel its impact on real people, and to take concrete steps toward making things right.

Acknowledging Harm

The first step in genuine accountability is acknowledgment. This is not merely saying the words "I did it" but truly recognizing the full extent of the harm caused. This recognition has multiple dimensions.

There is the physical harm—the injuries inflicted, the property damaged or destroyed, the financial losses incurred. There is the emotional harm—the fear, the anger, the grief, the sense of violation that victims carry long after the incident itself. There is the relational harm—the trust broken, the connections severed, the community fabric torn. And there is the social harm—the ripple effects that spread outward to affect families, neighborhoods, and the broader society.

To acknowledge harm is to see it in all these dimensions, to understand that one's actions have consequences far beyond what one might have intended or imagined. This acknowledgment requires what psychologists call "perspective-taking"—the ability to see the situation from another's point of view, to imagine what they have experienced and continue to experience.

This is where empathy enters the accountability process. Empathy is not merely feeling sorry for oneself or feeling bad about getting caught. It is the capacity to feel *with* the victim—to share, at least in some measure, their pain and suffering. When offenders develop this empathy, they are no longer looking at their actions from the outside, as abstract wrongs, but from the inside, as wounds to real people.

The theological dimension of this acknowledgment is profound. In the Hebrew scriptures, when David is confronted by the prophet Nathan after his sin with Bathsheba, he does not merely admit to the facts but enters into the depth of his wrongdoing: "I have sinned against the Lord" (2 Samuel 12:13). The Psalms of lament and confession—Psalm 51 most famously—give voice to this deep acknowledgment of sin and its effects. "Against you, you only, have I sinned and done what is evil in your sight"

(Psalm 51:4). This is not merely admitting guilt but recognizing the relational breach that sin creates.

Taking Responsibility

Acknowledgment must lead to taking responsibility. This means moving beyond excuses and justifications—beyond "I couldn't help it" or "They had it coming" or "Everyone does it"—to owning one's actions fully. It means saying, "I did this. This was my choice. These consequences flow from my actions."

Taking responsibility also means recognizing the moral and ethical dimensions of what one has done. It is not merely that one broke a rule or violated a law but that one harmed another human being, that one acted in ways that are wrong, that one failed to live up to the moral standards that govern human community.

This moral accountability is central to the biblical understanding of sin. Sin is not merely transgression of arbitrary rules but violation of relationship—with God and with neighbor. When the prodigal son in Jesus's parable comes to himself, he does not merely calculate that he would be better off as a hired hand; he confesses, "Father, I have sinned against heaven and before you" (Luke 15:18). He takes responsibility not only for his actions but for the relational breach they have caused.

Making Amends

The final step in accountability is making amends. Acknowledgment and responsibility, however genuine, are incomplete if they do not issue in action. The offender must do something to repair the harm, to make things right as far as possible.

This may take various forms. Financial restitution compensates victims for material losses. Community service gives something back to the community that has been harmed. Direct apologies, offered face to face, acknowledge the personal dimension of harm. Participation in restorative processes—circles, conferences, mediation—demonstrates commitment to restoration.

Making amends requires active participation from all parties. It is not something done *to* the victim or *for* the offender but something done *with* both, in collaboration. The victim's needs shape what amends are appropriate. The offender's capacities shape what amends are possible. The community's support enables the process to move forward.

This collaborative dimension reflects the biblical understanding of restitution. The law of Moses required not merely compensation but restoration—sometimes multiple times over what was taken (Exodus 22). When Zacchaeus encounters Jesus, he does not merely express remorse but commits to action: "Behold, Lord, the half of my goods I give to the poor. And if I have defrauded anyone of anything, I restore it fourfold" (Luke 19:8). His repentance issues in reparation.

The Significance of Accountability in Restorative Justice

Why is accountability so central to restorative justice? Because without it, neither healing nor restoration is possible.

Promoting Personal Growth and Rehabilitation

The process of taking responsibility is itself transformative. When offenders engage in genuine self-reflection—examining not only what they did but why they did it, what led to their actions, what patterns of thought and behavior contributed to the harm—they open themselves to change.

This self-reflection is not merely introspective navel-gazing but active engagement with the consequences of one's actions. Hearing from victims directly, learning how one's behavior affected real people, facing the community's response—all of these challenge the defenses and justifications that offenders may have constructed. They create cognitive dissonance, the psychological discomfort that arises when our self-understanding conflicts with evidence of the harm we have caused. And cognitive dissonance, when properly managed, can motivate genuine change.

The goal is not merely to avoid future punishment but to become a different kind of person—one who does not want to cause harm, who has internalized the values that prevent wrongdoing. This is what psychologists call "internalization"—the process by which external norms become internal guides. When offenders take genuine responsibility, they are not merely complying with external demands but incorporating those demands into their own moral framework.

This is precisely what the biblical tradition means by repentance—*metanoia*, a change of mind and heart that leads to transformed life. It is not merely feeling sorry but turning around, going in a new direction. Ezekiel captures this when he reports God's word: "Cast away from you all the transgressions that you have committed, and make yourselves a new heart and a new spirit" (Ezekiel 18:31). Repentance is not static but dynamic, not passive but active, not merely emotional but behavioral.

Fostering Healing for Victims

Accountability also serves victims' healing. When offenders acknowledge the harm they have caused, it validates victims' experiences. Victims hear that what happened to them mattered, that someone else recognizes its significance, that they are not alone in their understanding of the harm.

This validation is profoundly important psychologically. Victims of crime often experience what researchers call "secondary victimization"—the sense that the justice system does not take their suffering seriously, that they are merely evidence in a case, that their needs are secondary to the state's interest in punishment. When offenders acknowledge harm directly, it counters this secondary victimization. It says to victims, "You matter. Your suffering is real. I see it."

The process of making amends can also restore trust. Trust is built through experience—through seeing that others are reliable, that they keep commitments, that they care about our well-being. When offenders follow through on agreements to make amends, they demonstrate that they can be trusted, at least to some degree. This does not erase the harm or restore full trust overnight, but it begins the process.

Theologically, this validation echoes God's own response to human suffering. The Psalms are filled with cries for God to see, to hear, to acknowledge. "O Lord, you have searched me and known me" (Psalm 139:1). When offenders acknowledge harm, they participate in this divine attentiveness to suffering.

Restoring Social Harmony

Finally, accountability serves the restoration of social harmony. Crime disrupts not only individual relationships but the entire social fabric. When offenders take responsibility and make amends, they help repair that fabric.

This repair occurs at multiple levels. At the interpersonal level, relationships between victims and offenders can be restored—not necessarily to what they were before, but to some new place of mutual respect and peaceful coexistence. At the community level, trust is rebuilt as members see that harm can be addressed constructively, that offenders can change, that justice can heal rather than wound.

This social dimension of accountability reflects the biblical vision of *shalom*—the peace that comes when all things are in right relationship. *Shalom* is not merely the absence of conflict but the presence of wholeness, flourishing, and harmony. When offenders take responsibility and make amends, they contribute to the restoration of *shalom*.

Facilitating Accountability through Restorative Practices

Restorative justice employs various practices specifically designed to facilitate genuine accountability.

Victim-Offender Mediation

In victim-offender mediation, a trained facilitator brings victim and offender together in a structured environment. The offender hears directly from the victim about the impact of the crime—not filtered through police reports or prosecutor's summaries but in the victim's own words, with all the emotion and particularity that direct communication allows.

This direct encounter makes abstract harm concrete. The offender cannot remain detached; they must face the human consequences of their actions. They see the victim's pain, hear their questions, witness their struggle. This encounter, when properly facilitated, can evoke genuine empathy and remorse.

From this encounter, mutually agreed outcomes can emerge. The victim may want specific restitution—compensation for losses, help with repairs, an apology. The offender may offer what they can. Together, they work out an agreement that addresses the harm and charts a path forward.

Restorative Circles

Restorative circles expand participation beyond victim and offender to include community members. In the circle, all have equal opportunity to speak, using a talking piece that passes from person to person. This structure ensures that every voice can be heard.

For the offender, the circle provides multiple perspectives on their actions. They hear not only from the victim but from neighbors, family members, community leaders—all of whom may have been affected in different ways. This collective witness can deepen understanding of the harm's full scope.

The circle also emphasizes collective accountability. The offender is accountable not only to the victim but to the community as a whole. And the community, in turn, is accountable to support both victim and offender in the restorative process. This mutual accountability reflects the interconnectedness that restorative justice affirms.

Family Group Conferencing

Family group conferencing brings together the victim, offender, and their respective families and support networks. This approach recognizes that families are deeply affected by crime and have crucial roles to play in accountability and healing.

The presence of family provides both support and accountability. Offenders are supported by loved ones who want to see them change; they are also accountable to those loved ones, who will live with the consequences of their actions. Victims are supported by their families, who can help them articulate their needs and cope with the emotions that arise.

Family group conferencing also includes private family time—a period when the offender's family meets alone to develop a plan for making amends. This provision respects family autonomy and creativity, allowing those who know the offender best to design interventions that are likely to work.

Community Restorative Boards

Community restorative boards consist of trained community volunteers who meet with offenders to discuss the harm caused and develop restorative agreements. These boards represent the community's direct involvement in the justice process.

For offenders, appearing before a board of their neighbors makes accountability concrete and personal. These are not distant officials but people they may see at the store, at community events, on the street. The board's expectations carry the weight of community norms.

The agreements developed by restorative boards typically include specific actions the offender will take to address the harm and contribute positively to the community. The board may also provide ongoing support and monitoring to ensure that agreements are fulfilled.

Challenges and Considerations in Promoting Accountability

Promoting genuine accountability is not without challenges. Several considerations must be addressed.

Ensuring Genuine Accountability

For accountability to be meaningful, participation in restorative processes must be voluntary. When offenders are coerced or pressured, their expressions of responsibility may be insincere—merely going through the motions to avoid worse consequences. This undermines the entire restorative endeavor.

Facilitators must be alert to signs of inauthentic engagement—offenders who say what they think others want to hear, who go through the motions without genuine understanding, who make promises they have no intention of keeping. Creating conditions for authentic engagement requires skill, patience, and attention to the offender's readiness.

Addressing Power Imbalances

Power imbalances can distort the accountability process. An offender who is more articulate, more confident, or more socially skilled may dominate the conversation, minimizing their responsibility or manipulating others' perceptions. A victim who is traumatized, intimidated, or marginalized may be unable to speak freely or advocate for their needs.

Facilitators must be trained to recognize and address these imbalances. This may involve meeting separately with parties beforehand, providing support persons during the process, ensuring that all voices are heard, and intervening when necessary to maintain balance. Creating a safe and equitable environment is essential for genuine accountability.

Measuring Accountability

Measuring the success of accountability in restorative justice is challenging. Completion of reparative actions is one measure, but not the only one. Personal growth—changes in attitude, understanding, and behavior—is equally important but harder to quantify. Victim healing—the restoration of well-being and sense of safety—is another crucial outcome.

Ongoing monitoring and support are often necessary to ensure that offenders follow through on commitments and that intended outcomes are achieved. This requires resources and infrastructure that may not always be available.

Reparation: Making Amends and Repairing Harm

If accountability is the process of taking responsibility, reparation is the substance of making things right. Reparation is what offenders do to address the harm they have caused—concrete actions that demonstrate their commitment to restoration.

Understanding Reparation in Restorative Justice

Reparation in restorative justice goes far beyond mere compensation. It is a holistic approach to addressing harm that encompasses material, emotional, and relational dimensions.

Acknowledging Harm

As with accountability, reparation begins with acknowledgment. Offenders must understand the full extent of the harm they have caused—not only the obvious, immediate damage but the ripple effects that continue through time.

This acknowledgment has multiple dimensions. There is the physical dimension: injuries inflicted, property damaged, environments disrupted. There is the emotional dimension: fear, anger, grief, shame. There is the psychological dimension: trauma, anxiety, depression, loss of trust. There is the relational dimension: broken relationships, severed connections, community fragmentation. And there is the spiritual dimension: for many victims, crime shakes their sense of meaning, their faith in goodness, their trust in God.

To acknowledge harm is to see it in all these dimensions, to recognize that one's actions have consequences far beyond what one might have intended. This acknowledgment opens the possibility of genuine reparation.

Making Amends

From acknowledgment flows action—concrete steps to make amends. These may be material: financial restitution, repair of damaged property, replacement of stolen goods. They may be service-oriented: community service that gives back to the community, work that benefits those affected. They may be communicative: direct apologies, letters of explanation, participation in restorative processes.

The key is that these actions are meaningful—they address real needs and demonstrate genuine commitment. A restitution payment that covers a victim's medical expenses is meaningful. Community service that benefits the neighborhood where harm occurred is meaningful. An apology offered face to face, with genuine emotion and commitment to change, is meaningful.

But reparation also includes symbolic acts—actions whose meaning transcends their material value. A public apology acknowledges the community dimension of harm. Participation in a reconciliation ceremony signals commitment to restored relationship. Symbolic acts communicate what words alone cannot: that the offender understands, that they care, that they are changed.

Promoting Healing

The ultimate goal of reparation is healing—not only for victims but for offenders and communities as well. Reparation aims to restore what was broken, to mend what was torn, to heal what was wounded.

This healing is holistic. It addresses the material needs of victims—the practical losses that crime causes. It addresses their emotional needs—the pain, fear, and grief that crime inflicts. It addresses their relational needs—the trust and connection that crime severs. And it addresses their spiritual needs—the meaning and hope that crime can shatter.

For offenders, reparation promotes healing by enabling them to make things right, to demonstrate their changed commitment, to be restored to community. The shame of wrongdoing is not removed by punishment alone; it is addressed by doing good, by contributing positively, by being seen as someone capable of change.

For communities, reparation heals the social fabric, rebuilding trust and strengthening bonds. When harm is addressed constructively, when offenders make amends, when victims are supported, communities grow stronger and more resilient.

The Significance of Reparation in Restorative Justice

Reparation is significant for multiple reasons, touching every dimension of the restorative endeavor.

Addressing Victims' Needs

First and foremost, reparation addresses victims' needs. Victims have been harmed; they deserve to have that harm addressed. They deserve restitution for their losses—not as charity but as justice. They deserve acknowledgment of their suffering—not as pity but as validation. They deserve support in their healing—not as an afterthought but as a priority.

When reparation is provided, victims experience validation. Their suffering is acknowledged as real and significant. They are not invisible; they matter. This validation is itself healing, countering the isolation and marginalization that victims often feel.

When reparation is provided, victims experience empowerment. They have a voice in determining what will make things right. They are not passive recipients of whatever the system provides but active participants in shaping outcomes. This empowerment restores a measure of control that crime took away.

Promoting Offender Rehabilitation

Reparation also promotes offender rehabilitation. The process of making amends requires offenders to engage actively with the consequences of their actions, to take responsibility, to contribute positively. This engagement is itself transformative.

When offenders provide restitution, they experience what it means to give rather than take. When they perform community service, they experience what it means to contribute rather than harm. When they offer apologies, they practice empathy and vulnerability. These experiences shape character, building the virtues that prevent future offending.

Reparation also supports reintegration. When offenders make amends, they demonstrate to themselves and others that they are capable of positive contribution. They are seen not merely as wrongdoers but as people who can do good. This changed perception opens doors to community acceptance and support.

Restoring Social Harmony

Finally, reparation restores social harmony. Trust, once broken, must be rebuilt. Reparation provides the means: concrete actions that demonstrate changed commitment, visible evidence that offenders are taking responsibility, tangible contributions that benefit the community.

When reparation occurs, the community experiences justice being done—not abstract justice but concrete restoration. This experience builds confidence in the possibility of healing, in the capacity of communities to address harm constructively, in the hope that even serious wrongs can be made right.

Facilitating Reparation through Restorative Practices

Restorative practices are designed to facilitate reparation in multiple ways.

Victim-Offender Mediation

In victim-offender mediation, reparation is a central focus. Through dialogue, victims and offenders explore what would constitute meaningful amends. The victim's needs shape the discussion: What losses need to be addressed? What would help the victim heal? What would demonstrate genuine accountability?

From this dialogue, mutually agreed outcomes emerge. These may include financial restitution, community service, apologies, or other reparative actions. The agreement is not imposed but developed together, ensuring that it addresses what victims actually need and what offenders can actually provide.

Restorative Circles

Restorative circles expand participation, allowing community members to contribute to reparation. The circle may identify community needs that offenders can address through service. It may provide resources to support restitution. It may witness and affirm the offender's reparative actions.

The circle also emphasizes collective reparation. Offenders make amends not only to individual victims but to the community as a whole. And the community, in turn, participates in supporting both victim and offender, contributing to the healing process.

Family Group Conferencing

Family group conferencing brings families into the reparation process. Families may contribute resources to support restitution. They may help offenders identify meaningful ways to make amends. They may provide ongoing support to ensure that reparative actions are completed.

The family's involvement also reinforces accountability. When families are part of developing and supporting reparative agreements, they have a stake in seeing them fulfilled. Their ongoing presence provides motivation and support for offenders to follow through.

Community Restorative Boards

Community restorative boards develop formal restorative agreements that specify reparative actions. These agreements are tailored to the particular case, addressing the harm caused and the needs of those affected.

The board may also monitor compliance, providing oversight to ensure that agreements are fulfilled. This monitoring supports accountability while also offering encouragement and assistance when needed.

Types of Reparation

Reparation can take many forms, each addressing different aspects of harm.

Financial Restitution

Financial restitution compensates victims for material losses—medical expenses, property damage, lost income, and other costs resulting from the offense. While money cannot undo the harm, it can address practical needs and serve as tangible acknowledgment of responsibility.

The symbolic value of restitution should not be underestimated. When offenders pay compensation, they are giving something of themselves, demonstrating commitment to making things right. This giving contrasts with the taking that characterized the offense.

Community Service

Community service allows offenders to give back to the community they have harmed. By contributing their time and labor to projects that benefit others, they demonstrate their capacity for positive contribution. This can be particularly meaningful when the service is connected to the nature of the offense—for example, someone who vandalized a park helping to restore it.

Community service also helps restore community trust. When community members see offenders working for the common good, their perceptions shift. The offender is no longer merely a threat but a contributor. This changed perception supports reintegration.

Direct Apologies and Reconciliation

Direct apologies, offered face to face, are among the most powerful forms of reparation. In an apology, the offender acknowledges the harm, expresses remorse, and asks for forgiveness. This direct communication can be profoundly healing for victims, who hear that their suffering is recognized and regretted.

Apologies also open the door to reconciliation. When an apology is accepted, a new relationship becomes possible—not erasing what happened but transcending it. Victim and offender can move forward together, no longer bound by the past.

Symbolic Acts

Symbolic acts—public apologies, reconciliation ceremonies, memorial contributions—address the communal and spiritual dimensions of harm. These acts acknowledge that harm affects not only individuals but the broader community, and that healing requires collective as well as individual response.

Symbolic acts can be particularly important in cases of severe harm, where material restitution seems inadequate. A ceremony of reconciliation, witnessed by community members, can mark a turning point, creating new possibilities for relationship and trust.

Challenges and Considerations in Promoting Reparation

Promoting genuine reparation involves several challenges.

Ensuring Meaningful Reparation

For reparation to be meaningful, it must be voluntary. Coerced restitution is not genuine reparation; it is merely payment extracted under threat. Facilitators must ensure that offenders are genuinely committed to making amends, not merely going through the motions.

Meaningful reparation also requires authentic engagement. Offenders must understand why they are doing what they do, must connect their actions to the harm they caused. Without this understanding, reparation becomes empty ritual.

Addressing Power Imbalances

Power imbalances can distort reparation. Offenders with greater resources may be able to provide more generous restitution, creating inequities between cases. Victims who are marginalized may have difficulty articulating their needs or advocating for what would truly help.

Facilitators must work to create equitable conditions, ensuring that all voices are heard and all needs considered. This may require providing support and advocacy for vulnerable participants, helping them identify and communicate what they need.

Measuring Reparation

Measuring the success of reparation is challenging. Completion of agreed actions is one measure, but not the only one. The healing that reparation produces—for victims, offenders, and communities—is equally important but harder to quantify.

Ongoing monitoring and support are often necessary to ensure that reparative actions are completed and that they achieve their intended effects. This requires resources and commitment over time.

Community Involvement: The Significance of Community Participation in the Justice Process

We turn now to the third core principle of restorative justice: community involvement. This principle recognizes that crime is not merely an individual matter but a community concern, and that communities have essential roles to play in responding to harm.

Understanding Community Involvement in Restorative Justice

Community involvement in restorative justice means actively engaging community members in the justice process—not as spectators but as participants, not as recipients of decisions made elsewhere but as contributors to decisions made together.

Community as Stakeholders

The first premise of community involvement is that communities are stakeholders in justice. Crime affects not only direct victims but the broader community. The sense of safety is diminished. Trust between neighbors is eroded. The fabric of community life is torn.

Because communities are affected, they have a stake in how harm is addressed. They need to see that justice is done, that victims are supported, that offenders are held accountable, that conditions for safety are restored. They need to be part of the solution, not merely bystanders to problems.

This understanding reflects the communitarian philosophy we explored in Chapter 2. Communities are not mere collections of individuals but networks of relationship, shared identity, and mutual responsibility. Justice, therefore, must be concerned with the health of communities, not merely the fate of individuals.

Roles of Community Members

Community members play multiple roles in restorative justice. They provide support for victims—emotional comfort, practical assistance, ongoing presence. They help victims feel less isolated, more connected, more able to heal.

Community members also hold offenders accountable. Their presence in restorative processes communicates that the community cares about what happened, that the offender's actions have social consequences, that restoration to community requires meeting community expectations.

Trained community members may serve as facilitators or mediators, guiding restorative processes and ensuring they are fair and effective. This community facilitation brings local knowledge and relationships to the process, enhancing its relevance and legitimacy.

The Significance of Community Participation

Community participation is significant for multiple reasons.

Enhancing the Justice Process

When communities are involved, decisions reflect community values and needs. Outcomes are not imposed by distant authorities but developed by those who will live with them. This enhances legitimacy and support.

Community involvement also promotes shared responsibility. When communities participate in justice, they share the burden of addressing harm. The formal justice system is not alone in responding to crime; communities contribute their resources, relationships, and wisdom.

Promoting Healing and Support

Community members provide vital support networks for victims. They offer practical help—transportation, childcare, meals. They offer emotional comfort—listening, validating, caring. They offer social connection—including victims in community life, preventing isolation.

For offenders, community participation creates a supportive environment for accountability and change. Offenders are not merely processed by the system but engaged by people who know them, who care about them, who have a stake in their future. This engagement can motivate genuine change.

Strengthening Social Cohesion

Community involvement builds trust. When community members participate in justice processes, they see that the system can work, that harm can be addressed, that healing is possible. This builds confidence in both the justice system and the community itself.

Community involvement also strengthens social bonds. People who work together to address harm develop relationships, learn to trust one another, build the social capital that makes communities resilient. These bonds serve them well beyond any particular case.

Facilitating Community Involvement through Restorative Practices

Restorative practices are designed to facilitate meaningful community involvement.

Restorative Circles

Restorative circles bring community members together with victims and offenders. In the circle, all have equal opportunity to speak, to share their perspectives, to contribute to the resolution. This inclusive structure ensures that community voices are heard and valued.

The circle also emphasizes collective decision-making. The community helps develop and support reparative actions, ensuring that outcomes reflect community values and have community backing.

Family Group Conferencing

Family group conferencing brings together victims, offenders, and their families and support networks. This approach recognizes that families are the most immediate communities for many people, and that their involvement is essential for effective accountability and healing.

The conference includes private family time, during which the offender's family develops a plan for making amends. This provision respects family autonomy while ensuring community input.

Community Restorative Boards

Community restorative boards consist of trained community volunteers who meet with offenders to develop restorative agreements. These boards represent the community's direct involvement in the justice process, holding offenders accountable and supporting their efforts to make amends.

The boards also provide ongoing monitoring and support, ensuring that agreements are fulfilled and that offenders have the help they need to succeed.

Victim-Offender Mediation with Community Support

Even in victim-offender mediation, community members may participate as support persons. Their presence provides additional perspectives and ensures that solutions have community endorsement. Victims and offenders alike benefit from this broader support.

Benefits of Community Involvement

Community involvement benefits all parties.

For Victims

Victims receive enhanced support from their community. They are not alone in their suffering but surrounded by people who care. They experience validation as community members witness and acknowledge their harm. They gain satisfaction from knowing that their community is engaged in addressing what happened.

Research confirms that victims who participate in community-involved restorative processes report higher satisfaction than those whose cases are handled entirely by formal systems. They feel heard, respected, and supported.

For Offenders

Offenders receive reintegration support from their community. They are not merely released from supervision but welcomed back into relationship. This support can be crucial for successful reentry and sustained change.

Offenders also experience accountability to their community, not merely to abstract authorities. Knowing that neighbors, family members, and community leaders are watching and caring can motivate genuine change.

For the Community

Communities benefit from strengthened social bonds. Working together to address harm builds relationships and trust. People learn that they can rely on one another, that collective action is possible, that problems can be solved together.

Communities also develop increased trust in the justice system. When they are involved in processes and see positive outcomes, they gain confidence that the system can work for them. This trust supports future cooperation and engagement.

Challenges and Considerations in Promoting Community Involvement

Promoting meaningful community involvement involves several challenges.

Ensuring Meaningful Participation

For community involvement to be meaningful, participation must be voluntary. People should not be pressured or coerced into participating. They should be genuinely interested and committed.

Inclusivity is also essential. Efforts must be made to ensure that all voices in the community are heard—including marginalized or underrepresented groups. Communities are not homogeneous; they contain diverse perspectives and experiences. All should have opportunity to contribute.

Addressing Power Imbalances

Power imbalances within the community can affect restorative processes. Some individuals or groups may have more influence, more resources, more voice. Others may be marginalized or silenced.

Facilitators must work to create equitable conditions, ensuring that all participants can speak and be heard. This may require providing support and advocacy for vulnerable community members, helping them articulate their perspectives.

Sustaining Community Engagement

Sustaining community engagement over time requires ongoing effort. Trust must be built and maintained. Relationships must be nurtured. A sense of collective responsibility must be cultivated.

Investing in community capacity building—training, resources, infrastructure—can enhance the community's ability to participate effectively. Communities with strong capacity are better able to sustain engagement over the long term.

Empathy and Healing: Fostering Empathy and Emotional Healing

The fourth core principle of restorative justice is empathy and healing—the recognition that emotional wounds must be addressed if true restoration is to occur.

Understanding Empathy in Restorative Justice

Empathy—the ability to understand and share the feelings of others—is crucial in restorative justice. It enables offenders to recognize the impact of their actions. It helps victims feel heard and validated. It creates the conditions for genuine reconciliation.

Defining Empathy

Empathy has multiple dimensions. Cognitive empathy is the intellectual understanding of another's feelings and perspectives—being able to see the world from their point of view. Emotional empathy is the capacity to feel what another is experiencing—to share, at least in part, their emotional state. Compassionate empathy adds the desire to help—to respond to another's need with care and action.

All three dimensions are important in restorative justice. Cognitive empathy helps offenders understand victims' experiences. Emotional empathy connects them to victims' pain. Compassionate empathy motivates them to make amends.

The Role of Empathy in Restorative Justice

Empathy builds understanding. When offenders develop empathy for victims, they grasp the real impact of their actions. They move beyond abstract awareness of wrongdoing to concrete recognition of harm. This understanding is essential for genuine accountability.

Empathy promotes reconciliation. When victims and offenders connect on a human level, barriers of anger and resentment can begin to break down. Victims may see offenders as more than their worst actions; offenders may see victims as more than obstacles to their own interests. This mutual recognition opens the possibility of reconciliation.

Empathy enhances healing. For victims, having their emotions understood and validated is itself healing. They are not alone in their pain; someone else recognizes it. For offenders, experiencing empathy can be transformative, awakening moral awareness and motivating change.

The Significance of Healing in Restorative Justice

Healing is the central goal of restorative justice. All the principles we have explored—accountability, reparation, community involvement—serve the ultimate purpose of healing.

Types of Healing

Healing has multiple dimensions. Emotional healing addresses the pain, fear, anger, and grief that crime causes. Victims need to move beyond these emotions, to find peace and hope. Offenders need to address the shame and guilt that accompany wrongdoing, to find new ways of being.

Psychological healing addresses deeper wounds—trauma, anxiety, depression, loss of trust. These wounds may persist long after the immediate harm, affecting victims' ability to function and flourish. Healing requires addressing them directly.

Social healing restores trust and harmony within the community. When relationships are broken, the entire community suffers. Healing requires rebuilding those relationships, restoring the social fabric.

The Role of Healing in Restorative Justice

Healing restores victims' well-being. The goal is not merely to process cases but to help victims move beyond trauma, to regain a sense of security and peace, to rebuild their lives. This requires attention to their emotional and psychological needs.

Healing rehabilitates offenders. The goal is not merely to punish but to change—to address underlying issues, to promote positive development, to enable offenders to become contributing members of society. This requires attention to their emotional and psychological needs as well.

Healing rebuilds communities. The goal is not merely to resolve individual cases but to strengthen the social fabric, to build resilience, to create conditions in which harm is less likely to occur. This requires collective attention to the health of the whole.

Facilitating Empathy and Healing through Restorative Practices

Restorative practices are designed to facilitate empathy and promote healing.

Victim-Offender Mediation

In victim-offender mediation, direct dialogue creates conditions for empathy. Victims share their experiences, their emotions, their needs. Offenders listen, respond, express remorse. This exchange, when facilitated skillfully, can evoke genuine empathy on both sides.

The mediation also provides space for emotional expression. Victims can say what they need to say, ask what they need to ask. Offenders can express their feelings, their regrets, their hopes. This expression is itself healing.

Restorative Circles

Restorative circles bring together multiple participants, creating opportunities for shared experience and mutual understanding. As participants share their stories, they build empathy for one another. The circle becomes a container for collective healing.

The circle's structure—with its talking piece, its emphasis on listening, its commitment to respect—creates a safe space for emotional expression. Participants can share what is in their hearts, knowing they will be heard and not judged.

Family Group Conferencing

Family group conferencing brings together the victim, offender, and their families. This extended involvement provides broader emotional support and understanding. Families can help victims feel less alone; they can help offenders recognize the impact of their actions on those they love.

The conference's supportive environment encourages emotional expression and fosters empathy. With family present, participants may feel safer sharing vulnerable feelings. This sharing can deepen understanding and promote healing.

Community Restorative Boards

Community restorative boards involve community members in the justice process. Their presence provides additional perspectives and support for empathy and healing. Community members may share how the offense affected them, broadening offenders' understanding. They may also offer support and encouragement for victims' healing.

Restorative agreements developed by boards may include actions specifically designed to promote healing—counseling, participation in support groups, engagement with healing resources.

Strategies for Fostering Empathy and Healing

Several strategies can be employed to foster empathy and promote healing.

Active Listening

Active listening—listening with full attention, without judgment, with the intent to understand—is essential for empathy and healing. Facilitators create safe spaces where participants can speak freely, knowing they will be heard. They validate participants' emotions, reinforcing that their feelings matter.

Narrative Sharing

Encouraging participants to share their personal stories builds empathy and understanding. Stories make abstract harm concrete; they connect statistics to lived experience. When participants share their narratives, they reveal their humanity, making connection possible.

Narrative sharing also promotes mutual recognition. As victims and offenders hear each other's stories, they may recognize shared humanity, shared pain, shared hope. This recognition can be profoundly healing.

Emotional Support

Providing access to counseling and therapeutic support helps participants process their emotions and begin healing. Some harms are too deep to be addressed solely through restorative processes; professional support may be needed.

Peer support groups offer another form of emotional support. Connecting with others who have similar experiences can reduce isolation and provide practical wisdom for healing.

Reparative Actions

Symbolic acts of contrition—apologies, reconciliation ceremonies—play a significant role in acknowledging harm and promoting healing. These acts communicate what words alone cannot: that the offender understands, that they care, that they are changed.

Concrete reparative actions—restitution, community service—also contribute to healing. They demonstrate commitment to making amends, providing tangible evidence of change.

Benefits of Empathy and Healing

Fostering empathy and promoting healing benefit all parties.

For Victims

Victims receive emotional validation. Their suffering is acknowledged, their feelings are understood, their experiences are taken seriously. This validation is itself healing, countering the isolation and marginalization that victims often feel.

Victims also experience recovery and resilience. The healing process helps them move beyond trauma, rebuild their lives, and develop strength for the future. They are not merely survivors but thrivers.

For Offenders

Offenders experience moral growth. Empathy awakens them to the impact of their actions, fostering genuine remorse and commitment to change. This growth is the foundation of rehabilitation.

Offenders also receive support for healing. Addressing underlying issues—trauma, addiction, mental health problems—enables them to change more fully. They are not merely punished but transformed.

For the Community

Empathy and healing strengthen social bonds. When community members participate in healing processes, they develop deeper connections with one another. They learn to trust, to care, to support.

Community involvement in healing also builds trust and cooperation. People see that the community can address harm constructively, that healing is possible, that they can rely on one another. This trust supports ongoing community health and resilience.

Challenges and Considerations in Fostering Empathy and Healing

Fostering empathy and promoting healing involve several challenges.

Ensuring Genuine Empathy

For empathy to be genuine, participation must be voluntary. Coerced empathy is not empathy at all but performance. Facilitators must create conditions in which participants can authentically engage.

Authentic engagement requires that participants be genuinely interested in understanding one another, not merely going through motions. Facilitators must be alert to signs of inauthenticity and work to create genuine connection.

Addressing Emotional Barriers

Participants may have emotional barriers that hinder empathy or healing. Victims may be too angry, too traumatized, too guarded to open themselves to connection. Offenders may be too defensive, too ashamed, too disconnected to feel for others.

Facilitators must be skilled in addressing these barriers—creating safety, building trust, pacing the process appropriately. Access to counseling and support can help participants work through emotional obstacles.

Creating Safe Spaces

Creating a safe and supportive environment is crucial for empathy and healing. Participants must feel secure enough to share vulnerable feelings, to take emotional risks. They must trust that the space will hold them, that they will not be harmed by participating.

Confidentiality and trust are essential for creating safe spaces. Participants must know that what they share will not be used against them, that they can speak freely without fear. Facilitators must establish and maintain this trust throughout the process.

The Interconnection of Principles

As we have explored each of these core principles—accountability, reparation, community involvement, empathy, and healing—we have seen how they interrelate and support one another. Accountability without reparation is empty; reparation without accountability is meaningless. Community involvement without empathy becomes bureaucratic; empathy without community involvement becomes isolated. All work together to create the transformative potential of restorative justice.

This interconnection reflects the holistic nature of restorative justice. It does not address harm in fragments but as a whole, recognizing that all dimensions of harm—material, emotional, relational, social—must be addressed together. It does not treat victims, offenders, and communities separately but brings them together, recognizing that all are affected and all must be involved in healing.

The theological vision underlying this interconnection is the vision of *shalom*—the peace that comes when all things are in right relationship. In *shalom*, individuals are at peace with themselves, with one another, with God, with creation. Justice is not merely the absence of conflict but the presence of wholeness, flourishing, and harmony. Restorative justice, with its integrated principles and values, offers a path toward this *shalom*.

The Psychological Foundations of These Principles

The principles we have explored are not merely philosophical commitments; they are grounded in psychological research about what promotes healing and change.

Research on trauma shows that healing requires safety, acknowledgment, and connection. Victims need to feel safe before they can begin to heal. They need their suffering acknowledged by others. They need connection with people who care. Restorative practices, with their emphasis on safe space, validation, and community support, provide these conditions.

Research on offender rehabilitation shows that change requires cognitive and emotional engagement. Offenders must understand the impact of their actions and feel genuine remorse. They must develop new skills and new ways of thinking. Restorative practices, with their emphasis on dialogue, empathy, and active participation, promote this engagement.

Research on community resilience shows that strong social bonds protect against crime and promote well-being. Communities where people know and trust one another, where they work together to solve problems, are safer and healthier. Restorative practices, with their emphasis on community involvement and collective responsibility, build these bonds.

The Theological Foundations of These Principles

For those who approach restorative justice from a faith perspective, these principles have deep theological roots.

Accountability reflects the biblical understanding of sin and repentance. Sin is real; it has consequences; it must be addressed. But God's desire is not the death of the sinner but their turning and living (Ezekiel 18:23). Accountability serves repentance, not merely punishment.

Reparation reflects the biblical emphasis on restitution and restoration. The law of Moses required making amends. The prophets called for justice that rolls down like waters. Jesus's teaching and example embodied restorative action. Reparation is not optional but essential to genuine repentance.

Community involvement reflects the biblical understanding of covenant and body. God's people are called together, formed as community, responsible for one another. When one suffers, all suffer; when one rejoices, all rejoice. Justice is the work of the whole community, not merely of officials or institutions.

Empathy and healing reflect the character of God, who is "gracious and merciful, slow to anger and abounding in steadfast love" (Psalm 145:8). God enters into human suffering, shares human pain, works for human healing. Those who participate in restorative justice participate in this divine work.

The Legal Dimensions of These Principles

Restorative principles also have implications for legal systems. Accountability, understood as taking responsibility, differs from legal guilt. Reparation, understood as making amends, differs from punitive damages. Community involvement, understood as participatory justice, differs from state-centered prosecution.

Legal systems that embrace restorative principles must find ways to incorporate them while maintaining fairness, consistency, and protection of rights. This requires careful attention to how restorative processes relate to legal proceedings, how restorative agreements are enforced, and how rights are protected.

Many jurisdictions have made progress in this integration. New Zealand's Family Group Conferencing operates within the legal system while maintaining restorative character. Canada's youth justice legislation encourages restorative approaches while protecting legal rights. European Union directives promote restorative justice while ensuring procedural safeguards.

As restorative justice continues to develop, its integration with legal systems will remain an important frontier. The principles we have explored in this chapter provide guidance for this integration, ensuring that restorative values are not lost in legal translation.

As we move forward into the remaining chapters, we will build on these core principles. We will explore the various models and practices through which restorative justice is implemented. We will consider case studies and real-world applications. We will examine benefits and challenges. We will explore restorative justice in legal systems, international contexts, and social justice movements. And we will look to the future, imagining how restorative justice might continue to transform our world.

The principles we have explored in this chapter—accountability, reparation, community involvement, empathy, and healing—are not merely abstract ideals. They are living values that can guide our responses to harm, our relationships with one another, and our vision for a more just and compassionate society. They are the foundation on which a restorative society can be built—a society where healing justice transforms our world.

CHAPTER 04

RESTORATIVE PRACTICES AND MODELS

Having explored the philosophical foundations and core principles of restorative justice, we now turn to the practical question: How is restorative justice actually done? What are the practices and models that bring these principles to life? In this chapter, dear reader, we will examine the primary restorative practices that have been developed and refined over decades of experience. We will see how each practice embodies restorative principles, how it facilitates accountability and healing, and how it engages victims, offenders, and communities in the work of restoration.

The practices we will explore—victim-offender mediation, family group conferencing, circle processes, and community restorative boards—are not rigid formulas to be applied mechanically. They are flexible frameworks that can be adapted to different contexts, cultures, and situations. What they share is a commitment to the core restorative values we have explored: accountability, reparation, community involvement, empathy, and healing. What distinguishes them is the particular way they structure participation and dialogue.

As we journey through these practices, I invite you to imagine yourself in each setting—as a victim finding voice, as an offender facing the consequences of your actions, as a community member supporting healing, as a facilitator guiding the process. For restorative justice is not merely something to be studied; it is something to be experienced, embodied, and lived.

Victim-Offender Mediation: The Process and Benefits of Direct Mediation

Let us begin with the practice that, in many ways, launched the modern restorative justice movement: victim-offender mediation. This practice brings together those most directly affected by crime—the victim and the offender—in a facilitated dialogue aimed at addressing harm, promoting accountability, and fostering healing.

Understanding Victim-Offender Mediation

Victim-offender mediation (VOM) is a structured process in which a trained mediator facilitates a face-to-face meeting between victim and offender. The goal is not to determine guilt or innocence—that has typically been established already—but to address the harm that has occurred and to find ways to make things right.

Direct Dialogue

At the heart of VOM is direct dialogue. Victim and offender sit together, sometimes with support persons present, and speak directly to one another about what happened. This is not a conversation mediated by lawyers or filtered through court proceedings but a genuine human encounter between the person who caused harm and the person who was harmed.

This directness is essential to the restorative power of VOM. When victims speak directly to offenders, they are not testifying to a third party but confronting the person responsible. When offenders respond directly to victims, they are not pleading to a judge but answering to the person they have harmed. This direct encounter has a power that no mediated communication can replicate.

Restorative Goals

The goals of VOM are fundamentally restorative. The process seeks to address the harm caused by the offense—not in the abstract but in concrete terms that matter to the actual victim. It seeks to promote accountability—not the passive acceptance of punishment but the active taking of responsibility. And it seeks to facilitate healing—for both victim and offender—through genuine dialogue and mutual understanding.

These goals distinguish VOM from other forms of alternative dispute resolution. Mediation in civil cases aims at settlement—resolving the dispute so that both parties can move on. VOM aims at something deeper: transformation of the relationship between victim and offender, healing of the wounds that crime has inflicted, restoration of the humanity of both parties.

Key Principles of Victim-Offender Mediation

Several key principles guide the practice of victim-offender mediation.

Voluntary Participation

Participation in VOM must be voluntary for both parties. No one should be coerced or pressured into meeting with the person who harmed them or whom they have harmed. This voluntariness is essential to the integrity of the process. When participation is coerced, the dialogue that follows cannot be genuine. The victim's voice may be silenced by fear; the offender's expressions of remorse may be mere performance.

Voluntariness also means that participants can withdraw at any time. The process belongs to them, not to the mediator or the referring agency. If at any point a participant feels unable to continue, they should be free to end the session without penalty.

Confidentiality

The mediation process is confidential. What is said in the session stays in the session. This confidentiality allows participants to speak openly and honestly without fear that their words will be used against them in other contexts. Victims can express their anger, their pain, their fears without worrying that these emotions will be reported to others. Offenders can admit wrongdoing, express remorse, and make commitments without fear that these admissions will lead to additional charges.

Confidentiality has limits, of course. If someone discloses an intention to cause future harm, the mediator may have a duty to report. But within these bounds, confidentiality creates the safe space necessary for genuine dialogue.

Neutral Facilitation

A trained mediator facilitates the session, ensuring that the dialogue remains balanced and respectful. The mediator is not a judge; they do not determine who is right or what should happen. They are not an advocate; they do not take sides or push for particular outcomes. Their role is to create conditions in which victims and offenders can speak and listen to one another, to guide the conversation when it falters, to ensure that both parties have opportunity to be heard.

This neutrality is essential to the fairness of the process. Victims need to know that the mediator is not aligned with the offender. Offenders need to know that the mediator is not aligned with the victim. Both need to trust that the mediator will hold the process fairly, ensuring that each can speak and be heard.

The Process of Victim-Offender Mediation

Victim-offender mediation typically proceeds through several stages, each designed to build trust, promote understanding, and facilitate resolution.

Referral and Intake

The process begins with referral. Cases may be referred to VOM by various sources: the justice system (prosecutors, judges, probation officers), community organizations, or the parties themselves. Some programs accept referrals only after guilt has been established; others accept cases at earlier stages, as diversion from prosecution.

Once a referral is received, the mediator conducts an intake assessment. This assessment determines whether the case is suitable for mediation. The mediator evaluates the willingness of both parties to participate, assesses any potential risks or safety concerns, and gathers basic information about the offense and its impact.

Not all cases are suitable for VOM. Cases involving extreme power imbalances, ongoing intimidation, or parties who are unwilling or unable to participate safely may need to be handled through other means. The intake assessment helps identify these situations and ensure that only appropriate cases proceed.

Preparation

If the case is accepted, the mediator meets separately with victim and offender to prepare them for the mediation session. These pre-mediation meetings are crucial to the success of the process. They build trust between the mediator and each party. They explain the process in detail, answering questions and addressing concerns. They help each party think through what they want to say and what they hope to achieve.

In these meetings, the mediator also establishes ground rules for the mediation session. These rules typically include expectations of respect, honesty, and confidentiality. Both parties must agree to these ground rules before the session can proceed.

The preparation phase also allows the mediator to assess each party's readiness. A victim who is too traumatized, too angry, or too fearful may not be ready for direct encounter. An offender who is still in denial, who blames the victim, who shows no sign of remorse may not be ready either. The mediator may recommend postponing the session until both parties are ready, or may determine that mediation is not appropriate at this time.

Mediation Session

The mediation session itself is the heart of the process. The mediator brings victim and offender together in a neutral, comfortable setting. The session begins with the mediator explaining the purpose and ground rules, ensuring that both parties understand how the session will proceed.

The mediator then invites the victim to speak. This is often the first time the victim has had opportunity to tell their story directly to the person responsible. They may describe what happened, how it has affected them, what they have experienced since. They may express anger, fear, grief—whatever emotions are present. The mediator ensures that the victim can speak without interruption, that their words are heard.

When the victim has finished, the mediator invites the offender to respond. The offender may acknowledge what the victim has said, may express remorse, may offer explanations—though not excuses. They may ask questions, seeking to understand more fully the impact of their actions.

This dialogue continues, with the mediator guiding as needed, until both parties feel they have said what they need to say and heard what they need to hear. The conversation may range widely—from the specifics of the offense to the broader context of both parties' lives, from the immediate harm to the possibilities for repair.

If the dialogue leads to a desire for reparation, the mediator helps the parties develop a plan. This plan may include financial restitution, community service, apologies, or other actions. The plan must be mutually agreed upon—not imposed by the mediator or by one party on the other. It must be specific, achievable, and responsive to the victim's needs.

Follow-Up

After the session, the mediator follows up with both parties to ensure that any agreements are being implemented and to provide ongoing support if needed. This follow-up may be brief or extended, depending on the complexity of the case and the needs of the parties.

If difficulties arise—if the offender fails to complete agreed actions, if the victim experiences new difficulties—the mediator may arrange additional sessions or refer the parties to other resources. The goal is to support the healing process beyond the initial meeting.

Benefits of Victim-Offender Mediation

The benefits of victim-offender mediation are extensive, touching victims, offenders, and communities in profound ways.

Benefits for Victims

For victims, VOM offers empowerment. In the conventional justice system, victims are often marginalized, reduced to the role of witness, their needs secondary to the state's interest in punishment. In VOM, victims are central. They have a voice; they can tell their story directly to the person responsible. They have a role; they can participate in determining what will make things right. This empowerment counteracts the powerlessness that crime often creates.

VOM also facilitates emotional healing. Victims have opportunity to confront the offender, to ask questions that have haunted them, to receive answers that can bring closure. They may learn why they were targeted, whether the offender understands what they have done, whether the offender feels remorse. These answers, when offered sincerely, can be profoundly healing.

The opportunity to negotiate restitution and reparation addresses victims' material needs. They may receive compensation for losses, help with repairs, or other forms of practical support. This restitution cannot undo the harm, but it can address its practical consequences.

Research consistently shows high levels of victim satisfaction with VOM. Victims who participate report feeling heard, respected, and satisfied with the process. They are more likely to feel that justice has been done than victims whose cases go through conventional channels.

Benefits for Offenders

For offenders, VOM encourages genuine accountability. Facing the person they have harmed, hearing directly about the impact of their actions, they cannot remain abstractly detached. The harm becomes real, personal, undeniable. This encounter often evokes remorse and a genuine desire to make amends.

The process also promotes personal growth and rehabilitation. Offenders who participate in VOM often develop empathy—the capacity to understand and share the feelings of others. This empathy is a powerful protective factor against future offending. They also develop a sense of responsibility and a commitment to making things right—attitudes that support pro-social behavior.

Research indicates that participation in VOM can reduce recidivism. Offenders who meet their victims, who understand the harm they have caused, who make commitments to repair that harm, are less likely to reoffend than those who simply go through the conventional system. The encounter changes them in ways that punishment alone cannot.

Benefits for the Community

VOM also benefits the broader community. By addressing the underlying harm caused by crime and promoting reconciliation between victim and offender, it helps restore social harmony. Conflicts that might otherwise fester are resolved. Relationships that might remain broken are healed.

The process also fosters community involvement in justice. When VOM is supported by community organizations, when community members serve as mediators or support persons, the community takes ownership of the justice process. This involvement reinforces collective responsibility and builds social capital.

Finally, VOM offers an alternative to the traditional justice system—one that is more humane, more effective, and more restorative. By demonstrating that justice can be done differently, it opens possibilities for broader reform.

Case Studies and Examples

Let us consider some real-world examples that illustrate the power of victim-offender mediation.

Juvenile Offenders

In a case from a restorative justice program in California, a teenage boy was referred for vandalizing a local park. He had spray-painted graffiti on playground equipment, causing significant damage and upsetting community members who used the park.

Through VOM, the boy met with several community members who used the park regularly. They described how the vandalism had affected them—the disappointment of children who couldn't use the equipment, the anger of parents who felt their neighborhood was being disrespected, the cost of repairs that would have to be paid by the community.

The boy, who had initially dismissed his actions as "just graffiti," was visibly affected by these stories. He expressed genuine remorse and agreed to participate in cleaning up the park and repainting the damaged equipment. He also agreed to meet with a youth mentor who would help him find positive ways to express himself.

The outcome was transformative. The community members felt heard and respected. They supported the boy's rehabilitation, greeting him by name when they saw him working in the park. The boy developed a sense of connection to his community and a commitment to contributing positively. He did not reoffend.

Property Crimes

In a burglary case from a program in England, a woman's home had been broken into while she was at work. The offender had stolen electronics, jewelry, and other valuables. The woman was left feeling violated and unsafe in her own home.

Through VOM, she met with the offender. She was able to tell him how the burglary had affected her—the fear she felt coming home alone, the sleepless nights, the sense that her private space had been invaded. She asked why he had chosen her home, whether he had watched her, whether he might return.

The offender, a young man struggling with addiction, explained that he hadn't chosen her specifically; he had been looking for easy targets to support his drug habit. He expressed deep remorse for the fear he had caused. He had already been convicted and was serving a sentence, but he wanted to make amends.

Together, they developed a plan. The offender, through his work in prison, would earn money to provide restitution. He would also participate in drug treatment and, upon release, would volunteer with a community safety program. The woman, while still fearful, felt some closure. She had confronted the person who harmed her, received answers to her questions, and seen genuine remorse.

Violent Crimes

Perhaps most remarkably, VOM has been used in cases of violent crime. In a case from a program in Texas, a man who had been assaulted in a bar fight met with the man who had attacked him. The assault had left him with lasting physical injuries and psychological trauma.

The mediation was carefully prepared, with extensive pre-mediation meetings and support persons present. The victim described the ongoing effects of the assault—the pain, the difficulty working, the fear of crowded places. The offender, who had been drinking heavily that night, expressed profound remorse. He had no memory of the assault but accepted responsibility for what he had done.

Together, they developed an agreement. The offender would pay restitution to cover medical expenses. He would complete an anger management program. He would also speak to youth groups about the dangers of alcohol and violence, sharing his story to prevent others from making similar choices.

The victim reported that the mediation had been healing. He no longer felt like a victim but like someone who had contributed to preventing future violence. The offender reported that facing his victim had changed him in ways that prison never could.

Challenges and Considerations in Victim-Offender Mediation

While VOM offers significant benefits, it also presents challenges that must be addressed.

Ensuring Voluntary Participation

The most fundamental challenge is ensuring that participation is truly voluntary. Victims may feel pressured to participate—by family, by community, by the justice system. Offenders may feel that participation is their only chance for leniency. These pressures can undermine the authenticity of the process.

Mediators must be vigilant in assessing voluntariness. They must ensure that participants understand that they can withdraw at any time without penalty. They must create conditions in which participants feel free to say no.

Addressing Power Imbalances

Power imbalances between victims and offenders can distort the mediation process. An offender who is more articulate, more confident, or more socially skilled may dominate the conversation. A victim who is traumatized, intimidated, or marginalized may be unable to speak freely.

Mediators must be trained to recognize and address these imbalances. This may involve meeting separately with parties beforehand, providing support persons during the session, ensuring that both have opportunity to speak, and intervening when necessary to maintain balance.

Safety and Emotional Well-Being

Ensuring the physical and emotional safety of all participants is paramount. Mediators must screen cases for safety concerns, ensure that the setting is secure, and be prepared to intervene if emotions become overwhelming.

Providing access to emotional support and counseling is also important. Participants may experience strong emotions during and after the session. Having support available can help them process these emotions and continue their healing journey.

Cultural Sensitivity

VOM must be culturally sensitive and appropriate for the participants involved. Different cultures have different norms around communication, conflict, and relationship. What is respectful in one culture may be disrespectful in another.

Mediators should be trained in cultural competence and should engage with community leaders and members to ensure that their practices are respectful and responsive. Adapting the process to fit cultural contexts while maintaining restorative principles is essential.

Family Group Conferencing: Involving Family and Community in the Resolution Process

We turn now to a practice that expands participation beyond victim and offender to include their families and support networks: family group conferencing. This model recognizes that families are deeply affected by crime and have crucial roles to play in accountability and healing.

Understanding Family Group Conferencing

Family group conferencing (FGC) originated in New Zealand, drawing on Maori traditions of family and community involvement in justice. It has since been adopted in various forms around the world, particularly in youth justice systems.

Inclusive Process

FGC brings together the victim, the offender, their families, and other supportive community members in a structured meeting. The goal is to address the harm caused, develop a plan for making amends, and support the offender's rehabilitation and reintegration.

The inclusion of family is not merely symbolic. Families have knowledge of the offender that no professional can match. They have relationships that can support or undermine change. They have a stake in outcomes that outsiders do not share. By involving them directly, FGC harnesses these resources for restorative purposes.

Restorative Goals

The goals of FGC are the same as those of restorative justice generally: to address harm, promote accountability, and foster healing. But FGC pursues these goals through the distinctive mechanism of family and community engagement. The plan that emerges from an FGC is not imposed by professionals but developed by those who know the offender best and will live with the consequences.

Key Principles of Family Group Conferencing

Several key principles guide the practice of family group conferencing.

Family and Community Involvement

FGC recognizes that families and communities are essential to justice. They are not merely sources of information or support but active participants in the process. Their involvement ensures that decisions reflect the values and needs of those closest to the situation.

Collective Decision-Making

Decisions in FGC are made collaboratively, with input from all participants. No single party—not the victim, not the offender, not the professionals—has veto power. The goal is to reach consensus on a plan that addresses the harm and supports rehabilitation.

Empowerment

FGC empowers families and communities to take an active role in justice. Rather than having decisions made for them by distant authorities, they are given responsibility for developing and implementing plans. This empowerment builds capacity and strengthens community bonds.

The Process of Family Group Conferencing

The FGC process typically proceeds through several stages.

Referral and Preparation

Cases are referred to FGC by the justice system, social services, or community organizations. A coordinator assesses suitability, considering the willingness of parties to participate and any safety concerns.

Preparation meetings are held separately with the victim, the offender, and their families. These meetings explain the process, address concerns, and prepare participants for the conference. They also gather information that will be shared during the conference.

The Conference

The conference itself begins with an opening by the facilitator, who outlines the purpose and ground rules. All participants are introduced, and the facilitator explains how the session will proceed.

The victim is then invited to speak about the impact of the offense. Family and community members may also share their perspectives. The offender is given opportunity to respond, to acknowledge the harm, and to express remorse.

After this sharing, the family and supporters of the offender meet privately to develop a plan. This private family time is a distinctive feature of FGC. It allows the family to discuss frankly what they can offer, what they need, and what should be included in the plan. The facilitator remains available for questions but does not participate in the discussion.

When the family has developed a draft plan, the full conference reconvenes. The plan is presented and discussed. The victim must agree that the plan adequately addresses the harm; if not, the plan is revised. When consensus is reached, the plan is finalized and commitments are made.

Follow-Up

After the conference, the facilitator and community members monitor implementation of the plan. Follow-up meetings may be held to review progress and address any challenges. The goal is to ensure that agreements are kept and that the healing process continues.

Benefits of Family Group Conferencing

FGC offers numerous benefits for victims, offenders, and communities.

Benefits for Victims

Victims in FGC have opportunity to express their feelings, ask questions, and participate in developing the plan. They are not passive recipients of justice but active contributors. This participation can be empowering and healing.

The presence of family and community provides additional support. Victims are not alone in facing the offender; they have their own supporters present. This support can make the process feel safer and more manageable.

Victims may also receive tangible restitution and support from the offender's family. Families may contribute resources, offer practical assistance, or provide ongoing support that goes beyond what the offender alone could provide.

Benefits for Offenders

FGC encourages offenders to take responsibility in the presence of those who matter most to them. Facing not only the victim but also their own family, they cannot hide behind excuses or justifications. The shame of disappointing loved ones can be a powerful motivator for change.

The involvement of family provides a supportive environment for rehabilitation. Families can offer encouragement, accountability, and practical help. They can monitor progress and intervene when problems arise. This ongoing support is often more effective than professional supervision alone.

The process also promotes personal growth. Offenders who participate in FGC often develop empathy, remorse, and commitment to change. They see the impact of their actions on those they love and want to make things right.

Benefits for the Community

FGC strengthens relationships within families and communities. The process brings people together, fosters communication, and builds trust. Families learn that they can work together to address problems. Communities learn that they have resources to respond to harm.

The process also restores social harmony by addressing the underlying harm and promoting reconciliation. Conflicts that might otherwise divide families and communities are resolved constructively. Relationships are healed, not further damaged.

Finally, FGC offers an alternative to the traditional justice system—one that is more community-based, more restorative, and often more effective, particularly for young offenders.

Case Studies and Examples

Let us consider some examples of FGC in practice.

Youth Offenses

In a case from New Zealand, a teenage boy was referred for vandalism. He had spray-painted graffiti on several buildings in his neighborhood, causing significant damage and anger among residents.

An FGC was convened, bringing together the boy, his parents, the victims (representatives of the affected businesses and residents), and a youth justice coordinator. The victims described how the vandalism had affected them—the cost of repairs, the sense of disrespect, the fear that their neighborhood was becoming unsafe.

The boy's parents were visibly distressed. They had not known about their son's activities and were shocked by the impact. They expressed their disappointment and their determination to support him in making things right.

During private family time, the family developed a plan. The boy would apologize personally to each victim. He would participate in cleaning up the graffiti under supervision. He would also complete a course on art and community, learning how to express himself constructively. His parents would monitor his activities and ensure he stayed out of trouble.

The victims accepted the plan. They appreciated the personal apologies and the visible work of cleaning up. The boy, seeing the impact on his parents and the victims, expressed genuine remorse. He completed his commitments and did not reoffend.

Domestic Disputes

In a case from a program in England, a family was in crisis after an incident of domestic violence. A teenage son had assaulted his mother during an argument. The mother was traumatized; the father was angry; the son was defensive and ashamed.

An FGC was convened, bringing together the son, his parents, his grandparents, and a community support worker. The mother described the fear and pain she had experienced. The father expressed his anger and his concern for the family. The grandparents shared their sorrow at seeing the family torn apart.

The son, hearing his mother's words and seeing his family's distress, broke down. He acknowledged what he had done and expressed genuine remorse. He wanted to make things right but didn't know how.

During private family time, the family developed a comprehensive plan. The son would move temporarily to his grandparents' home to give everyone space. He would participate in anger management counseling. The family would attend counseling together. Regular family meetings would be held to address issues before they escalated.

The plan was implemented with support from the community worker. Over time, relationships healed. The son returned home, and the family developed new patterns of communication. The process, though painful, had brought them closer together.

School-Based Incidents

In a school setting in Pennsylvania, an FGC was used to address a bullying incident. Several students had been systematically harassing a classmate, causing significant emotional distress.

The conference brought together the victims, the offenders, their parents, teachers, and school administrators. The victims described the pain of being excluded, mocked, and threatened. The offenders initially minimized their actions, but hearing the victims' stories and seeing their parents' disappointment, they began to understand the impact.

During private family time, each offender's family developed plans for accountability and change. These included apologies, participation in peer mentoring, and community service at the school. The families also committed to monitoring their children's behavior and maintaining communication with the school.

The plan was accepted by all parties. The offenders completed their commitments, and the bullying stopped. The victims reported feeling safer and more supported. The school implemented ongoing restorative practices to prevent future incidents.

Challenges and Considerations in Family Group Conferencing

FGC presents several challenges that must be addressed.

Ensuring Voluntary Participation

As with VOM, participation in FGC must be voluntary. Families may feel pressured to participate, particularly if the alternative is formal court processing. Facilitators must ensure that all participants understand their rights and feel free to decline.

Addressing Power Imbalances

Power imbalances can affect FGC as well. Within families, parents may dominate, children may be silenced. Between families and victims, differences in social status, education, or confidence can distort the process. Facilitators must be skilled in recognizing and addressing these imbalances.

Creating a Safe Environment

Ensuring safety is paramount, particularly in cases involving domestic violence or ongoing conflict. Facilitators must assess safety concerns carefully and create conditions in which all participants feel secure.

Cultural Sensitivity

FGC must be culturally appropriate. The model originated in Maori culture and may need adaptation for other contexts. Engaging with community leaders and members can help ensure that the process respects local norms and values.

Circle Processes: The Role of Restorative Circles in Conflict Resolution

We turn now to one of the most ancient and powerful restorative practices: circle processes. Rooted in indigenous traditions, circles have been adapted for diverse contexts—from schools to prisons, from communities to workplaces.

Understanding Circle Processes

Restorative circles bring together all those affected by a conflict or harm in a structured, inclusive dialogue. The circle format itself is significant: seated in a circle, all participants are visible to one another, all are equal, none is at the head.

Structured Dialogue

Circle processes follow a structured format designed to ensure that all voices are heard. A talking piece is passed from person to person; only the person holding the piece may speak. This simple mechanism prevents domination by the loudest or most powerful and ensures that even the quietest have opportunity to speak.

The facilitator, often called a keeper, guides the process but does not control it. The circle belongs to all participants; the keeper's role is to hold the space, to ensure that the process remains respectful, and to intervene when necessary.

Restorative Goals

The goals of circle processes are the same as those of restorative justice generally: to address harm, promote accountability, and facilitate healing and reconciliation. But circles pursue these goals through the distinctive mechanism of collective dialogue and shared responsibility.

Key Principles of Circle Processes

Several key principles guide circle processes.

Equality and Respect

In the circle, all participants are equal. No one has more authority, more power, more right to speak than anyone else. This equality is symbolized by the circle itself and reinforced by the talking piece.

Respect is fundamental. Participants commit to speaking and listening respectfully, to honoring one another's experiences, to treating each other with dignity even when they disagree.

Inclusivity and Participation

Circle processes are inclusive. All those affected by the conflict or harm are invited to participate—not only the direct parties but also family members, friends, neighbors, professionals, anyone with a stake in the outcome. This inclusivity ensures that multiple perspectives are heard and that solutions reflect the needs of all.

Shared Responsibility

The circle emphasizes shared responsibility for addressing harm and finding solutions. The problem belongs to the community, not merely to individuals. The solution must be found together, not imposed by authorities. This shared responsibility builds community capacity and strengthens social bonds.

The Process of Circle Processes

Circle processes typically proceed through several stages.

Preparation

The keeper identifies all those who should be invited—all who have been affected, all who have a stake in the outcome. This may include the direct parties, their families, community members, professionals, and others.

The keeper meets individually with participants to explain the process, address concerns, and prepare them for the circle. These preparation meetings are essential for building trust and ensuring that participants understand what to expect.

Ground rules are established. These typically include respect, confidentiality, use of the talking piece, and commitment to the process. All participants must agree to these rules.

Opening the Circle

The circle begins with an opening ceremony or statement that sets the tone. This may include a reading, a moment of silence, a prayer, or simply words of welcome. The purpose is to create a sacred space, separate from ordinary life, where honest dialogue can occur.

Participants introduce themselves. The keeper explains the purpose of the circle and reviews the ground rules. The talking piece is introduced.

Facilitated Dialogue

The keeper poses a question or invites sharing on a particular topic. The talking piece passes around the circle; each person speaks when they hold the piece, others listen. This continues through multiple rounds, each focusing on a different aspect of the situation.

Participants share their stories, their feelings, their perspectives. They describe how the conflict or harm has affected them. They listen as others do the same. Over time, understanding deepens, empathy grows, and common ground emerges.

When the dialogue has run its course, the keeper invites participants to explore solutions. What would make things right? What is needed for healing? What can each person contribute? Again, the talking piece passes, and ideas are shared.

Developing Agreements

Through dialogue, consensus begins to emerge. The keeper helps participants articulate agreements—specific actions that will address the harm, promote healing, and prevent recurrence. These agreements are recorded and reviewed to ensure that all are clear about what has been decided.

All participants commit to the agreements. The circle affirms their commitment, often with a ceremony or closing ritual.

Closing the Circle

The circle closes with a reflection on the process and expressions of gratitude. Participants may share what the experience has meant to them, what they have learned, what they will take forward. The keeper ensures that everyone feels heard and respected before the circle ends.

Follow-up plans are outlined. The keeper or other participants may monitor implementation of agreements and provide ongoing support.

Benefits of Circle Processes

Circle processes offer numerous benefits for victims, offenders, and communities.

Benefits for Victims

Victims in circles have opportunity to speak and be heard in the presence of their community. They are not isolated with their pain but surrounded by people who care. The collective response validates their experience and supports their healing.

The circle also gives victims a voice in determining outcomes. They participate in developing agreements that address their needs. This participation can be empowering, restoring a sense of control that crime took away.

Benefits for Offenders

Offenders in circles face not only the victim but also their community. They hear multiple perspectives on the impact of their actions. This collective witness can deepen understanding and motivate genuine change.

The circle also provides support for rehabilitation. Community members may offer encouragement, accountability, and practical help. Offenders are not cast out but held, supported in their efforts to change.

Benefits for the Community

Circles strengthen community bonds. People who participate in circles develop relationships, build trust, and learn to work together. These bonds serve them well beyond any particular conflict.

The process also builds community capacity to address conflicts constructively. Communities that use circles become more resilient, more able to solve their own problems without relying on outside authorities.

Case Studies and Examples

Let us consider some examples of circle processes in practice.

School-Based Circles

In a school in Minnesota, a circle was used to address ongoing conflict between two groups of students. Tensions had been building for months, with occasional fights and constant hostility. The school climate was suffering.

The circle included the students involved, their friends, teachers, administrators, and parents. Over several sessions, participants shared their perspectives, their fears, their hopes. They began to understand how the conflict had affected everyone—not just those directly involved.

Through dialogue, they developed agreements: the students would participate in a peer mediation program; teachers would facilitate regular check-ins; the school would implement restorative practices school-wide. The conflict de-escalated, and relationships slowly improved.

Community Disputes

In a neighborhood in Ontario, a circle was convened to address ongoing disputes between neighbors. Complaints about noise, property lines, and parking had escalated into harassment and threats.

The circle brought together the neighbors, other community members, and a community police officer. Using a talking piece, each person shared their experience of the conflict—not accusations but stories of how the situation affected their lives.

Over several hours, understanding grew. The neighbors discovered that some of their complaints were based on misunderstandings. They also discovered shared concerns about the neighborhood's safety and well-being.

Together, they developed a community agreement: guidelines for noise, respect for property, communication protocols for addressing future issues. They also planned a neighborhood gathering to build positive relationships. The conflicts subsided, and neighbors began to look out for one another.

Family Conflicts

In a family in Colorado, a circle was used to address conflict between a teenage daughter and her parents. The daughter was rebelling against rules she saw as unfair; the parents were frustrated by her defiance.

The circle included the daughter, her parents, her grandparents, and a family friend. Each shared their perspective—the daughter's need for autonomy, the parents' fear for her safety, the grandparents' concern for family unity.

Through dialogue, they came to understand one another's positions more deeply. The daughter saw that her parents' rules came from love, not control. The parents saw that their daughter needed more responsibility, not less.

They developed a family agreement: the daughter would have more freedom but also more accountability; the parents would trust her more but also maintain appropriate boundaries; all would commit to regular family meetings to address issues before they escalated. The family relationships improved, and conflicts decreased.

Challenges and Considerations in Circle Processes

Circle processes present several challenges.

Ensuring Voluntary Participation

As with other restorative practices, participation must be voluntary. Participants should not be coerced or pressured. The keeper must ensure that all are free to participate or withdraw as they choose.

Addressing Power Imbalances

Power imbalances can affect circles as well. Some participants may dominate; others may be silenced. The keeper must be skilled in recognizing and addressing these imbalances, using the talking piece and other interventions to ensure equitable participation.

Creating a Safe Environment

Ensuring safety is paramount. Participants must feel physically and emotionally safe to share honestly. The keeper must assess safety concerns, create appropriate conditions, and be prepared to intervene if necessary.

Cultural Sensitivity

Circles must be culturally appropriate. The practice originated in indigenous cultures and should be adapted with respect for those traditions. Engaging with community leaders and members can help ensure that circles are respectful and responsive to local norms.

Community Restorative Boards: Community-Driven Justice Practices

Finally, we consider community restorative boards—practices that place community members at the center of the justice process.

Understanding Community Restorative Boards

Community restorative boards (CRBs) are composed of trained community volunteers who meet with offenders to address harm and develop restorative agreements. These boards represent the community's direct involvement in justice.

Community-Driven Process

CRBs are community-driven. Board members are volunteers from the community where the offense occurred. They bring local knowledge, relationships, and values to the process. They represent the community's stake in justice and its capacity to respond to harm.

Restorative Goals

The goals of CRBs are the same as those of restorative justice generally: to address harm, promote accountability, and facilitate healing and reintegration. But CRBs pursue these goals through the distinctive mechanism of community engagement and oversight.

Key Principles of Community Restorative Boards

Several key principles guide CRBs.

Community Involvement

CRBs embody the principle that communities should be involved in justice. Board members are not professionals imported from outside but neighbors and fellow citizens. Their involvement ensures that justice reflects community values and that outcomes have community support.

Collective Responsibility

CRBs operate on the principle of collective responsibility. The community, through its representatives, takes responsibility for addressing harm and supporting rehabilitation. This collective responsibility strengthens community bonds and builds capacity.

Restorative Justice

CRBs are grounded in restorative justice principles. They focus on repairing harm, restoring relationships, and promoting healing. They seek outcomes that address the needs of victims, hold offenders accountable, and strengthen the community.

The Process of Community Restorative Boards

CRBs typically proceed through several stages.

Referral and Intake

Cases are referred to CRBs by the justice system, schools, social services, or community organizations. The board assesses suitability, considering the willingness of parties to participate and any safety concerns.

Board members conduct an intake assessment, gathering information about the case and the perspectives of those involved. This assessment prepares them for the board meeting.

Preparation

Board members meet to discuss the case, establish ground rules, and plan the meeting. They ensure that all participants understand the process and are prepared to engage constructively.

The facilitator contacts the victim, offender, and relevant community members to explain the process, address concerns, and invite them to the meeting.

The Board Meeting

The meeting begins with introductions and an explanation of the purpose and ground rules. The facilitator ensures that all participants understand how the session will proceed.

Participants share their perspectives on the offense, its impact, and their feelings. The board facilitates open communication and mutual understanding, ensuring that all voices are heard.

Together, participants explore solutions—ways to address the harm and promote healing. The board encourages creative thinking and collaborative problem-solving.

The board works with participants to develop a restorative agreement. This agreement outlines specific actions the offender will take to make amends and support their rehabilitation. It may include restitution, community service, apologies, counseling, or other elements.

Follow-Up

Board members monitor implementation of the restorative agreement. They provide support and address any challenges that arise. Follow-up meetings may be held to review progress and make adjustments if necessary.

Benefits of Community Restorative Boards

CRBs offer numerous benefits for victims, offenders, and communities.

Benefits for Victims

Victims in CRBs have opportunity to express their feelings, ask questions, and participate in developing the agreement. They are not passive recipients of justice but active contributors.

The presence of community members provides additional support and validation. Victims know that their community cares about what happened and is committed to making things right.

Benefits for Offenders

Offenders in CRBs face community members who represent the values and expectations of their neighbors. This encounter can be more powerful than facing a distant judge or probation officer. It communicates that the community is watching, that it cares, that it expects accountability.

The board also provides support for rehabilitation. Members may offer encouragement, connect offenders with resources, and monitor progress. This ongoing support can be crucial for successful reintegration.

Benefits for the Community

CRBs strengthen community bonds. Board members develop relationships with one another and with the participants they serve. Communities learn that they have the capacity to address harm themselves.

The process also builds trust in the justice system. When communities are involved in justice, they see that the system can work for them. This trust supports future cooperation and engagement.

Case Studies and Examples

Let us consider some examples of CRBs in practice.

Juvenile Offenses

In a community in Vermont, a juvenile offender was referred to a CRB after vandalizing a neighbor's property. The board included several community volunteers, including a teacher, a business owner, and a retired police officer.

In the board meeting, the neighbor described the impact of the vandalism—the cost of repairs, the sense of violation, the fear that her property was not safe. The offender, a teenager, initially seemed indifferent, but as he heard the neighbor's story and saw the board members' serious attention, he began to understand.

Together, they developed an agreement. The offender would apologize personally to the neighbor. He would repair the damage under the neighbor's supervision. He would also complete community service at a local park and meet with a mentor from the board for ongoing support.

The offender completed his commitments. The neighbor reported feeling satisfied with the outcome. The board members continued to check in with the offender, who did not reoffend.

Neighborhood Disputes

In a community in Oregon, a CRB was convened to address ongoing disputes between neighbors. Complaints about noise, trash, and parking had escalated into harassment and threats.

The board brought together the neighbors, other community members, and a community police officer. In the meeting, each person shared their experience of the conflict. The board facilitated dialogue, helping participants move beyond accusations to genuine communication.

Through this process, the neighbors discovered that some of their complaints were based on misunderstandings. They also discovered shared concerns about the neighborhood's safety and well-being.

Together, they developed a community agreement: guidelines for noise and trash, respect for parking, communication protocols for addressing future issues. The board agreed to monitor implementation and reconvene if necessary. The conflicts subsided, and neighbors began to look out for one another.

School Incidents

In a school in Colorado, a CRB addressed a conflict involving several students and staff members. The board included students, teachers, parents, and community members.

The meeting brought together all those involved in the conflict. Each shared their perspective—the students described feeling disrespected; the teachers described feeling undermined; parents described their concern for their children's education.

Through facilitated dialogue, understanding grew. The students recognized that their behavior had made it difficult for teachers to teach; the teachers recognized that their approach had alienated students. Both wanted the same thing—a positive learning environment.

Together, they developed a plan. The students would participate in a peer mediation program. The teachers would receive training in restorative practices. The school would implement regular circles to build community and address issues before they escalated. The board agreed to monitor progress and reconvene if needed.

Challenges and Considerations in Community Restorative Boards

CRBs present several challenges.

Ensuring Voluntary Participation

Participation must be voluntary. Offenders should not be coerced into appearing before a board; victims should not be pressured to participate. The board must ensure that all participants understand their rights and feel free to choose.

Addressing Power Imbalances

Power imbalances can affect board meetings. Offenders may feel intimidated by a panel of adults; victims may feel silenced by their own trauma. Board members must be trained to recognize and address these imbalances, creating conditions for equitable participation.

Creating a Safe Environment

Ensuring safety is paramount. Board members must assess safety concerns, create appropriate conditions, and be prepared to intervene if necessary. Emotional support should be available for participants who need it.

Cultural Sensitivity

CRBs must be culturally appropriate. Board composition should reflect community diversity. Processes should respect cultural differences in communication, relationship, and conflict resolution. Engaging with community leaders and members can help ensure cultural sensitivity.

The Integration of Practices

As we have explored these four restorative practices—victim-offender mediation, family group conferencing, circle processes, and community restorative boards—we have seen how each embodies restorative principles in distinctive ways. VOM focuses on direct encounter between victim and offender. FGC expands participation to include families and support networks. Circles engage the broader community in collective dialogue. CRBs place community members at the center of decision-making.

These practices are not mutually exclusive. They can be combined, adapted, and integrated to meet the needs of particular situations. A case might begin with a circle to engage the community, move to mediation for direct victim-offender dialogue, and conclude with a restorative board to monitor agreements. The key is fidelity to restorative principles, not rigid adherence to any particular model.

The Psychological Foundations of Restorative Practices

The practices we have explored are grounded in psychological research about what promotes healing and change.

Trauma-Informed Practice

All restorative practices must be trauma-informed. Many victims (and some offenders) have experienced trauma that affects their ability to participate safely and effectively. Facilitators must understand trauma, recognize its signs, and create conditions that support rather than retraumatize participants.

Research on trauma shows that safety, choice, and control are essential for healing. Restorative practices that emphasize voluntary participation, informed consent, and participant control over outcomes align with these principles.

Procedural Justice

Research on procedural justice shows that people's satisfaction with legal processes depends not only on outcomes but on how those outcomes are reached. When people perceive that they have been treated fairly—with respect, with voice, with neutrality—they are more satisfied even with unfavorable outcomes.

Restorative practices excel on procedural justice dimensions. Participants have voice; they can tell their stories and express their views. They are treated with respect by facilitators and other participants. The process is neutral and transparent. This procedural justice contributes to the legitimacy and effectiveness of restorative outcomes.

Empathy and Moral Development

Research on empathy and moral development supports restorative approaches. Empathy can be cultivated through experience and practice. Restorative practices that bring victims and offenders into direct dialogue create powerful opportunities for empathy development.

Studies of moral development show that higher stages of moral reasoning involve greater capacity for perspective-taking and consideration of multiple viewpoints. Restorative dialogue, which requires participants to consider multiple perspectives and reason together about just outcomes, may support moral development.

The Theological Foundations of Restorative Practices

For those who approach restorative justice from a faith perspective, these practices have deep theological significance.

Encounter and Reconciliation

The biblical vision of reconciliation involves direct encounter between those who have been estranged. Jesus teaches that if you are offering your gift at the altar and remember that your brother has something against you, leave your gift there and first be reconciled to your brother (Matthew 5:23-24). This reconciliation requires direct engagement, not merely good intentions.

Restorative practices create the conditions for such encounter. They bring together those who have been separated by harm, creating space for truth-telling, acknowledgment, and the possibility of reconciliation.

Community and Covenant

The biblical understanding of community as covenant—a binding relationship between God and people, and among people themselves—provides a foundation for community-involved practices. When harm occurs, it breaches covenant. Restoration requires rebuilding covenant relationships.

Practices like circles and family group conferencing engage the community in this covenantal work. They bring together those bound by relationship to repair what has been broken, to restore what has been lost.

Justice and Mercy

The biblical vision holds justice and mercy together. God is both just and merciful; God's justice is not opposed to mercy but fulfilled in it. Restorative practices embody this integration. They hold offenders accountable while extending mercy; they address harm while offering hope for restoration.

Hospitality and Inclusion

The biblical practice of hospitality—welcoming the stranger, including the outsider—informs restorative inclusion. Practices that bring together victims, offenders, and community members embody hospitality, creating space for all to be heard and valued.

The Legal Dimensions of Restorative Practices

Restorative practices also have implications for legal systems.

Integration with Legal Processes

Restorative practices can be integrated with legal processes at various points: as diversion before formal charging, as a supplement to traditional processing, as part of sentencing, as a condition of probation, as part of reentry planning. Each point of integration requires careful attention to legal rights and procedural safeguards.

Many jurisdictions have developed protocols for integrating restorative practices. These protocols address issues such as confidentiality, admissibility of statements made in restorative processes, enforcement of restorative agreements, and relationship between restorative and legal outcomes.

Rights and Protections

Restorative practices must respect the legal rights of all participants. Victims have rights to information, participation, and protection. Offenders have rights to due process, to avoid self-incrimination, to legal counsel. These rights must be honored even as restorative processes proceed.

Facilitators must be trained to recognize when legal issues arise and to ensure that participants' rights are protected. They may need to work with legal professionals to ensure that restorative processes complement rather than conflict with legal requirements.

Policy and Legislation

Many jurisdictions have enacted legislation supporting restorative practices. New Zealand's Children, Young Persons, and Their Families Act 1989 made family group conferencing mandatory for most youth offenses. Canada's Youth Criminal Justice Act 2003 encourages restorative approaches. European Union directives promote restorative justice member-wide.

These legislative frameworks provide resources and guidance for implementing restorative practices while protecting participants' rights. They represent important steps toward integrating restorative justice into mainstream legal systems.

As we move forward into the remaining chapters, we will build on these practical foundations. We will examine case studies and real-world applications of restorative practices. We will explore benefits and challenges. We will consider restorative justice in legal systems, international contexts, and social justice movements. And we will look to the future, imagining how restorative practices might continue to transform our world.

The practices we have explored in this chapter—victim-offender mediation, family group conferencing, circle processes, and community restorative boards—are not merely techniques. They are embodiments of restorative values, expressions of restorative philosophy, instruments of restorative transformation. They are the means by which the vision of a restorative society can be realized, one encounter at a time.

CHAPTER 05

CASE STUDIES AND REAL-WORLD APPLICATIONS

We have journeyed together through the philosophical foundations of restorative justice, explored its core principles and values, and examined the practices and models that bring these principles to life. Now, dear reader, we arrive at a crucial question: Does restorative justice actually work? What happens when these principles and practices are implemented in real-world settings? How do they affect the lives of victims, offenders, and communities?

In this chapter, we will explore case studies and real-world applications of restorative justice across four key domains: the criminal justice system, schools and educational settings, workplaces and organizations, and community programs. Through these examples, we will see restorative justice in action—its successes, its challenges, and its transformative potential. We will draw on research and evaluation findings to understand what works, why it works, and under what conditions.

As we examine these cases, I invite you to consider not only the outcomes but the processes—the ways in which restorative principles were embodied, the challenges that arose, and the lessons learned. For restorative justice is not a formula to be applied mechanically but a living practice that must be adapted to each unique context.

Criminal Justice System: Implementation of Restorative Practices in Criminal Justice

Let us begin with the domain where restorative justice first gained modern prominence: the criminal justice system. Here, restorative practices have been implemented at every stage—from diversion before formal charging to post-sentencing programs within prisons. The results have been remarkable, though not without challenges.

Understanding Restorative Practices in Criminal Justice

Restorative justice in the criminal justice system represents a fundamental shift in how we understand and respond to crime. Rather than focusing solely on punishment, restorative practices prioritize healing, accountability, and the restoration of relationships. They aim to address the harm caused by crime and to rehabilitate offenders while involving the community in the justice process.

Key Principles of Restorative Practices

Three key principles guide restorative practices in criminal justice.

First is the victim-centered approach. Restorative practices focus on addressing the needs and experiences of victims, providing them with a voice and an opportunity for healing. This contrasts sharply with conventional justice, where victims are often marginalized, their needs secondary to the state's interest in punishment.

Research in victimology consistently shows that victims want more than punishment. They want acknowledgment of their suffering, answers to their questions, and opportunities to participate in determining what justice requires. Restorative practices respond to these needs.

Second is offender accountability. Offenders are encouraged to take responsibility for their actions, understand the impact of their behavior, and actively participate in making amends. This accountability is not passive acceptance of punishment but active engagement in restoration.

Psychological research on desistance—the process by which people stop offending—shows that internal motivation is more powerful than external coercion. When offenders understand the harm they have caused and choose to make amends, they are more likely to change than when they merely serve time.

Third is community involvement. The community plays a vital role in supporting victims, holding offenders accountable, and fostering social cohesion and healing. This involvement recognizes that crime affects not only individuals but the broader community, and that community resources are essential for restoration.

Sociological research on social capital demonstrates that communities with strong networks and collective efficacy are better able to prevent crime and support healing. Restorative practices build this social capital.

Types of Restorative Practices in Criminal Justice

Several types of restorative practices are used in criminal justice settings.

Victim-Offender Mediation (VOM) brings victims and offenders together in facilitated dialogue to address harm, promote understanding, and agree on reparative actions. This practice, which we explored in detail in Chapter 4, is one of the most widely used restorative interventions.

Restorative Circles involve victims, offenders, and community members in inclusive meetings to discuss the impact of the crime and develop a plan for resolution. Circles draw on indigenous traditions and are particularly effective for building community engagement.

Family Group Conferencing (FGC) brings together the victim, offender, their families, and community members to collaboratively address harm and support rehabilitation. Originating in New Zealand, FGC has been adopted in many jurisdictions, particularly for youth offenses.

Community Restorative Boards (CRBs) are community-driven boards that facilitate restorative processes and monitor the implementation of agreements. These boards embody the principle of community involvement in justice.

Benefits of Restorative Practices in Criminal Justice

The integration of restorative practices into criminal justice systems offers numerous benefits for victims, offenders, and communities.

Benefits for Victims

For victims, restorative practices provide empowerment and voice. Victims have opportunity to express their feelings, ask questions, and participate in the justice process. This participation counteracts the powerlessness that crime often creates and the marginalization that conventional justice can reinforce.

Research consistently shows that victims who participate in restorative processes report higher satisfaction than those whose cases go through conventional channels. They feel heard, respected, and involved in ways that traditional justice rarely provides.

Restorative practices also facilitate emotional healing. Victims receive emotional support and validation, helping them recover from the trauma of crime. The opportunity to confront the offender, to ask questions, and to receive answers can bring closure that punishment alone cannot provide.

Victims may also receive restitution and reparation through restorative processes. They can negotiate for compensation, apologies, or other forms of making amends that address their material and emotional needs. This restitution is not imposed by the state but agreed upon by the parties, making it more meaningful.

Benefits for Offenders

For offenders, restorative practices encourage genuine accountability. Facing the person they have harmed, hearing directly about the impact of their actions, they cannot remain abstractly detached. The harm becomes real, personal, undeniable.

Research on offender rehabilitation shows that this encounter can be transformative. Offenders who participate in restorative processes often develop empathy, remorse, and a genuine desire to change. This internal motivation is far more powerful than external coercion in producing lasting behavioral change.

Restorative practices also promote personal growth and rehabilitation. The process of taking responsibility, making amends, and being restored to community builds pro-social identity and commitment. Offenders see themselves differently—not as irredeemable criminals but as people capable of good.

Most importantly, restorative practices reduce recidivism. Multiple meta-analyses have found that restorative justice programs produce statistically significant reductions in reoffending compared to conventional processing. These effects are particularly strong for violent offenses—precisely the cases where one might expect restorative approaches to be least appropriate.

Finally, restorative practices support reintegration. Offenders receive support from their community, aiding their rehabilitation and reintegration into society. They are not cast out but welcomed back, their restoration celebrated rather than feared.

Benefits for the Community

For communities, restorative practices strengthen social bonds. By involving community members in the justice process, they build relationships, foster mutual support, and develop collective responsibility. These strengthened bonds make communities more resilient and better able to address future challenges.

Restorative practices also restore social harmony. By addressing the underlying harm and promoting reconciliation between victims, offenders, and the community, they heal the rifts that crime creates. Conflicts are resolved, not merely processed; relationships are restored, not further damaged.

Finally, restorative practices offer an alternative to the traditional justice system—one that is more humane, more effective, and more community-based. By demonstrating that justice can be done differently, they open possibilities for broader reform.

Case Studies and Examples

Let us now examine specific examples of restorative practices in criminal justice systems around the world.

New Zealand's Restorative Justice Programs

New Zealand has been a pioneer in integrating restorative justice into its criminal justice system. The country's approach is rooted in Maori traditions of family and community involvement in justice, which were formalized in the Children, Young Persons, and Their Families Act 1989.

The centerpiece of New Zealand's restorative approach is Family Group Conferencing (FGC). FGC is used extensively in cases involving juvenile offenders, and increasingly for adults as well. The process brings together the victim, the offender, their families, and community representatives to discuss the harm caused and develop a plan for making amends.

The FGC process follows a structured format. After preparation meetings with all parties, the conference convenes. The facilitator explains the purpose and ground rules. The victim describes the impact of the offense. The offender responds, often expressing remorse. Family and community members share their perspectives. The family then meets privately to develop a plan, which is presented to the full conference for discussion and agreement. The plan may include apologies, restitution, community service, or other actions.

Research on New Zealand's FGC program has documented impressive outcomes. Studies show higher levels of victim satisfaction compared to conventional court processing. Victims report feeling heard, respected, and involved in ways that traditional justice rarely provides.

Recidivism rates are also reduced. Young offenders who go through FGC are less likely to reoffend than those processed through conventional courts. The encounter with victims, the involvement of family, and the opportunity to make amends appear to promote genuine change.

The New Zealand experience demonstrates that restorative justice can be integrated into a mainstream criminal justice system at scale. FGC is not a marginal experiment but a central component of youth justice, handling thousands of cases each year. This integration required legislative change, substantial investment in training, and ongoing commitment from justice officials—but the results have justified the investment.

Canada's Victim-Offender Mediation Programs

Canada has implemented victim-offender mediation (VOM) programs in various jurisdictions, focusing on both juvenile and adult offenders. These programs draw on Canada's diverse cultural traditions, including indigenous practices of healing and reconciliation.

VOM sessions in Canada are facilitated by trained mediators who prepare both parties thoroughly before the meeting. The mediation itself provides a structured environment for victims to describe the impact of the offense and for offenders to respond, ask questions, and express remorse. Together, they develop a plan for reparation that addresses the victim's needs and the offender's capacities.

Research on Canadian VOM programs has shown impressive results. Victims report high levels of satisfaction, feeling that their voices were heard and their needs addressed. Offenders demonstrate increased accountability, understanding the impact of their actions in ways that conventional processing rarely achieves.

Recidivism rates are lower for offenders who participate in VOM compared to those processed through conventional courts. The encounter with victims, the opportunity to make amends, and the experience of being restored to community appear to promote lasting change.

Canada's experience also highlights the importance of cultural adaptation. Programs have been developed specifically for indigenous communities, incorporating traditional practices and involving elders in the process. These culturally adapted programs have been particularly effective, demonstrating that restorative justice must be responsive to local contexts.

United States Community Restorative Boards

Community Restorative Boards (CRBs) have been established in several states across the United States to address minor offenses and support offender rehabilitation. These programs embody the principle of community involvement in justice.

CRBs are composed of trained community volunteers who meet with offenders to discuss the harm caused and develop restorative agreements. The boards represent the community's stake in justice and its capacity to respond to harm. Offenders appear before their neighbors, not distant officials, making accountability concrete and personal.

The CRB process begins with referral from the justice system, typically for minor offenses that might otherwise result in probation or short jail sentences. Board members conduct an intake assessment, then meet with the offender to discuss the offense and its impact. Together, they develop a restorative agreement specifying actions the offender will take to make amends—restitution, community service, apologies, counseling. The board monitors implementation and reports back to the referring court.

Evaluation research on CRBs has documented positive outcomes. Recidivism rates are lower for offenders who go through CRBs compared to those processed conventionally. Victims report satisfaction with the process, particularly the opportunity to have their needs addressed. Community members value the opportunity to be involved in justice and report stronger connections to their neighbors.

CRBs also demonstrate the potential for restorative justice to reduce the burden on formal justice systems. By diverting minor cases from courts and probation, they free resources for more serious offenses. And by involving community volunteers, they leverage resources that would otherwise be unavailable.

South Africa's Truth and Reconciliation Commission

Perhaps the most ambitious application of restorative principles in criminal justice is South Africa's Truth and Reconciliation Commission (TRC), established to address the atrocities committed during apartheid.

The TRC was not a conventional court. It did not prosecute or punish perpetrators in the usual sense. Instead, it provided a forum for victims and perpetrators to share their experiences, seek forgiveness, and agree on reparative actions. Perpetrators who fully disclosed their political crimes could receive amnesty; victims could tell their stories and receive acknowledgment and reparations.

The TRC was grounded in the concept of *Ubuntu*—the African philosophy that emphasizes interconnectedness and shared humanity. Archbishop Desmond Tutu, who chaired the commission, explained that Ubuntu means "my humanity is caught up, is inextricably bound up, in yours." This philosophical foundation shaped the TRC's restorative approach.

The TRC's work was not without controversy. Some criticized the amnesty provisions as letting perpetrators off too easily. Others questioned whether truth-telling alone could constitute justice for victims of horrific violence. The commission faced enormous practical challenges, including limited resources, political pressure, and the sheer scale of the atrocities to be addressed.

Yet the TRC's achievements were remarkable. It provided a platform for thousands of victims to tell their stories, to be heard, to have their suffering acknowledged. It created a public record of apartheid-era atrocities, countering denial and establishing a foundation for historical truth. It demonstrated that restorative approaches could be applied at societal scale, in the aftermath of massive human rights violations.

The TRC has influenced subsequent truth commissions in countries around the world, from Rwanda to Sierra Leone to Canada. It stands as a powerful example of restorative justice in transitional contexts—a model for addressing systemic injustice and promoting national healing.

Challenges and Considerations in Implementing Restorative Practices

While restorative practices offer significant benefits, their implementation in criminal justice systems presents several challenges.

Ensuring Voluntary Participation

The most fundamental challenge is ensuring that participation is truly voluntary. Victims may feel pressured to participate—by family, by community, by the justice system. Offenders may feel that participation is their only chance for leniency. These pressures can undermine the authenticity of the process.

Programs must be designed to protect voluntariness. Participants must be fully informed about the process and its potential outcomes before agreeing to participate. They must understand that they can withdraw at any time without penalty. Facilitators must be vigilant in assessing whether participation is genuinely voluntary.

Addressing Power Imbalances

Power imbalances between victims and offenders can distort restorative processes. An offender who is more articulate, more confident, or more socially skilled may dominate the conversation. A victim who is traumatized, intimidated, or marginalized may be unable to speak freely.

Facilitators must be trained to recognize and address these imbalances. This may involve meeting separately with parties beforehand, providing support persons during the process, ensuring that both have opportunity to speak, and intervening when necessary to maintain balance. Creating a safe and equitable environment is essential for genuine dialogue.

Creating a Safe Environment

Ensuring the physical and emotional safety of all participants is paramount. Facilitators must screen cases for safety concerns, ensure that the setting is secure, and be prepared to intervene if emotions become overwhelming.

Providing access to emotional support and counseling is also important. Participants may experience strong emotions during and after restorative encounters. Having support available can help them process these emotions and continue their healing journey.

Cultural Sensitivity

Restorative practices must be culturally sensitive and appropriate for the participants involved. Different cultures have different norms around communication, conflict, and relationship. What is respectful in one culture may be disrespectful in another.

Facilitators should be trained in cultural competence and should engage with community leaders and members to ensure that their practices are respectful and responsive. Adapting processes to fit cultural contexts while maintaining restorative principles is essential.

Sustainability and Integration

Successful implementation of restorative practices requires institutional support. This includes training for facilitators, funding for programs, and policies that integrate restorative approaches into the criminal justice system. Without this support, programs may struggle to survive.

Ongoing evaluation is also essential. Regular assessment of restorative programs ensures their effectiveness, identifies challenges, and supports continuous improvement. Evaluation findings can also demonstrate the value of restorative approaches to funders, policymakers, and the public.

Schools and Educational Settings: Restorative Justice in Schools and Its Impact on Students

We turn now to another domain where restorative justice has been transformative: schools and educational settings. Here, restorative practices address disciplinary issues, improve school climate, and build supportive learning communities.

Understanding Restorative Justice in Schools

Restorative justice in schools involves practices that prioritize repairing harm, fostering understanding, and promoting a positive school climate. These practices aim to address disciplinary issues, improve student behavior, and build a supportive school community where all members can thrive.

Key Principles of Restorative Justice in Schools

Three key principles guide restorative practices in schools.

First is respect and dignity. Restorative practices emphasize treating all students with respect and dignity, recognizing their inherent worth. This contrasts with punitive approaches that can shame and stigmatize students, damaging their sense of self and connection to school.

Research in educational psychology shows that students who feel respected and valued are more engaged, more motivated, and more likely to succeed academically. Restorative practices create the conditions for this engagement.

Second is accountability and responsibility. Students are encouraged to take responsibility for their actions, understand the impact of their behavior, and make amends. This accountability is not about punishment but about learning and growth.

Developmental psychology research shows that adolescents are particularly responsive to opportunities for moral reflection and responsibility-taking. Restorative practices tap into this developmental potential.

Third is community and relationships. Building strong, positive relationships within the school community is a central focus. When students feel connected to teachers and peers, they are more likely to behave pro-socially and less likely to engage in harmful behavior.

Research on school climate consistently shows that positive relationships are the foundation of effective schools. Restorative practices build these relationships.

Types of Restorative Practices in Schools

Several types of restorative practices are used in schools.

Restorative circles are regularly scheduled gatherings where students and teachers discuss issues, resolve conflicts, and build community. Circles may be used proactively to strengthen relationships or responsively to address specific incidents.

Peer mediation involves trained student mediators who help their peers resolve conflicts through guided dialogue and problem-solving. Peer mediation empowers students to take ownership of conflict resolution and builds leadership skills.

Restorative conferences are facilitated meetings involving students, teachers, and sometimes parents to address specific incidents of harm and develop plans for resolution. Conferences are typically used for more serious incidents that affect the whole school community.

Restorative dialogue refers to one-on-one or small group discussions to address conflicts and misunderstandings, promoting empathy and understanding. These informal conversations can prevent conflicts from escalating.

Benefits of Restorative Justice in Schools

Implementing restorative practices in schools offers numerous benefits for students, teachers, and the broader school community.

Benefits for Students

For students, restorative practices improve behavior. By encouraging reflection on actions and their impact, they help students develop internal controls rather than merely complying with external rules. Students learn to make better choices, not just avoid punishment.

Research on school discipline shows that punitive approaches often fail to change behavior and may actually increase it by alienating students and reinforcing negative identities. Restorative practices, by contrast, promote genuine behavioral change.

Restorative practices also enhance social and emotional skills. Students learn empathy—understanding and sharing the feelings of others. They learn active listening—hearing what others say without judgment. They learn conflict resolution—finding solutions that address everyone's needs. These skills serve them throughout life.

Students also experience increased engagement. When school feels safe, supportive, and respectful, students are more motivated to attend and participate. They feel that they belong, that they matter, that their voices are heard. This engagement translates into better academic performance and higher graduation rates.

Finally, restorative practices reduce bullying. By addressing underlying causes—social dynamics, power imbalances, lack of empathy—rather than merely punishing individual incidents, they create a culture where bullying is less likely to occur. Students learn to treat one another with respect and to intervene when they see harm.

Benefits for Teachers

For teachers, restorative practices provide tools for better classroom management. Rather than relying on rewards and punishments, teachers can use restorative approaches to address behavioral issues constructively. This reduces disruptions and creates a more positive learning environment.

Teachers also build stronger relationships with students. When conflicts are addressed through dialogue rather than punishment, trust grows. Students see teachers as allies in their development, not adversaries to be resisted. These relationships make teaching more rewarding and effective.

Implementing restorative practices also involves ongoing professional development. Teachers learn new skills—facilitation, dialogue, conflict resolution—that enhance their practice. They become more confident in handling challenging situations and more effective in their work.

Benefits for the School Community

For the school community as a whole, restorative practices contribute to a positive school climate. Students feel safe, respected, and valued. Teachers feel supported and effective. Parents feel confident that their children are in good hands.

Restorative practices also engage parents and community members in the school. When families are involved in restorative processes, they become partners in education, not just consumers of services. This engagement strengthens the whole community.

Finally, restorative practices offer an alternative to punitive discipline. Suspensions and expulsions, which disproportionately affect students of color and those with disabilities, are reduced. Students remain in school, engaged in learning, rather than pushed out into the streets. This is not only more humane but more effective for promoting student success.

Case Studies and Examples

Let us examine specific examples of restorative practices in schools.

Restorative Circles at Edward W. Brooke Charter School

Edward W. Brooke Charter School in Boston, Massachusetts, implemented restorative circles to address behavioral issues and build a positive school culture. The school serves a diverse student population, many from historically marginalized communities.

The school scheduled regular restorative circles in every classroom. Students and teachers sat in a circle, used a talking piece, and followed structured protocols for sharing. Circles addressed a range of topics—academic challenges, interpersonal conflicts, community issues. They built relationships and created a sense of shared responsibility.

When conflicts arose, responsive circles were convened to address them. The affected students, their peers, and teachers came together to discuss what happened, how it affected everyone, and what needed to happen to make things right. These circles resolved conflicts constructively and restored relationships.

The results were impressive. Disciplinary referrals decreased significantly. Suspensions dropped dramatically. Students reported feeling safer and more connected to school. Teachers reported that classrooms were more peaceful and productive. The school climate improved markedly.

The Brooke Charter School experience demonstrates that restorative circles can be implemented effectively in urban schools serving challenging populations. It required commitment from leadership, training for staff, and patience as the approach was integrated into school culture—but the results justified the investment.

Peer Mediation Program at West Philadelphia High School

West Philadelphia High School introduced a peer mediation program to address conflicts and reduce violence among students. The school had experienced significant challenges with fighting and interpersonal violence, disrupting learning and creating an unsafe environment.

The program recruited and trained student mediators from diverse backgrounds. These students learned active listening, conflict resolution, and mediation skills. They practiced facilitating dialogue between peers in conflict, helping them understand each other's perspectives and find mutually acceptable solutions.

When conflicts arose, students could request mediation or be referred by teachers or administrators. The mediators, supervised by a coordinator, facilitated sessions in a neutral setting. They guided the parties through structured dialogue, ensuring that both could speak and be heard. They helped them develop agreements to resolve the conflict and prevent recurrence.

The results were striking. Fights and violent incidents decreased significantly. Students reported feeling safer and more supported. The mediators developed leadership skills and gained respect from peers. The school climate improved, and learning became more possible.

The West Philadelphia experience demonstrates the power of peer mediation. By empowering students to resolve their own conflicts, the program built ownership and capacity. Students learned skills that would serve them throughout life. And the school became a more peaceful, productive place.

Restorative Conferences at Denver Public Schools

Denver Public Schools implemented restorative conferences as part of their discipline policy to address serious behavioral incidents. The district had been struggling with high suspension rates, particularly among students of color, and was seeking more effective alternatives.

Under the new policy, restorative conferences were offered as an alternative to suspension for many offenses. When a serious incident occurred, the involved students, their families, teachers, and sometimes administrators would come together in a facilitated conference. They would discuss what happened, how it affected everyone, and what needed to happen to make things right.

The conferences followed a structured format. A trained facilitator prepared all parties beforehand. The conference opened with ground rules and introductions. The affected students described the impact of the incident. The responsible students responded, often expressing remorse. Families shared their perspectives. Together, they developed a plan for making amends and preventing recurrence.

Evaluation of the program showed impressive results. Suspensions and expulsions decreased significantly. Students who participated in conferences were less likely to reoffend than those who received traditional discipline. Families reported satisfaction with the process, feeling that their voices were heard and their needs addressed. School administrators appreciated having an alternative to suspension that kept students in school and addressed underlying issues.

The Denver experience demonstrates that restorative conferences can be integrated into school discipline policies at scale. It required training for facilitators, support from administrators, and commitment to the process—but the results justified the investment.

Whole-School Restorative Approach at Oakland Unified School District

Oakland Unified School District in California adopted a whole-school restorative approach to create a positive and supportive school climate. The district serves a diverse, largely low-income student population and had been struggling with high suspension rates and poor school climate.

The district's approach was comprehensive. They provided extensive training for all staff—teachers, administrators, counselors, security personnel—in restorative principles and practices. They integrated restorative practices into the curriculum, teaching students conflict resolution and communication skills. They engaged parents and community members in restorative processes, building partnerships for student success.

Schools in the district implemented restorative circles, peer mediation, restorative conferences, and other practices. They used data to track disciplinary incidents and outcomes, continuously improving their approaches. They built restorative culture over time, not overnight.

The results were remarkable. Disciplinary actions decreased dramatically. Suspensions and expulsions dropped, particularly among students of color who had been disproportionately affected. Academic outcomes improved—test scores, graduation rates, college attendance. Students reported feeling safer, more respected, more connected to school. Teachers reported that classrooms were more peaceful and productive.

The Oakland experience demonstrates that whole-school restorative approaches can transform educational environments. It required sustained commitment, substantial investment in training and support, and patience as culture shifted—but the results were transformative.

Challenges and Considerations in Implementing Restorative Practices

Implementing restorative practices in schools presents several challenges.

Ensuring Buy-In and Support

Successful implementation requires buy-in from both staff and students. Teachers may be skeptical of new approaches, particularly if they have experienced failed reforms in the past. Students may be wary of processes that feel unfamiliar or uncomfortable.

Building understanding and commitment to restorative principles is essential. This requires ongoing communication, opportunities for input, and visible support from leadership. When teachers and students understand why restorative practices matter and how they work, they are more likely to embrace them.

Leadership support is crucial. Principals and district administrators must provide resources, training, and policy changes to support restorative practices. They must model restorative values in their own interactions and hold the vision for school transformation.

Providing Training and Professional Development

Implementing restorative practices requires ongoing training for teachers, staff, and students. Facilitating circles, mediating conflicts, and conducting conferences are skills that must be learned and practiced. One-time workshops are insufficient; ongoing support and coaching are essential.

Schools must allocate resources for this training. This may require reallocating funds from other priorities, seeking grants, or partnering with community organizations. Without adequate training, restorative practices may be implemented poorly and produce disappointing results.

Addressing Power Imbalances

Power imbalances between students, teachers, and other participants can affect restorative processes. Teachers may dominate; students may be silenced. Facilitators must be skilled in recognizing and addressing these imbalances, creating conditions for equitable participation.

Providing support and advocacy for vulnerable students can help. Students who are marginalized—because of race, class, disability, or other factors—may need additional support to participate fully. Schools must ensure that restorative practices do not reproduce the inequalities they seek to address.

Creating a Safe Environment

Ensuring physical and emotional safety is paramount. Participants must feel secure enough to share honestly. Facilitators must create safe and respectful environments for restorative dialogue.

Providing access to emotional support and counseling can help students process their feelings and engage more fully. Some conflicts involve deep trauma that requires professional support. Schools must have resources available to meet these needs.

Cultural Sensitivity

Restorative practices must be culturally sensitive and appropriate for diverse student populations. Different cultures have different norms around communication, conflict, and relationship. Practices that work well in one cultural context may be ineffective or even harmful in another.

Facilitators should be trained in cultural competence and should engage with families and community members to ensure that practices are respectful and responsive. Adapting practices to fit cultural contexts while maintaining restorative principles is essential.

Workplace and Organizations: Restorative Approaches in Resolving Workplace Conflicts

We turn now to a third domain where restorative practices are increasingly being applied: workplaces and organizations. Here, restorative approaches address conflicts, improve employee relations, and build positive organizational cultures.

Understanding Restorative Approaches in the Workplace

Restorative approaches in the workplace focus on repairing harm, promoting understanding, and restoring relationships. These methods are used to address various conflicts, ranging from interpersonal disputes to systemic issues within the organization.

Key Principles of Restorative Approaches

Three key principles guide restorative approaches in the workplace.

First is respect and dignity. Treating all employees with respect and recognizing their inherent worth is fundamental. When conflicts arise, this respect must be maintained even as harm is addressed.

Research in organizational psychology shows that employees who feel respected are more engaged, more productive, and more loyal. Restorative practices build this respect.

Second is accountability and responsibility. Employees are encouraged to take responsibility for their actions and their impact on others. This accountability is not about blame but about learning and growth.

Organizational research shows that cultures of accountability—where people own their mistakes and work to correct them—are more effective than cultures of blame, where people hide errors and deflect responsibility. Restorative practices build accountability.

Third is community and relationships. Building strong, positive relationships within the workplace fosters a sense of belonging and mutual support. When relationships are strong, conflicts are less likely to arise and easier to resolve when they do.

Research on organizational culture consistently shows that positive relationships are the foundation of effective organizations. Restorative practices build these relationships.

Types of Restorative Practices in the Workplace

Several types of restorative practices are used in workplace settings.

Restorative circles are facilitated meetings where employees can discuss issues, resolve conflicts, and build community. Circles may be used proactively to strengthen relationships or responsively to address specific incidents.

Mediation involves a neutral third party who helps conflicting parties reach a mutually acceptable resolution through guided dialogue. Mediation is particularly useful for interpersonal conflicts that are not affecting the broader organization.

Restorative conferences are structured meetings involving the parties in conflict, their supporters, and a facilitator to address harm and develop a plan for making amends. Conferences are typically used for more serious incidents that affect multiple people.

Restorative dialogue refers to one-on-one or small group discussions to address conflicts and misunderstandings, promoting empathy and understanding. These informal conversations can prevent conflicts from escalating.

Benefits of Restorative Approaches in the Workplace

Implementing restorative practices in the workplace offers numerous benefits for employees, managers, and organizations.

Benefits for Employees

For employees, restorative practices improve relationships. By addressing conflicts constructively, they help repair and strengthen connections among colleagues. This makes work more pleasant and productive.

Employees also develop enhanced communication and conflict resolution skills. Through participation in restorative processes, they learn to express themselves clearly, listen actively, and find solutions that work for everyone. These skills benefit them throughout their careers.

Restorative practices also increase engagement and morale. When employees feel that conflicts will be addressed fairly and constructively, they are more committed to their work and their organization. Turnover and absenteeism decrease.

Finally, restorative practices provide a platform for addressing workplace harassment and discrimination. Rather than ignoring these issues or handling them through formal complaints that can be adversarial and traumatizing, restorative approaches create space for dialogue, understanding, and resolution. This can be particularly valuable for addressing subtle or systemic issues that formal processes struggle to handle.

Benefits for Managers

For managers, restorative approaches provide tools for effective conflict resolution. Rather than spending excessive time on unresolved disputes or relying on formal processes that can be costly and damaging, managers can use restorative practices to address issues early and constructively.

Managers who use restorative practices also build trust and credibility with their teams. When employees see that conflicts are handled fairly and that relationships matter, they trust their leaders more. This trust makes teams more cohesive and productive.

Implementing restorative practices also involves ongoing professional development for managers. They learn facilitation, communication, and conflict resolution skills that enhance their leadership. They become more confident and effective in their roles.

Benefits for the Organization

For organizations, restorative practices contribute to improved organizational culture. When employees feel valued, respected, and heard, culture becomes more positive. This positivity attracts talent, retains employees, and enhances performance.

Restorative practices also enhance productivity. When conflicts are resolved quickly and constructively, teams can focus on their work rather than being distracted by interpersonal issues. A harmonious workplace is a productive workplace.

Organizations also reduce legal risks by addressing conflicts through restorative practices. When issues are resolved informally, they are less likely to escalate to formal complaints, grievances, or lawsuits. This saves time, money, and reputational damage.

Finally, organizations that implement restorative practices demonstrate commitment to ethical and socially responsible business practices. This enhances their reputation with customers, investors, and the public. It positions them as leaders in creating positive workplaces.

Case Studies and Examples

Let us examine specific examples of restorative practices in workplace settings.

Restorative Circles at Google

Google, the technology giant, implemented restorative circles to address interpersonal conflicts and improve team dynamics within its diverse workforce. The company recognized that even highly skilled employees could struggle with collaboration when conflicts arose.

Trained mediators facilitated restorative circles for teams experiencing difficulties. In these circles, team members sat together, used a talking piece, and followed structured protocols for sharing. They discussed challenges, expressed feelings, and worked collaboratively to find solutions.

The circles created safe space for honest communication. Team members who had been in conflict could express their perspectives and hear those of others. Misunderstandings were clarified, hurts were acknowledged, and relationships began to heal.

The results were positive. Communication improved within teams. Relationships strengthened. Employee satisfaction and engagement increased. Teams became more cohesive and productive.

The Google experience demonstrates that restorative circles can be effective even in fast-paced, high-pressure corporate environments. It required commitment from leadership, skilled facilitation, and willingness from employees to engage—but the benefits justified the investment.

Mediation Program at Coca-Cola

Coca-Cola introduced a mediation program to resolve workplace conflicts and promote a positive organizational culture. The company recognized that unresolved conflicts were costing time, money, and employee morale.

Trained mediators, drawn from within the organization and from external providers, facilitated confidential mediation sessions for employees in conflict. The mediators guided parties through structured dialogue, helping them understand each other's perspectives and develop mutually acceptable resolutions.

The mediation program addressed a wide range of conflicts—interpersonal disputes, team disagreements, management-employee tensions. It provided an alternative to formal complaints and grievances, resolving issues before they escalated.

The results were impressive. Formal grievances and disciplinary actions decreased significantly. Employee relations improved. Job satisfaction increased. The program saved time and money while building a more positive workplace culture.

The Coca-Cola experience demonstrates that mediation can be integrated into corporate human resources practices at scale. It required training mediators, promoting the program to employees, and ensuring confidentiality and trust—but the results were substantial.

Restorative Conferences at Kaiser Permanente

Kaiser Permanente, the healthcare giant, implemented restorative conferences to address incidents of workplace harassment and discrimination. The organization recognized that traditional complaint processes were often inadequate for addressing these complex issues.

When harassment or discrimination occurred, affected employees could request a restorative conference. Trained facilitators brought together the parties involved, their supporters, and sometimes organizational representatives. In structured meetings, they discussed the impact of the behavior, explored underlying issues, and developed plans for making amends and preventing recurrence.

The conferences provided a alternative to formal complaints. Rather than an adversarial process focused on determining blame and imposing punishment, they offered a collaborative process focused on understanding, accountability, and healing. This was particularly valuable in cases where the parties had ongoing working relationships.

The results were encouraging. Harassment complaints decreased. Workplace climate improved. Trust between employees and management increased. Participants reported that the conferences helped them understand each other and move forward constructively.

The Kaiser experience demonstrates that restorative conferences can be effective for addressing serious workplace issues like harassment and discrimination. It required skilled facilitation, careful preparation, and commitment to the process—but the outcomes justified the effort.

Whole-Organization Restorative Approach at Patagonia

Patagonia, the outdoor clothing company known for its commitment to social and environmental responsibility, adopted a whole-organization restorative approach to create a supportive and inclusive workplace culture. The company recognized that its values should be reflected in how it handled conflicts and relationships.

The company provided extensive training for all staff in restorative principles and practices. It integrated restorative approaches into its policies and procedures, ensuring that conflicts would be addressed constructively. It engaged employees in regular restorative circles and dialogues, building relationships and addressing issues before they escalated.

The whole-organization approach meant that restorative practices were not just a program but a way of being. Employees at all levels learned to communicate openly, address conflicts directly, and support one another. The culture became more collaborative, more supportive, more inclusive.

The results were impressive. Employee engagement increased. Retention rates improved. The organizational culture became stronger and more cohesive. Patagonia's reputation as a great place to work was enhanced.

The Patagonia experience demonstrates that whole-organization restorative approaches can transform workplace culture. It required sustained commitment, substantial investment in training, and patience as culture shifted—but the results were transformative.

Challenges and Considerations in Implementing Restorative Practices

Implementing restorative practices in workplaces presents several challenges.

Ensuring Buy-In and Support

Successful implementation requires buy-in from both employees and management. Employees may be skeptical of new approaches, particularly if they have experienced failed initiatives in the past. Managers may be resistant to processes that feel unfamiliar or time-consuming.

Building understanding and commitment to restorative principles is essential. This requires ongoing communication, opportunities for input, and visible support from leadership.

When employees and managers understand why restorative practices matter and how they work, they are more likely to embrace them.

Leadership support is crucial. Organizational leaders must provide resources, training, and policy changes to support restorative practices. They must model restorative values in their own interactions and hold the vision for cultural transformation.

Providing Training and Professional Development

Implementing restorative practices requires ongoing training for employees and managers. Facilitating circles, mediating conflicts, and conducting conferences are skills that must be learned and practiced. One-time workshops are insufficient; ongoing support and coaching are essential.

Organizations must allocate resources for this training. This may require reallocating funds from other priorities, investing in external providers, or building internal capacity. Without adequate training, restorative practices may be implemented poorly and produce disappointing results.

Addressing Power Imbalances

Power imbalances between employees, managers, and other participants can affect restorative processes. Managers may dominate; employees may be silenced. Facilitators must be skilled in recognizing and addressing these imbalances, creating conditions for equitable participation.

Providing support and advocacy for vulnerable employees can help. Those who are marginalized—because of race, gender, position, or other factors—may need additional support to participate fully. Organizations must ensure that restorative practices do not reproduce the inequalities they seek to address.

Creating a Safe Environment

Ensuring physical and emotional safety is paramount. Participants must feel secure enough to share honestly. Facilitators must create safe and respectful environments for restorative dialogue.

Providing access to emotional support and counseling can help employees process their feelings and engage more fully. Some conflicts involve deep trauma that requires professional support. Organizations must have resources available to meet these needs.

Cultural Sensitivity

Restorative practices must be culturally sensitive and appropriate for diverse employee populations. Different cultures have different norms around communication, conflict, and relationship. Practices that work well in one cultural context may be ineffective or even harmful in another.

Facilitators should be trained in cultural competence and should engage with employees from diverse backgrounds to ensure that practices are respectful and responsive. Adapting practices to fit cultural contexts while maintaining restorative principles is essential.

Community Programs: Successful Community-Based Restorative Justice Programs

Finally, we turn to community-based restorative justice programs—initiatives that engage community members directly in addressing harm, supporting victims, and rehabilitating offenders.

Understanding Community-Based Restorative Justice Programs

Community-based restorative justice programs emphasize the active involvement of community members in the justice process. These programs are rooted in the belief that the community plays a vital role in maintaining social harmony and addressing harm.

Key Principles of Community-Based Restorative Justice

Three key principles guide community-based restorative justice.

First is community involvement. The active participation of community members is essential in addressing harm and supporting the justice process. Communities have knowledge, relationships, and resources that outsiders lack. Their involvement makes justice more effective and more legitimate.

Second is restorative justice. These programs focus on repairing harm, promoting accountability, and facilitating healing for all parties involved. They embody the restorative principles we have explored throughout this book.

Third is collective responsibility. Community-based programs encourage a sense of collective responsibility, where the community works together to support victims and offenders. This responsibility strengthens community bonds and builds capacity to address future challenges.

Types of Community-Based Restorative Justice Programs

Several types of community-based restorative justice programs exist.

Restorative circles bring together community members, victims, and offenders to discuss issues, resolve conflicts, and build community. Circles draw on indigenous traditions and are particularly effective for engaging diverse participants.

Community Restorative Boards are composed of community volunteers who facilitate restorative processes and monitor the implementation of agreements. These boards represent the community's direct involvement in justice.

Family Group Conferencing involves the victim, offender, their families, and community members in meetings to collaboratively address harm and support rehabilitation. Conferencing harnesses family and community resources for restorative purposes.

Victim-Offender Mediation provides facilitated dialogues between victims and offenders to address harm, promote understanding, and agree on reparative actions. When embedded in community programs, mediation benefits from community support and oversight.

Benefits of Community-Based Restorative Justice Programs

Implementing restorative justice at the community level offers numerous benefits for victims, offenders, and communities.

Benefits for Victims

For victims, community-based programs provide empowerment and voice. Victims have opportunity to express their feelings, ask questions, and participate actively in the justice process. This participation counteracts the powerlessness that crime often creates.

The supportive environment of community programs contributes to emotional healing. When offenders acknowledge harm in the presence of community members, victims feel validated. Their suffering is recognized as real and significant.

Victims may also receive tangible restitution and support from offenders and the community. Community members may contribute resources, offer practical assistance, or provide ongoing support that addresses victims' material and emotional needs.

Benefits for Offenders

For offenders, community-based programs encourage accountability and responsibility. Facing not only the victim but also community members, they cannot hide behind excuses or justifications. The harm becomes real and undeniable.

The involvement of community members provides a supportive environment for rehabilitation and reintegration. Offenders are not cast out but held, supported in their efforts to change. Community members may offer encouragement, accountability, and practical help.

The process promotes personal growth, empathy, and positive behavioral change. Offenders who participate in community-based programs often develop new understanding and commitment to pro-social behavior. Recidivism is reduced.

Benefits for the Community

For communities, these programs strengthen social bonds. When community members work together to address harm, they develop relationships, build trust, and learn to rely on one another. These bonds make communities more resilient.

Community-based programs also restore social harmony. By addressing underlying harm and promoting reconciliation, they heal the rifts that crime creates. Conflicts are resolved, not merely processed; relationships are restored, not further damaged.

Finally, these programs offer an alternative to the traditional justice system—one that is more restorative, more community-based, and often more effective. By demonstrating that communities can address their own problems, they build capacity and confidence.

Case Studies and Examples

Let us examine specific examples of community-based restorative justice programs.

Community Restorative Boards in Vermont

Vermont has implemented Community Restorative Boards (CRBs) as part of its statewide restorative justice initiatives. The program involves community volunteers in addressing low-level offenses, diverting cases from conventional court processing.

CRBs are composed of trained volunteers from the local community. When an offender is referred, board members meet with them to discuss the offense and its impact. Together, they develop a restorative agreement specifying actions the offender will take to make amends—restitution, community service, apologies, counseling. The board monitors implementation and reports back to the referring court.

The process involves victims as well. Victims are invited to participate, to share their perspectives, and to contribute to the agreement. Their involvement ensures that the agreement addresses their needs.

Evaluation of Vermont's CRBs has documented impressive outcomes. Recidivism rates are lower for offenders who go through CRBs compared to those processed conventionally. Victims report satisfaction with the process, feeling that their voices were heard and their needs addressed. Community members value the opportunity to be involved in justice and report stronger connections to their neighbors.

The Vermont experience demonstrates that CRBs can be implemented statewide, serving diverse communities from rural to urban. It requires training for volunteers, coordination with courts, and ongoing support—but the results justify the investment.

Restorative Circles in Brazil

Brazil has adopted restorative circles in various communities to address conflicts and promote social harmony. The program, implemented in partnership with community organizations and the justice system, brings restorative practices to neighborhoods affected by violence and crime.

Trained mediators facilitate restorative circles in community settings. The circles bring together those affected by conflicts—victims, offenders, family members, neighbors—to discuss what happened, share feelings, and collaboratively find solutions. The process is inclusive, participatory, and focused on healing.

The circles address a wide range of issues—neighborhood disputes, family conflicts, school-based incidents, even more serious crimes. They provide an alternative to violence and formal justice, engaging communities in solving their own problems.

Evaluation of the Brazilian program has shown promising results. Communication improves within communities. Relationships strengthen. Conflicts are resolved constructively. Violence and crime decrease. Participants report satisfaction with the process and its outcomes.

The Brazilian experience demonstrates that restorative circles can be effective in diverse cultural contexts, including communities affected by significant violence and poverty. It requires skilled facilitation, community engagement, and patience—but the results are transformative.

Family Group Conferencing in New Zealand

We have already discussed New Zealand's Family Group Conferencing program in the context of criminal justice. But FGC is also a community-based program, rooted in Maori traditions and implemented with community involvement.

FGC brings together victims, offenders, their families, and community representatives to address harm and develop plans for making amends. The process is collaborative, inclusive, and focused on restoration. Families are given private time to develop plans, ensuring that their knowledge and resources are fully engaged.

The community involvement in FGC is essential. Community representatives bring local knowledge and relationships. They offer support to both victims and offenders. They ensure that agreements reflect community values and have community backing.

Research on New Zealand's FGC program has documented impressive outcomes. Victims report high levels of satisfaction. Recidivism rates are reduced. Offenders are rehabilitated and reintegrated. Communities are strengthened.

The New Zealand experience demonstrates that FGC can be implemented at scale, serving as a central component of the justice system rather than a marginal alternative. It required legislative change, substantial investment, and ongoing commitment—but the results have been transformative.

Victim-Offender Mediation in Canada

Canada's victim-offender mediation programs, which we discussed earlier, are also community-based. Many are implemented by community organizations, with community volunteers serving as mediators and supporters.

These programs bring victims and offenders together in facilitated dialogue to address harm and develop reparative agreements. The process is voluntary, confidential, and focused on healing. Community involvement ensures that outcomes have local support and that resources are available for implementation.

Canadian VOM programs have been particularly effective in indigenous communities, where they are often integrated with traditional healing practices. Elders may participate, ceremonies may be incorporated, and the process may be adapted to fit cultural norms. These culturally adapted programs have been especially successful.

Research on Canadian VOM programs shows high levels of victim satisfaction, increased offender accountability, and reduced recidivism. The community-based nature of the programs contributes to these outcomes by ensuring local relevance and support.

The Canadian experience demonstrates that VOM can be implemented effectively in diverse community contexts, with adaptations to fit local needs and cultures. It requires skilled facilitators, community engagement, and ongoing support—but the results are substantial.

Challenges and Considerations in Implementing Community-Based Programs

Implementing community-based restorative justice programs presents several challenges.

Ensuring Voluntary Participation

As with all restorative practices, participation must be truly voluntary. Community members should not be pressured to participate; offenders should not feel coerced. Programs must be designed to protect voluntariness and ensure informed decision-making.

Addressing Power Imbalances

Power imbalances within communities can affect restorative processes. Some individuals or groups may have more influence, more resources, more voice. Others may be marginalized or silenced. Facilitators must be skilled in recognizing and addressing these imbalances.

Creating a Safe Environment

Ensuring safety is paramount. Community settings may lack the security of formal institutions. Facilitators must assess safety concerns, create appropriate conditions, and be prepared to intervene if necessary.

Cultural Sensitivity

Community-based programs must be culturally appropriate. Different communities have different norms, values, and traditions. Programs must be adapted to fit local contexts while maintaining restorative principles. Engaging community leaders and members in program design is essential.

Sustainability and Integration

Community-based programs require institutional support to survive. This includes training for facilitators, funding for operations, and policies that integrate restorative approaches into the broader justice system. Without this support, programs may struggle to maintain momentum.

Ongoing evaluation is also essential. Regular assessment ensures effectiveness, identifies challenges, and supports continuous improvement. Evaluation findings can also demonstrate value to funders, policymakers, and the community.

The Integration of Law, Psychology, Philosophy, and Theology

As we have explored these case studies and real-world applications, we have seen how restorative justice draws on multiple disciplines to achieve its transformative potential.

Legal Integration

In each domain—criminal justice, schools, workplaces, communities—restorative practices must be integrated with legal frameworks. This requires attention to rights, procedures, and outcomes. In criminal justice, restorative processes must respect victims' rights, offenders' due process, and the public's interest in safety. In schools, they must align with education laws and policies. In workplaces, they must comply with employment regulations. In communities, they must work alongside formal justice systems.

Successful integration requires collaboration between restorative practitioners and legal professionals. Judges, prosecutors, defense attorneys, and police must understand restorative principles and support restorative processes. Policies must be developed that authorize restorative approaches while protecting participants' rights. Legislation may be needed to provide funding and legitimacy.

Psychological Foundations

The case studies we have examined also demonstrate the psychological foundations of restorative justice. Victims heal when they are heard, validated, and empowered. Offenders change when they understand harm, develop empathy, and make amends. Communities strengthen when they work together to address problems.

Research in trauma, moral development, procedural justice, and desistance supports these observations. Restorative practices align with what psychology tells us about human healing and change. They work with the grain of human nature, not against it.

Philosophical Underpinnings

The philosophical principles we explored in earlier chapters—relational ethics, communitarianism, virtue ethics, restorative ontology, ethical responsibility, dialogical ethics—are not merely abstract ideas. They are lived in these case studies. When victims and offenders meet in mediation, they embody relational ethics. When communities gather in circles, they practice communitarianism. When offenders take responsibility and make amends, they develop virtue. When healing occurs, restorative ontology is confirmed.

Theological Dimensions

For those who approach restorative justice from a faith perspective, these case studies also demonstrate theological truths. The biblical vision of *shalom*—peace, wholeness, right relationship—is realized when victims heal, offenders change, and communities strengthen. The reconciling work of God in Christ is mirrored when those who have been estranged are brought together. The hospitality of God's kingdom is practiced when communities welcome back those who have caused harm.

The South African TRC, with its grounding in *Ubuntu* and its commitment to truth and reconciliation, exemplifies this theological dimension. The Maori-influenced FGC in New Zealand embodies indigenous spiritual traditions. The circles in Brazil draw on deep human values that transcend particular religions. Restorative justice, while not dependent on any particular faith, resonates with the deepest teachings of many traditions.

As we move forward into the remaining chapters, we will build on these real-world applications. We will examine the benefits and challenges of restorative justice more systematically. We will explore its relationship to legal systems, international contexts, and social justice. And we will look to the future, imagining how restorative justice might continue to transform our world.

The case studies we have examined in this chapter demonstrate that restorative justice is not merely a theory but a practice—a way of responding to harm that has been tested in diverse contexts and found effective. From New Zealand to Canada, from schools to workplaces, from community programs to truth commissions, restorative practices are healing wounds, restoring relationships, and building stronger, more just communities. This is the promise of restorative justice—a promise being fulfilled, one case at a time, around the world.

CHAPTER 06

BENEFITS AND CHALLENGES

We have journeyed together through the philosophical foundations of restorative justice, explored its core principles and values, examined the practices and models that bring these principles to life, and studied real-world applications across multiple domains. Now, dear reader, we arrive at a critical juncture: the honest assessment of benefits and challenges. For restorative justice, like any transformative endeavor, is not without its complexities, limitations, and controversies. A mature understanding requires us to look clearly at both its remarkable achievements and the obstacles it faces.

In this chapter, we will explore the positive outcomes that restorative justice produces for victims, offenders, and communities—outcomes that are supported by a growing body of research and real-world evidence. We will then examine the common challenges that arise in implementing restorative practices, along with strategies for overcoming them. Finally, we will engage honestly with the criticisms and controversies that surround restorative justice, addressing concerns with evidence and reasoned argument.

Throughout this exploration, I invite you to hold two truths together: restorative justice has demonstrated extraordinary potential to heal harm and transform lives, and it faces real challenges that must be acknowledged and addressed. Neither truth diminishes the other; together, they point toward the ongoing work of refinement and growth that any vital movement requires.

Positive Outcomes: Evidence of the Benefits of Restorative Justice for Victims, Offenders, and Communities

Let us begin with the good news—the abundant evidence that restorative justice produces meaningful, measurable benefits for all those affected by crime and conflict. These benefits are not merely anecdotal; they are documented by decades of research across multiple countries and contexts.

Positive Outcomes for Victims

Restorative justice practices prioritize the needs and experiences of victims in ways that conventional justice systems rarely do. The benefits for victims are profound and multifaceted.

Empowerment and Voice

In conventional criminal justice, victims are often marginalized. They may testify as witnesses, but they have no formal role in determining outcomes. Their needs and perspectives are secondary to the state's interest in punishment. This marginalization can compound the trauma of victimization, leaving victims feeling powerless and unheard.

Restorative justice changes this fundamentally. Victims are given an active voice in the process. They have the opportunity to express their feelings directly to the person who harmed them—to describe the impact of the crime, to ask questions that have haunted them, to articulate what they need to heal. This active participation counteracts the powerlessness that crime creates.

The psychological significance of this cannot be overstated. Research on procedural justice consistently shows that people's satisfaction with legal processes depends heavily on whether they feel they have been heard and treated with respect. When victims have voice, they perceive the process as fairer and more legitimate, regardless of the specific outcome.

Victims also experience validation when their experiences and emotions are acknowledged by the offender and the community. This acknowledgment says, in effect, "Your suffering matters. What happened to you is real and significant. You are not alone in recognizing this." This validation can be profoundly healing, countering the isolation that victims often feel.

Emotional Healing

Restorative justice facilitates emotional healing in ways that conventional justice cannot. Victims often carry deep emotional wounds—anger, fear, grief, shame—that punishment alone does not address. These wounds may persist long after the offender has been sentenced and incarcerated.

Participating in restorative processes helps victims achieve closure. They may learn, through direct dialogue, the reasons behind the offender's actions. They may receive apologies that acknowledge the harm and express genuine remorse. They may see the offender take concrete steps to make amends. These experiences can bring a sense of resolution that punishment cannot provide.

The supportive and empathetic environment of restorative justice also helps reduce trauma. Victims are surrounded by people who care—family members, community supporters, trained facilitators. They are not alone in their pain. This support can buffer the effects of trauma and promote recovery.

Research on victim satisfaction bears this out. Studies consistently show that victims who participate in restorative processes report higher levels of satisfaction than those whose cases go through conventional channels. They feel heard, respected, and involved. They are more likely to feel that justice has been done.

Restitution and Support

Restorative justice also addresses victims' practical needs. Through dialogue and negotiation, victims can secure material restitution—financial compensation for losses, return of stolen property, help with repairs or medical expenses. This restitution addresses the tangible harms that crime causes.

But the support victims receive goes beyond the material. The involvement of community members in restorative processes provides a network of support that can help victims rebuild their lives. Community members may offer practical assistance, emotional comfort, ongoing friendship. This support helps victims regain a sense of security and belonging.

The theological dimension of this victim-centered approach is significant. The Hebrew scriptures consistently emphasize God's concern for victims—the widow, the orphan, the stranger, the poor. The prophets call for justice that protects the vulnerable and addresses their needs. Restorative justice, in its focus on victims, aligns with this biblical vision.

Positive Outcomes for Offenders

Restorative justice also produces significant benefits for offenders—benefits that extend far beyond the avoidance of punishment.

Accountability and Responsibility

In conventional justice, accountability means accepting punishment. Offenders are passive recipients of sanctions imposed by the state. They may serve their time, but they often emerge unchanged, still lacking understanding of the harm they caused and still lacking motivation to change.

Restorative justice offers a different kind of accountability. Offenders are encouraged to acknowledge the harm they have caused and to understand its impact on the victim and the community. This acknowledgment is not merely cognitive but emotional—they come to feel the weight of what they have done.

Taking responsibility in restorative justice means active participation in making amends. Offenders are not passive recipients of punishment but active agents in restoration. They help develop plans for reparation, they carry out agreed actions, they demonstrate through their behavior that they are committed to change.

This active responsibility-taking is transformative. Psychological research on moral development shows that internal motivation is far more powerful than external coercion in producing lasting change. When offenders choose to make amends because they understand the harm and want to repair it, they are fundamentally different from offenders who merely serve their time.

Personal Growth and Rehabilitation

Restorative justice fosters personal growth in ways that conventional punishment rarely does. Through dialogue with victims, offenders develop empathy—the capacity to understand and share the feelings of others. They come to see victims not as abstract categories but as real people with real pain.

This empathy often evokes genuine remorse. Offenders feel sorrow not just for getting caught but for the harm they have caused. This remorse is not merely emotional but motivational—it drives them to change.

The focus on rehabilitation and personal growth encourages behavioral change. Offenders who participate in restorative processes are more likely to address underlying issues—addiction, mental health problems, lack of skills—that contributed to their offending. They are more likely to develop pro-social identities and commitments.

The evidence for reduced recidivism is compelling. Multiple meta-analyses have found that restorative justice programs produce statistically significant reductions in reoffending compared to conventional processing. These effects are particularly strong for violent offenses—precisely the cases where one might expect restorative approaches to be least appropriate.

The theological dimension of offender transformation is profound. The biblical concept of repentance—*metanoia*—involves a fundamental turning around, a change of heart and life. Restorative justice creates conditions for this kind of transformation. Offenders are not merely punished but invited to become different people.

Supportive Reintegration

Restorative justice also supports offenders' reintegration into society. Offenders receive support from the community and from restorative justice facilitators, aiding their transition back into community life. This support can include practical help—housing, employment, education—as well as emotional encouragement and accountability.

The involvement of community members in restorative processes helps reduce the social stigma associated with offending. When community members see offenders taking responsibility and making amends, their perceptions shift. Offenders are no longer seen merely as threats but as people capable of change, worthy of support.

Restorative processes often include elements of skills development and counseling. Offenders may be connected with resources to address underlying issues, to develop employment skills, to build positive relationships. These supports help offenders build a positive future.

The biblical vision of restoration includes this kind of reintegration. The prodigal son, having squandered his inheritance, is welcomed home not with condemnation but with celebration. The community's embrace is part of his restoration.

Positive Outcomes for Communities

Restorative justice benefits not only individuals but entire communities.

Strengthened Social Bonds

Restorative justice involves community members in the justice process, fostering a sense of collective responsibility and mutual support. When communities work together to address harm, they build relationships, develop trust, and learn to rely on one another.

This strengthened social fabric has benefits beyond any particular case. Communities with strong social bonds are more resilient—better able to withstand challenges, more capable of solving problems collectively. They are also safer; research on collective efficacy shows that communities where neighbors know and trust one another have lower crime rates.

The collaborative and inclusive nature of restorative practices helps rebuild trust within the community. When people see that harm can be addressed constructively, that offenders can change, that healing is possible, they regain confidence in their community and its institutions.

Reduced Crime Rates

Restorative justice contributes to safer communities through multiple mechanisms. The focus on rehabilitation and accountability reduces recidivism among offenders who participate in restorative processes. These individuals are less likely to reoffend, making communities safer.

Restorative practices can also address conflicts and minor offenses early, preventing escalation. A neighborhood dispute that is resolved through a restorative circle is less likely to escalate into violence. A school conflict that is addressed through peer mediation is less likely to lead to more serious incidents.

By addressing underlying causes of crime—relationship breakdowns, social isolation, unresolved conflicts—restorative practices can reduce the overall crime rate. Communities that embrace restorative approaches often see crime decline over time.

Improved Community Well-Being

Restorative justice promotes a culture of respect, empathy, and support within the community. This cultural shift enhances overall well-being. People feel safer, more connected, more valued. They are more likely to look out for one another, to intervene when they see problems, to support those in need.

Involving community members in the justice process empowers them to take an active role in maintaining social order and addressing harm. This empowerment builds confidence and capacity. Communities learn that they can solve their own problems, that they are not dependent on outside authorities to keep them safe.

The biblical vision of *shalom*—peace, wholeness, flourishing—is realized when communities are healthy in this way. Restorative justice contributes to *shalom* by healing the wounds that crime inflicts and building the social fabric that prevents future harm.

Evidence of Positive Outcomes

The positive outcomes of restorative justice are not merely asserted; they are supported by extensive research and real-world examples.

Research Findings

Research on victim satisfaction is remarkably consistent. Studies across multiple countries and contexts show that victims who participate in restorative processes report higher levels of satisfaction than those whose cases go through conventional channels. They feel heard, respected, and involved. They are more likely to feel that justice has been done.

Research on recidivism is equally compelling. Meta-analyses of restorative justice programs find statistically significant reductions in reoffending compared to conventional processing. Programs such as Family Group Conferencing in New Zealand and Victim-Offender Mediation in Canada have demonstrated significant reductions in reoffending rates.

Research on community relations shows improved trust and cooperation between community members and justice systems. When communities are involved in restorative processes, they develop confidence that the system can work for them. This trust supports future cooperation and engagement.

Real-World Examples

New Zealand's Family Group Conferencing program has shown high levels of victim satisfaction, reduced recidivism rates, and better rehabilitation outcomes for young offenders. The program, now in place for decades, has become a model for restorative justice worldwide.

Canada's Victim-Offender Mediation programs have resulted in high victim satisfaction, increased offender accountability, and lower recidivism rates compared to traditional justice processes. These programs demonstrate that restorative approaches can be effective with both juvenile and adult offenders.

South Africa's Truth and Reconciliation Commission facilitated national healing and reconciliation, providing a model for restorative justice in post-conflict societies. The TRC's work, despite its limitations, demonstrated that restorative approaches could address massive human rights violations and promote national healing.

Challenges in Measuring Positive Outcomes

While the evidence for restorative justice is strong, measuring its outcomes presents several challenges.

Subjective Experiences

Victims and offenders may have different perceptions of satisfaction and healing, making it difficult to quantify outcomes consistently. What counts as healing for one person may differ for another. Satisfaction is inherently subjective.

Cultural differences can also affect how restorative justice processes are perceived and experienced. A practice that works well in one cultural context may be experienced differently in another. Researchers must be attentive to these differences in interpreting findings.

Long-Term Impact

Measuring the long-term impact of restorative justice on behavior and community well-being requires ongoing evaluation and follow-up. Recidivism studies typically follow offenders for several years, but longer-term effects are harder to track. Community-level impacts—changes in social cohesion, trust, collective efficacy—are even more difficult to measure.

Assessing the broader impact of restorative justice on the criminal justice system and societal norms involves complex, multi-faceted analysis. Restorative justice may influence system practices, policy development, public attitudes—all of which are difficult to quantify.

Resource Allocation

Ensuring adequate funding and support for restorative justice programs is essential for their sustainability and effectiveness. Programs that are underfunded, understaffed, or poorly implemented cannot be expected to produce the same outcomes as well-resourced programs.

Ongoing training and professional development for facilitators and community members are crucial for maintaining the quality and integrity of restorative practices. Without investment in human capacity, programs may decline over time.

Common Challenges: Obstacles to Implementing Restorative Justice and Strategies to Overcome Them

Having explored the benefits of restorative justice, we must now honestly examine the challenges that arise in its implementation. These challenges are real and significant, but they are not insurmountable. With thoughtful strategies and committed effort, they can be addressed.

Common Challenges in Implementing Restorative Justice

Resistance to Change

Perhaps the most fundamental challenge is resistance to change. Many justice systems and institutions are deeply rooted in retributive approaches. Judges, prosecutors, defense attorneys, police officers, and corrections officials have been trained in these approaches and have built careers around them. Shifting to a restorative model requires significant cultural and institutional change, which inevitably encounters resistance.

This resistance is not merely stubbornness; it reflects genuine concerns. Practitioners may worry that restorative justice is too lenient, that it will not hold offenders accountable, that it will not protect public safety. They may be skeptical of approaches that seem unfamiliar or untested. Overcoming this resistance requires patient education, demonstration of effectiveness, and gradual integration rather than abrupt replacement.

There is also often a lack of awareness and understanding of restorative justice among the public, policymakers, and practitioners. People may have never heard of restorative justice, or they may have misconceptions about what it involves. This lack of awareness can lead to skepticism and resistance when restorative programs are proposed.

Resource Constraints

Implementing restorative justice programs requires funding for training, facilitation, and ongoing support. Facilitators must be trained and compensated. Space must be provided for meetings. Support services must be available for participants. All of this costs money.

Limited financial resources can hinder the establishment and sustainability of restorative programs. In an era of tight budgets for justice systems, finding funding for new initiatives can be challenging. Programs may be underfunded from the start, or they may struggle to maintain funding over time.

Adequately trained facilitators are essential for the success of restorative practices. Facilitation is a skilled activity that requires training, practice, and ongoing development. However, there is often a shortage of trained personnel, and providing comprehensive training can be resource-intensive. Programs may struggle to find and retain qualified facilitators.

Ensuring Voluntary Participation

For restorative justice to be effective, participation must be truly voluntary. Victims should not feel pressured to meet with offenders; offenders should not feel coerced into participating to avoid worse consequences. When participation is coerced, the authenticity of the process is undermined.

Ensuring genuine consent is challenging. Victims may feel pressure from family, community, or justice officials to participate. Offenders may feel that participation is their only chance for leniency. These pressures can be subtle but powerful.

Participants also need to be fully informed about the process and its potential outcomes to make a genuine choice to engage.

They need to understand what will happen, what will be expected of them, what the possible outcomes are. Providing this information in accessible form is essential but not always easy.

Addressing Power Imbalances

Power imbalances between victims and offenders, or within the community, can affect the fairness and effectiveness of restorative processes. These imbalances can stem from differences in social status, authority, education, confidence, or vulnerability.

An offender who is more articulate, more confident, or more socially skilled may dominate the conversation, minimizing their responsibility or manipulating others' perceptions. A victim who is traumatized, intimidated, or marginalized may be unable to speak freely or advocate for their needs.

Vulnerable participants—victims of severe trauma, marginalized individuals, those with limited education or language skills—may require additional support and advocacy to ensure their voices are heard and respected. Providing this support requires resources and skill.

Creating a Safe Environment

Ensuring the physical and emotional safety of all participants is paramount. Participants must feel secure and respected to engage fully in the process. If they fear for their safety—physically or emotionally—they cannot participate authentically.

Restorative justice processes can evoke strong emotions. Victims may express anger, grief, fear. Offenders may feel shame, remorse, defensiveness. These emotions are part of the healing process, but they can also be overwhelming. Facilitators must be prepared to manage emotional intensity and provide support as needed.

Creating safety also means being attentive to the physical environment. The setting should be neutral, comfortable, and secure. Participants should know that they can leave if they feel unsafe. Support persons should be available if needed.

Cultural Sensitivity

Restorative practices must be culturally sensitive and appropriate for the diverse populations they serve. Different cultures have different norms around communication, conflict, relationship, and authority. What is respectful in one culture may be disrespectful in another. What works in one cultural context may fail in another.

Failure to consider cultural differences can lead to misunderstandings and ineffective outcomes. Participants may feel disrespected or misunderstood. The process may not resonate with their values or experiences. Agreements may not be sustainable because they do not fit cultural norms.

Engaging community leaders and members in the design and implementation of restorative practices helps ensure cultural relevance and acceptance. Those who know the culture best are best positioned to adapt practices appropriately.

Sustainability and Integration

Successful implementation of restorative justice requires strong institutional support. This includes policies that integrate restorative approaches into existing justice systems, funding that ensures programs can survive, and leadership that champions restorative values.

Without this support, restorative programs may remain marginal—small experiments that never achieve scale, initiatives that flourish briefly and then fade. Integration into mainstream systems is essential for long-term impact.

Regular evaluation and assessment of restorative programs are also essential. Programs need to know whether they are achieving their goals, what challenges they face, how they can improve. Evaluation provides the feedback necessary for continuous improvement.

Strategies to Overcome Challenges

Each of these challenges can be addressed with thoughtful strategies.

Building Awareness and Support

Education and training are essential for building awareness and support. Justice professionals need to learn about restorative justice—its principles, its practices, its evidence base. Community leaders need to understand how restorative approaches can benefit their communities. The public needs to hear stories of restorative success.

Training programs should be comprehensive and ongoing. One-time workshops are insufficient; practitioners need opportunities to develop skills over time, to reflect on their practice, to learn from experienced mentors.

Advocating for policy changes that support restorative justice can help institutionalize these practices and secure necessary resources. This advocacy may target legislation, administrative rules, funding allocations, or system policies. It requires building coalitions, making evidence-based arguments, and engaging with decision-makers.

Securing Funding and Resources

Exploring diverse funding opportunities can provide the financial resources needed to support restorative justice programs. Government grants, private donations, community fundraising—all can contribute. Programs should not rely on a single funding source but should develop diverse streams of support.

Building partnerships with community organizations, educational institutions, and businesses can enhance resource availability and support for restorative practices. Partners may provide funding, in-kind contributions, volunteers, or political support. Collaborative relationships strengthen programs and build broader constituencies.

Ensuring Voluntary Participation

Providing clear, accessible information about the restorative process and its potential benefits and risks helps ensure that participation is genuinely voluntary. Participants need to know what they are agreeing to before they agree. Information should be provided in multiple formats and, where necessary, in multiple languages.

Ensuring that the environment is safe and supportive can encourage voluntary participation and engagement. When participants feel respected and cared for, they are more likely to participate authentically. Creating this environment requires attention to physical space, interpersonal dynamics, and emotional support.

Addressing Power Imbalances

Training facilitators to recognize and address power imbalances is crucial. Facilitators should be skilled in creating an equitable environment where all participants feel heard and respected. This may involve meeting separately with parties beforehand, providing support persons during the process, ensuring that both have opportunity to speak, and intervening when necessary to maintain balance.

Offering support services, such as counseling and advocacy, can help vulnerable participants engage more fully and confidently in the process. Victims may need advocates to help them articulate their needs; offenders may need support to manage shame and develop accountability. Providing these services enhances equity.

Creating a Safe Environment

Integrating trauma-informed practices into restorative processes can help ensure the physical and emotional safety of participants. Trauma-informed approaches recognize the prevalence of trauma, understand its effects, and create conditions that avoid retraumatization. Facilitators trained in trauma-informed practice can recognize signs of distress and respond appropriately.

Providing access to emotional support and counseling during and after restorative sessions can help participants manage intense emotions. Participants may need debriefing after emotionally charged sessions; they may need ongoing support to process what they have experienced. Making these services available enhances safety and healing.

Ensuring Cultural Sensitivity

Training facilitators and practitioners in cultural competence ensures that restorative practices are respectful and appropriate for diverse populations. Cultural competence involves knowledge of different cultural norms, awareness of one's own cultural assumptions, and skill in adapting practice to fit cultural contexts.

Involving community leaders and members in the development and implementation of restorative programs can enhance cultural relevance and acceptance. Those who know the culture best can advise on appropriate adaptations, can help engage community members, and can lend legitimacy to the process.

Promoting Sustainability and Integration

Integrating restorative justice into existing institutional frameworks, policies, and procedures can promote sustainability and long-term impact. When restorative approaches are embedded in standard practice—not just added on as an option—they are more likely to survive changes in leadership or funding.

Implementing regular evaluation and feedback mechanisms allows for continuous improvement and adaptation of restorative programs to meet evolving needs and challenges. Programs that learn from experience, that adjust based on feedback, that track outcomes and use data to inform practice—these programs are more likely to succeed and endure.

Real-World Examples of Overcoming Challenges

The experience of jurisdictions that have successfully implemented restorative justice offers valuable lessons.

New Zealand's Integrated Approach

New Zealand faced significant challenges in implementing restorative justice: resistance to change from justice professionals, resource constraints, and the need to integrate restorative approaches with existing legal frameworks.

The strategy New Zealand adopted was comprehensive. The government provided strong policy support through legislation—the Children, Young Persons, and Their Families Act 1989—that made Family Group Conferencing mandatory for most youth offenses. This legislative mandate gave restorative justice legitimacy and resources.

Comprehensive training was provided for facilitators, justice professionals, and community members. The government invested in building capacity, ensuring that there were skilled people to implement the process.

Community involvement was central. The process drew on Maori traditions and involved families and communities directly. This cultural grounding enhanced acceptance and effectiveness.

The result was widespread acceptance and successful outcomes. New Zealand's FGC program is now a model for restorative justice worldwide, demonstrating that thoughtful implementation can overcome initial challenges.

Canada's Victim-Offender Mediation Programs

Canadian VOM programs faced challenges around ensuring voluntary participation and addressing power imbalances. The strategy they adopted prioritized informed consent and created safe, supportive environments for participants.

Facilitators received extensive training in managing power dynamics and providing emotional support. They learned to recognize when power imbalances were affecting the process and to intervene appropriately. They developed skills for creating safety and supporting vulnerable participants.

Preparation was thorough. Participants met with facilitators beforehand to understand the process, to think through what they wanted to say, to address any concerns. This preparation ensured that when they came to the mediation, they were ready to participate authentically.

The result has been high levels of satisfaction and reduced recidivism rates. Canadian VOM programs demonstrate that attention to process—to the quality of participation and the safety of participants—produces positive outcomes.

South Africa's Truth and Reconciliation Commission

The TRC faced enormous challenges: addressing the deep trauma of apartheid, ensuring cultural sensitivity across diverse communities, creating safety for participants who had experienced horrific violence.

The strategy the TRC adopted was to involve community leaders and integrate cultural practices into the restorative process. Traditional leaders, religious figures, and community representatives were engaged in shaping and implementing the process. Cultural practices of truth-telling, acknowledgment, and reconciliation were incorporated.

Trauma-informed approaches were central. The commission recognized that participants would be dealing with deep pain and provided support accordingly. Counselors were available; processes were designed to avoid retraumatization; follow-up support was provided.

The result, while imperfect, was a process that facilitated significant healing and reconciliation. The TRC demonstrated that restorative approaches could address even the most severe harms when implemented with care, cultural sensitivity, and attention to trauma.

Criticisms and Controversies: Addressing Criticisms and Debating Contentious Issues

No honest exploration of restorative justice would be complete without engaging the criticisms and controversies that surround it. These challenges arise from legitimate concerns and deserve thoughtful response.

Major Criticisms of Restorative Justice

Perceived Leniency

One of the most persistent criticisms of restorative justice is that it is too lenient on offenders. Critics argue that restorative practices do not provide sufficient deterrence or punishment for serious crimes, potentially undermining public confidence in the justice system. The concern is that offenders will "get off easy" and that this will send the wrong message about the consequences of wrongdoing.

This criticism, while understandable, misunderstands what restorative justice seeks to accomplish. Restorative justice is not about avoiding consequences but about meaningful accountability. It focuses on offenders taking responsibility, making amends, and engaging in rehabilitative actions. This kind of accountability is often more demanding than passive acceptance of punishment.

Consider what restorative justice requires of offenders. They must face their victims directly, hear about the harm they have caused, acknowledge their responsibility, and take concrete steps to make amends. This is not easy; it requires genuine engagement and emotional work. Many offenders find it more challenging than serving a sentence.

The evidence supports the effectiveness of this approach. Studies have shown that restorative justice can lead to lower reoffending rates and better outcomes for both victims and offenders than punitive measures. The question should not be whether restorative justice is lenient but whether it is effective in achieving justice goals.

Theologically, this criticism raises questions about the nature of justice. Is justice primarily about making offenders suffer, or is it about making things right? The biblical vision, as we have seen, emphasizes restoration—making whole what has been broken. Restorative justice aligns with this vision.

Inconsistent Outcomes

Critics also argue that restorative justice can lead to inconsistent outcomes, as the process relies heavily on the discretion of facilitators and the willingness of participants. This variability can result in perceived injustices or unequal treatment. Two similar cases might produce very different agreements depending on who facilitates and who participates.

This concern about consistency is legitimate. Any process that relies on human judgment and participant input will produce variability. The question is whether this variability is acceptable and how it can be managed.

Restorative justice processes are designed to be flexible and responsive to the needs of the individuals involved. This flexibility is a strength—it allows outcomes to be tailored to particular situations rather than imposed uniformly. But flexibility must be balanced with fairness.

Establishing clear guidelines, training facilitators thoroughly, and monitoring practices can help ensure consistency and fairness. Programs can develop standards for what agreements should include, what factors should be considered, what outcomes are appropriate. Facilitators can be trained to apply these standards consistently.

The personalized nature of restorative justice allows for more tailored and effective resolutions. What serves one victim's healing may differ from what serves another's. What enables one offender's rehabilitation may differ from what enables another's. Flexibility allows these differences to be honored.

Victim Participation and Coercion

There are concerns that victims may feel pressured to participate in restorative justice processes, which could re-traumatize them or compromise their autonomy. Critics worry about the potential for coercion, especially in cases involving power imbalances.

This concern is serious and must be addressed. Victims should never be pressured to participate. Their healing and well-being must be paramount. If participation would cause additional harm, it should not be pursued.

Ensuring voluntary participation and providing comprehensive support for victims are essential. Facilitators must be trained to recognize when victims are being pressured and to protect their autonomy. Victims should have access to advocacy and counseling services to help them make informed decisions and to support them through the process.

Proper safeguards and ethical standards can protect victims' rights and well-being. Programs should have clear protocols for assessing victim readiness, for providing support, for ensuring that participation remains voluntary throughout. These safeguards are essential for ethical practice.

The biblical tradition consistently emphasizes care for the vulnerable. Victims must be protected, not further harmed by the processes designed to help them. Restorative justice, properly implemented, honors this commitment.

Suitability for Severe Crimes

Restorative justice is sometimes criticized for being inappropriate for severe crimes, such as sexual assault, domestic violence, or homicide. Critics argue that these offenses require a more formal legal response and that restorative practices may not provide adequate justice or protection for victims.

This criticism deserves careful consideration. Severe crimes involve profound harm, deep trauma, and significant power imbalances. Restorative processes must be implemented with extreme care in these contexts, if at all.

However, it is not accurate to say that restorative justice is never appropriate for severe crimes. In some cases, with appropriate safeguards, restorative processes can offer benefits that conventional justice cannot. Victims of severe crimes may have needs—for acknowledgment, for answers, for a sense of control—that restorative processes can address.

Each case must be carefully assessed to determine the appropriateness of restorative justice. Factors to consider include the victim's wishes, the offender's accountability, the power dynamics between them, and the availability of support services. When these factors align, restorative processes can be valuable even in severe cases.

The experience of truth commissions in addressing atrocities demonstrates that restorative approaches can be applied to the most severe harms. South Africa's TRC, despite its limitations, showed that truth-telling, acknowledgment, and reconciliation are possible even after genocide-level violence.

Integration with Formal Justice Systems

Integrating restorative justice with formal justice systems can be challenging, leading to concerns about the coherence and effectiveness of the overall justice system. Critics worry about potential conflicts between restorative and retributive approaches, about confusion regarding which cases should go which way, about inconsistency in outcomes.

Successful integration requires collaboration between restorative and formal justice systems. Restorative justice should not be seen as a replacement for conventional justice but as a complement—an alternative for some cases, a supplement for others. Clear policies can specify which cases are appropriate for restorative approaches and how restorative processes relate to conventional proceedings.

Restorative justice can complement traditional approaches by addressing the underlying causes of crime and promoting rehabilitation. Conventional justice provides a framework for accountability and public protection. Together, they can create a more comprehensive and effective justice system.

Clear policies, communication, and shared goals can enhance coherence and effectiveness. When restorative and conventional systems work together, each contributing its strengths, the whole is greater than the sum of its parts.

Debating Contentious Issues

Beyond these specific criticisms, several broader issues remain subject to ongoing debate.

Effectiveness in Reducing Recidivism

There is ongoing debate about the effectiveness of restorative justice in reducing recidivism compared to traditional punitive measures. While numerous studies show positive effects, some question the quality of the evidence or the generalizability of findings.

The evidence, on balance, supports the effectiveness of restorative justice. Meta-analyses have found that restorative justice programs typically result in lower reoffending rates. These effects are statistically significant and practically meaningful. However, the success of these programs depends on proper implementation and support. Poorly implemented programs will not produce good results.

Continued research is needed to understand what works, for whom, and under what conditions. Which program models are most effective? For which types of offenders? In which contexts? Answering these questions will allow restorative justice to be refined and improved.

Balancing Restorative and Retributive Justice

Balancing the principles of restorative and retributive justice is a contentious issue. Some argue for a pure restorative approach, others for pure retribution, still others for a hybrid that incorporates elements of both.

A balanced approach can leverage the strengths of both models. Restorative justice addresses the needs of victims and promotes offender rehabilitation. Retributive justice provides a formal structure for accountability and public protection. Combining these approaches can create a more comprehensive and effective justice system.

The key is to use each approach where it is most appropriate. Restorative processes may be ideal for many cases, particularly those involving minor offenses, first-time offenders, or victims who desire restorative encounter. Retributive processes may be necessary for cases involving serious violence, ongoing danger, or victims who do not wish to participate. The goal should be a system that offers both options, with clear criteria for when each is appropriate.

Restorative Justice in Schools and Workplaces

The application of restorative justice in schools and workplaces raises questions about its appropriateness and effectiveness in non-criminal contexts. Some wonder whether practices designed for criminal justice can be effectively adapted for these settings.

The evidence suggests that restorative justice can be highly effective in these settings. School-based programs have reduced disciplinary incidents, improved school climate, and enhanced student relationships. Workplace programs have resolved conflicts, improved employee relations, and built positive organizational cultures.

The key is appropriate adaptation. School-based restorative practices must fit the developmental levels of students and the structures of schools. Workplace practices must fit organizational cultures and employment relationships. With thoughtful adaptation, restorative principles can be applied effectively in diverse contexts.

Restorative Justice and Cultural Sensitivity

Ensuring cultural sensitivity in restorative justice practices is crucial, as cultural differences can influence perceptions of justice and conflict resolution. Practices that work well in one cultural context may be ineffective or even harmful in another.

Restorative justice must be adapted to fit the cultural context of the communities it serves. This requires engaging community leaders, incorporating cultural practices, and providing cultural competence training for facilitators. It means being humble about what we know and open to learning from those with different cultural perspectives.

When restorative justice is culturally adapted, it can be more effective and more accepted. Communities see themselves reflected in the process; they trust it because it respects their values and traditions. This cultural grounding enhances legitimacy and outcomes.

Victim Satisfaction and Restorative Justice

While restorative justice aims to prioritize victims' needs, there is debate about its ability to consistently achieve high levels of victim satisfaction. Some question whether the positive findings in research reflect selection bias—perhaps only victims who are already inclined to be satisfied choose to participate.

Research generally shows high levels of victim satisfaction with restorative justice processes. Victims feel heard and involved in the resolution. They appreciate the opportunity to tell their stories, to ask questions, to receive acknowledgment. These benefits appear to be genuine.

However, ensuring ongoing support and addressing any concerns throughout the process are vital for maintaining this satisfaction. Victims' needs may change over time; their experience of the process may evolve. Programs must be attentive to these dynamics and responsive to victims' ongoing needs.

Addressing Criticisms and Improving Restorative Practices

The criticisms and controversies surrounding restorative justice point toward the ongoing work of improvement.

Enhanced Training and Standards

Providing comprehensive training for facilitators and practitioners can improve the quality and consistency of restorative justice processes. Training should cover not only technical skills but also ethical principles, cultural competence, trauma-informed practice, and power dynamics. Ongoing professional development ensures that practitioners continue to grow.

Establishing clear standards and guidelines can help ensure fairness, transparency, and effectiveness in restorative practices. Standards should address facilitator qualifications, participant protections, agreement requirements, and outcome monitoring. Guidelines should provide direction while allowing flexibility for individual cases.

Ongoing Research and Evaluation

Conducting ongoing research and evaluation of restorative justice programs can identify strengths, weaknesses, and areas for improvement. Research should examine not only outcomes but also processes—what happens in restorative encounters, how participants experience them, what makes them effective.

Implementing evidence-based practices and adapting strategies based on research findings can enhance the effectiveness of restorative justice. As we learn more about what works, we can refine our approaches. As contexts change, we can adapt.

Community and Stakeholder Engagement

Engaging community members, victims, offenders, and stakeholders in the design and implementation of restorative justice programs can build trust and support. Those who will be affected by programs should have voice in how they are designed. Their input can improve relevance and effectiveness.

Collaborative approaches that involve all stakeholders can ensure that restorative justice meets the needs of the community and aligns with broader justice goals. When everyone has a seat at the table, programs are more likely to be supported and sustained.

Balancing Restorative and Retributive Approaches

Developing integrated models that combine restorative and retributive elements can create a more balanced and comprehensive justice system. These models recognize that different cases may require different responses, that different goals may be served by different approaches.

Advocating for policies that support the integration of restorative justice into formal justice systems can enhance coherence and effectiveness. Policy change can provide resources, legitimacy, and structure for restorative programs. It can ensure that restorative justice is not just an afterthought but a central component of justice.

Ensuring Victim-Centered Approaches

Providing comprehensive support services for victims, including counseling and advocacy, can ensure their needs are met throughout the restorative process. Victims should not be left to navigate the process alone; they should have access to people who can support them, advise them, and advocate for their interests.

Empowering victims to choose whether to participate and ensuring they have control over the process can enhance their satisfaction and well-being. Victims should be the primary decision-makers about their involvement. They should be able to set boundaries, to withdraw if they need to, to shape how the process unfolds.

The Integration of Law, Psychology, Philosophy, and Theology

As we have explored the benefits and challenges of restorative justice, we have seen how multiple disciplines inform our understanding.

Legal Perspectives

Law provides the framework within which restorative justice operates. Legal principles of due process, equal protection, and proportionality must be honored. Legal rights of victims and offenders must be protected. Legal institutions must be engaged if restorative justice is to be integrated into mainstream systems.

The challenges we have explored—ensuring voluntary participation, addressing power imbalances, creating safe environments, maintaining consistency—all have legal dimensions. Legal standards can guide practice; legal oversight can ensure accountability.

Psychological Insights

Psychology illuminates why restorative justice produces its effects and what conditions are necessary for success. Research on trauma shows why safety and support are essential. Research on procedural justice shows why voice and respect matter.

Research on moral development shows why empathy and accountability promote change.

The challenges we have explored—managing emotional intensity, supporting vulnerable participants, addressing power imbalances—all have psychological dimensions. Psychological knowledge can inform practice; psychological support can enhance outcomes.

Philosophical Foundations

Philosophy provides the ethical framework for restorative justice. Relational ethics explains why relationships matter. Communitarianism explains why community involvement is essential. Virtue ethics explains why character formation is important. Restorative ontology explains why healing is possible.

The criticisms we have explored—about leniency, consistency, victim participation—raise philosophical questions about the nature of justice, the purposes of punishment, the rights of victims, the responsibilities of offenders. Philosophical reflection can clarify these issues and guide practice.

Theological Dimensions

For those who approach restorative justice from a faith perspective, theology provides deeper grounding. The biblical vision of *shalom*—peace, wholeness, right relationship—is what restorative justice seeks. The reconciling work of God in Christ is what restorative practices embody. The hospitality of God's kingdom is what restorative communities practice.

The challenges we have explored—resistance to change, resource constraints, cultural sensitivity—are not merely practical problems but spiritual opportunities. They call us to patience, creativity, humility, and trust in God's ongoing work. They remind us that restorative justice is not our project but God's, and we are privileged to participate.

As we move forward into the remaining chapters, we will build on this honest assessment of benefits and challenges. We will explore restorative justice in legal systems, international contexts, and social justice movements. We will examine how restorative principles can be applied to systemic injustice and historical wrongs. And we will look to the future, imagining how restorative justice might continue to transform our world.

The benefits of restorative justice are real and significant. The challenges are real and significant as well. Neither cancels the other. The path forward is not to pretend that challenges don't exist but to address them honestly and creatively, learning from experience, adapting to contexts, and always keeping faith with restorative values. This is the work of building a restorative society—one encounter, one program, one system at a time.

CHAPTER 07

RESTORATIVE JUSTICE AND THE LEGAL SYSTEMS

We have journeyed together through the philosophical foundations of restorative justice, explored its core principles and values, examined the practices and models that bring these principles to life, studied real-world applications across multiple domains, and honestly assessed both the benefits and challenges of restorative approaches. Now, dear reader, we arrive at a crucial intersection: the relationship between restorative justice and the legal systems that have long dominated our response to crime and conflict.

This relationship is complex and multifaceted. Restorative justice did not emerge in a vacuum; it developed in dialogue with—and often in critique of—existing legal systems. Yet restorative justice is not simply an alternative to those systems; it can also complement and enhance them. Understanding this relationship is essential for anyone seeking to implement restorative practices within the framework of law.

In this chapter, we will explore how restorative justice can be integrated with traditional legal systems, examining models of integration, practical strategies, and real-world examples. We will then examine the legislative frameworks that support restorative justice, exploring laws and policies from various jurisdictions. Finally, we will consider the role of case law and judicial precedents in shaping the development of restorative justice.

Throughout this exploration, we will draw on insights from law, psychology, philosophy, and theology to illuminate the complex relationship between restorative justice and legal systems. We will see how these different perspectives can inform and enrich our understanding.

Integration with Traditional Justice: How Restorative Justice Can Complement Traditional Legal Systems

Let us begin by considering how restorative justice can work alongside—not instead of—traditional legal systems. The goal is not to replace one system with another but to create a more comprehensive approach that draws on the strengths of both.

Understanding the Traditional Legal System

To appreciate how restorative justice can complement traditional legal systems, we must first understand those systems themselves. The traditional legal system, often referred to as retributive justice, has deep historical roots and continues to shape our understanding of justice in profound ways.

Key Characteristics of Traditional Legal Systems

Traditional legal systems are characterized by several key features. First and foremost is the emphasis on retribution and deterrence. The primary purpose of punishment, in this view, is to ensure that offenders receive their "just deserts"—punishment proportional to the severity of their offenses. This punishment is also intended to deter future crimes, both by the individual offender (specific deterrence) and by others who might be tempted to offend (general deterrence).

This emphasis on retribution and deterrence reflects a particular understanding of justice. Justice is about balancing the scales, ensuring that wrongdoing is met with appropriate consequences. It is about maintaining social order by making clear that certain behaviors will not be tolerated and will be punished.

The traditional legal system also operates through an adversarial process. The state, representing the public interest, prosecutes offenders. Defense attorneys represent their clients. The two sides present their cases to a judge or jury, who determine guilt and impose punishment. This adversarial structure is designed to ensure fairness—both sides have opportunity to present their case, and a neutral decision-maker determines the outcome.

The focus throughout is on guilt and punishment. The central questions are: Did the offender commit the offense? If so, what punishment does the law prescribe? The process is designed to answer these questions accurately and fairly.

Limitations of Traditional Legal Systems

Despite its strengths, the traditional legal system has significant limitations. One of the most serious is limited victim involvement. Victims may testify as witnesses, but they have no formal role in determining outcomes. Their needs and perspectives are secondary to the state's interest in punishment. This can leave victims feeling excluded, marginalized, and dissatisfied with a process that is supposed to serve justice on their behalf.

The focus on punishment rather than rehabilitation and reparation can also be problematic. Punishment alone often fails to address the underlying causes of criminal behavior. Offenders may serve their sentences and emerge unchanged, still lacking understanding of the harm they caused and still lacking motivation to change. This contributes to high recidivism rates and insufficient support for offender reintegration.

Finally, traditional legal systems are often overburdened. Courts and correctional facilities face overwhelming caseloads, leading to delays, overcrowding, and strained resources. The system processes cases as efficiently as it can, but efficiency often comes at the expense of the individualized attention that justice requires.

These limitations create space for restorative approaches. By addressing needs that the traditional system neglects, restorative justice can complement and enhance legal responses to crime.

Complementary Role of Restorative Justice

Restorative justice addresses many of the limitations of traditional legal systems by focusing on repairing harm, promoting accountability, and facilitating healing.

Key Principles of Restorative Justice

As we have explored throughout this book, restorative justice is guided by several key principles. The first is repairing harm. Rather than focusing solely on punishing offenders, restorative justice seeks to address the harm caused by crime and to make amends. This means attending to the needs of victims, the obligations of offenders, and the health of communities.

The second principle is accountability and responsibility. Restorative justice encourages offenders to take responsibility for their actions and to engage in reparative actions. This accountability is not passive acceptance of punishment but active engagement in making things right.

The third principle is victim and community involvement. Restorative justice actively involves victims and community members in the justice process. Victims have voice and agency; communities have a role in supporting healing and promoting accountability.

Benefits of Integrating Restorative Justice with Traditional Legal Systems

When restorative justice is integrated with traditional legal systems, multiple benefits can result.

For victims, integration provides enhanced support. Victims have a voice and active role in the justice process, leading to higher levels of satisfaction and healing. They are not merely witnesses but participants, whose needs and perspectives shape outcomes.

For offenders, integration promotes effective rehabilitation. By focusing on accountability and responsibility, restorative practices encourage offenders to understand the harm they have caused and to make amends. This process reduces recidivism rates and supports successful reintegration.

For the justice system itself, integration offers resource efficiency. By offering alternative resolution mechanisms, restorative justice can alleviate the burden on courts and correctional facilities. Cases that can be resolved restoratively free up resources for those that require conventional processing.

For communities, integration strengthens social bonds. By involving community members in the justice process, restorative practices build collective responsibility and mutual support. This community cohesion contributes to social harmony and prevents future harm.

The theological dimension of this integration is significant. The biblical vision of justice includes both accountability and mercy, both judgment and restoration. The integration of restorative and retributive approaches reflects this holistic vision, holding offenders accountable while offering pathways to healing.

Models of Integration

There are various models for integrating restorative justice with traditional legal systems, each offering different levels of incorporation and collaboration.

Pre-Charge Diversion Programs

In pre-charge diversion programs, offenders are diverted to restorative justice programs before formal charges are filed. This allows for early intervention and resolution, often for minor offenses or first-time offenders.

The benefits of this model are significant. It reduces the burden on the court system by resolving cases without formal prosecution. It provides timely resolution, which can be important for both victims and offenders. And it offers opportunities for rehabilitation and reparation without the lasting consequences of a criminal record.

For offenders, this model provides an incentive to take responsibility and make amends. Successful completion of the restorative program can result in charges being dropped, avoiding the collateral consequences of a criminal conviction. For victims, it provides an opportunity to have their needs addressed without the delays and uncertainties of court proceedings.

Post-Charge but Pre-Sentencing Programs

In post-charge but pre-sentencing programs, restorative justice processes are initiated after charges are filed but before sentencing. Successful participation can influence sentencing decisions.

This model encourages offenders to engage in reparative actions before they are sentenced. Their participation demonstrates accountability and commitment to change, which can be considered by the court in determining an appropriate sentence. This may result in reduced sentences, community-based dispositions, or other outcomes that support rehabilitation.

For victims, this model provides an opportunity to participate in the justice process before a final disposition is reached. Their input can inform the court's decision, ensuring that their needs are considered.

Post-Sentencing Programs

In post-sentencing programs, restorative justice is integrated into the correctional system. Offenders may participate in restorative processes during incarceration or as part of their probation or parole conditions.

This model supports offender rehabilitation by providing opportunities for accountability and growth even after sentencing. Offenders may meet with victims, participate in restorative circles, or engage in other reparative activities. These experiences can be transformative, promoting personal change and preparing offenders for reintegration.

For victims, post-sentencing restorative processes can provide opportunities for healing that were not available earlier. They may receive answers to questions, hear expressions of remorse, or receive restitution that was not previously possible.

Parallel Systems

In the parallel systems model, restorative justice operates alongside the traditional legal system, offering complementary pathways for conflict resolution and harm reparation. Victims and offenders may choose which pathway to pursue, or cases may be directed to one system or the other based on established criteria.

This model provides flexibility and choice. Victims who desire restorative encounter can pursue it; those who prefer conventional processing can do that. Offenders who are motivated to take responsibility and make amends can access restorative options; those who contest guilt may need conventional adjudication.

The parallel systems model recognizes that different cases and different parties may benefit from different approaches. By offering both options, the justice system can better serve diverse needs and promote more holistic outcomes.

Practical Strategies for Effective Integration

Successful integration of restorative justice with traditional legal systems requires careful planning, collaboration, and support from various stakeholders.

Policy and Legislative Support

The first requirement is policy and legislative support. Developing policies and legislation that support the implementation of restorative justice practices within the legal system provides the framework for integration. This may include laws authorizing restorative programs, funding for implementation, and standards for practice.

Legislative support can also include incentives for participation. Offering reduced sentences or expungement of records upon successful completion of restorative programs encourages offenders to engage. These incentives must be carefully designed to ensure that participation remains voluntary and that outcomes are fair.

Training and Capacity Building

Effective integration requires training for legal professionals. Judges, prosecutors, defense attorneys, and law enforcement officers need to understand restorative justice principles and practices. They need to know when restorative options are appropriate, how to refer cases, and how to support restorative processes.

Building facilitator capacity is equally important. Skilled facilitators are essential for conducting restorative processes effectively and ethically. Training programs must be comprehensive and ongoing, ensuring that facilitators develop and maintain the necessary competencies.

Collaboration and Partnerships

Integration requires collaboration with community organizations. Partnering with victim advocacy groups, restorative justice practitioners, and community-based organizations brings diverse expertise and resources to the table. These partnerships ensure that restorative programs are grounded in community needs and have community support.

Interagency collaboration is also essential. Criminal justice agencies, social services, and restorative justice programs must work together to ensure coordinated and effective implementation. This requires communication, shared protocols, and mutual understanding of roles and responsibilities.

Monitoring and Evaluation

Finally, integration requires ongoing monitoring and evaluation. Implementing mechanisms for monitoring restorative justice programs allows for assessment of their effectiveness and identification of areas for improvement. This feedback loop supports continuous improvement.

Data collection and analysis are essential components of monitoring and evaluation. Collecting data on program outcomes—victim satisfaction, recidivism rates, cost-effectiveness—provides evidence that can inform policy and practice. This evidence can also demonstrate the value of restorative justice to funders, policymakers, and the public.

Case Studies and Examples

Examining real-world examples of successful integration highlights best practices and lessons learned.

New Zealand's Family Group Conferencing

New Zealand has successfully integrated Family Group Conferencing into its juvenile justice system, providing a restorative alternative to traditional prosecution. The Children, Young Persons, and Their Families Act 1989 made FGC mandatory for most youth offenses, embedding restorative practice in the legal framework.

In FGC, offenders, victims, and their families participate in facilitated meetings to discuss the harm and develop a plan for making amends. The process is collaborative and inclusive, drawing on Maori traditions of family and community involvement.

The outcomes have been impressive. FGC has led to high levels of victim satisfaction, reduced recidivism rates, and positive rehabilitation outcomes for young offenders. The program demonstrates that restorative justice can be integrated into a mainstream legal system at scale.

Canada's Restorative Justice Initiatives

Canada has implemented various restorative justice programs at different stages of the criminal justice process. These include pre-charge diversion programs, post-charge but pre-sentencing initiatives, and post-sentencing programs within corrections.

Programs involve victim-offender mediation, community restorative boards, and circles, providing opportunities for reconciliation and reparation. They draw on Canada's diverse cultural traditions, including indigenous practices of healing and reconciliation.

These initiatives have resulted in lower recidivism rates, increased victim satisfaction, and more effective resource utilization. They demonstrate that restorative justice can be integrated at multiple points in the justice process.

South Africa's Truth and Reconciliation Commission

The Truth and Reconciliation Commission was established to address the atrocities committed during apartheid and promote national healing and reconciliation. While not a typical criminal justice process, the TRC operated alongside the legal system, offering a restorative alternative to prosecution for those who fully disclosed their political crimes.

The TRC facilitated public hearings where victims and perpetrators could share their experiences, seek forgiveness, and agree on reparative actions. It provided a platform for truth-telling, acknowledgment, and reconciliation that conventional legal processes could not offer.

The TRC played a crucial role in promoting reconciliation and healing in South Africa, providing a model for integrating restorative justice in post-conflict societies. Its work demonstrates that restorative approaches can address even the most severe harms when implemented with care and commitment.

Challenges and Considerations

Integrating restorative justice with traditional legal systems presents several challenges that must be addressed.

Ensuring Voluntary Participation

Participation in restorative processes must be truly voluntary. Coercion or pressure to participate can undermine the sincerity and outcomes of the process. Victims should not feel pressured to meet with offenders; offenders should not feel coerced into participating to avoid worse consequences.

Providing clear, accessible information about the process and its potential benefits and risks helps ensure genuine consent. Participants need to understand what they are agreeing to before they agree. They need to know that they can withdraw at any time without penalty.

Maintaining Fairness and Consistency

Ensuring that restorative justice practices are applied equitably and consistently across cases is essential to prevent disparities and biases. Similar cases should be treated similarly; outcomes should not depend on the particular facilitator or the particular participants.

Establishing clear guidelines and standards for restorative processes helps maintain fairness and integrity. These guidelines should address case selection, facilitator qualifications, participant protections, and outcome requirements.

Balancing Restorative and Retributive Goals

Balancing restorative and retributive goals requires careful attention. Both have legitimate roles in a comprehensive justice system. Restorative justice addresses needs that retributive justice neglects; retributive justice provides structure and accountability that restorative justice may lack.

The key is context-specific application. The appropriateness of restorative justice must be assessed on a case-by-case basis, considering the severity and context of the offense, the wishes of the victim, the accountability of the offender, and the resources available.

Building Public Confidence

Ensuring transparency and accountability in the implementation of restorative justice is essential for building public trust and confidence. The public needs to understand what restorative justice is, how it works, and why it is effective. They need to see that restorative processes are fair, that outcomes are just, that public safety is protected.

Engaging the community in restorative justice initiatives fosters understanding and support. When community members participate in restorative processes, they see firsthand how they work and what they achieve. This experience builds confidence and support.

Legislative Frameworks: Laws and Policies Supporting Restorative Justice

Having explored how restorative justice can be integrated with traditional legal systems, we now turn to the legislative frameworks that make such integration possible. Laws and policies provide the structure, resources, and legitimacy that restorative programs need to thrive.

Understanding Legislative Frameworks for Restorative Justice

Legislative frameworks for restorative justice establish the legal basis for implementing restorative practices within the justice system. These frameworks provide guidelines, standards, and procedures to ensure consistency, fairness, and effectiveness.

Key Components of Legislative Frameworks

Effective legislative frameworks include several key components. First is legal recognition—formal acknowledgment of restorative justice practices within the legal system. This recognition may take the form of statutory provisions that authorize restorative programs, define their scope, and establish their relationship to conventional proceedings.

Second are standards and guidelines. Legislation may establish standards for the implementation and operation of restorative justice programs, including requirements for facilitator training, participant protections, and program evaluation. These standards ensure consistency and quality across programs.

Third is funding and resources. Legislation may allocate funding to support restorative justice initiatives, including resources for training, facilitation, and evaluation. Adequate funding is essential for program sustainability.

Fourth is training and professional development. Legislation may require or support training for practitioners and stakeholders, ensuring that restorative processes are facilitated competently and ethically.

Fifth is monitoring and evaluation. Legislation may establish mechanisms for monitoring and evaluating the effectiveness of restorative justice programs, ensuring accountability and supporting continuous improvement.

Types of Legislative Models

Different jurisdictions have adopted different legislative models for restorative justice. Some have enacted stand-alone legislation—specific laws dedicated to establishing and regulating restorative justice practices. These laws provide comprehensive frameworks, addressing all aspects of restorative program implementation.

Others have incorporated restorative justice provisions into existing laws. Amendments to criminal justice, juvenile justice, or community justice legislation can authorize restorative programs without creating entirely new statutory frameworks.

Still others have issued policy directives or guidelines to support the implementation of restorative justice programs without formal legislative changes. While less robust than legislation, these policy instruments can still provide guidance and support.

Examples of Legislative Frameworks

Examining specific examples from various jurisdictions illustrates how legislative frameworks can support restorative justice.

New Zealand: Children, Young Persons, and Their Families Act 1989

New Zealand's legislative framework for restorative justice is rooted in the Children, Young Persons, and Their Families Act

1989, which introduced Family Group Conferencing as a key component of the juvenile justice system. This Act was groundbreaking in its recognition of restorative principles and its mandate for restorative processes.

The Act requires the use of FGC for most youth offenses, with limited exceptions. It emphasizes the involvement of families and communities in the decision-making process, reflecting Maori cultural values. It establishes procedures for conducting conferences, protecting participants' rights, and implementing agreements.

The impact of this legislation has been profound. It has led to significant reductions in youth offending rates and high levels of victim and family satisfaction. It has made restorative justice a central component of youth justice, not a marginal alternative.

Canada: Youth Criminal Justice Act 2003

The Youth Criminal Justice Act of 2003 incorporates restorative justice principles into Canada's juvenile justice system. The Act encourages the use of extrajudicial measures—including restorative justice programs—to address youth crime, reserving formal court proceedings for more serious cases.

The YCJA emphasizes the importance of repairing harm and reintegrating young offenders into the community. It authorizes a range of restorative options, including victim-offender mediation, community service, and other reparative measures. It requires that these measures be proportionate to the offense and respectful of victims' rights.

The Act has contributed to a decline in youth incarceration rates and promoted the use of restorative justice practices across the country. It demonstrates that legislative frameworks can encourage restorative approaches while maintaining appropriate safeguards.

Australia: Crimes (Restorative Justice) Act 2004 (Australian Capital Territory)

The Crimes (Restorative Justice) Act 2004 provides a legislative framework for the use of restorative justice in the Australian Capital Territory. The Act allows for the referral of both juvenile and adult offenders to restorative justice programs at various stages of the criminal justice process.

The Act outlines procedures for conducting restorative conferences, including requirements for facilitator qualifications, participant preparation, and agreement development. It ensures the protection of participants' rights, including the right to legal representation and the right to withdraw from the process.

The legislation has facilitated the integration of restorative justice into the ACT's criminal justice system, resulting in positive outcomes for victims, offenders, and the community. It demonstrates that comprehensive legislative frameworks can support restorative programs for both youth and adults.

South Africa: Child Justice Act 2008

The Child Justice Act 2008 establishes a separate juvenile justice system in South Africa, incorporating restorative justice principles. The Act provides for diversion programs, including restorative justice measures, for children in conflict with the law.

The Act emphasizes the importance of rehabilitation, reintegration, and the participation of families and communities. It authorizes a range of restorative options, including family group conferencing, victim-offender mediation, and other reparative measures. It establishes safeguards to protect children's rights throughout the process.

The legislation has promoted the use of restorative justice in addressing youth crime and contributed to more effective and humane responses to juvenile offending. It demonstrates that restorative principles can be embedded in juvenile justice systems even in challenging post-conflict contexts.

Developing Effective Legislative Frameworks

Developing effective legislative frameworks for restorative justice requires careful attention to several factors.

Stakeholder Engagement

An inclusive process that engages a wide range of stakeholders is essential. Victims, offenders, community members, legal professionals, and restorative justice practitioners all have perspectives that should inform legislative development. Their input ensures that legislation addresses real needs and has broad support.

A collaborative approach that facilitates collaboration between government agencies, non-governmental organizations, and community groups strengthens legislative development. These partnerships bring diverse expertise and resources to the table and build constituencies for restorative justice.

Comprehensive Guidelines and Standards

Clear definitions and objectives are essential. Legislation should define key terms—restorative justice, restorative practices, restorative processes—to ensure clarity and consistency. It should articulate objectives—what restorative programs are intended to achieve—to guide implementation and evaluation.

Procedural safeguards protect the rights and well-being of participants. Legislation should address informed consent, confidentiality, the right to legal representation, and other protections. These safeguards ensure that restorative processes are fair and respectful.

Funding and Resource Allocation

Adequate funding is essential for program sustainability. Legislation should allocate sufficient funding to support the implementation of restorative justice programs, including resources for training, facilitation, and evaluation. Without adequate funding, programs cannot survive.

Resource support for community-based organizations and restorative justice practitioners is also important. Legislation should provide resources to build capacity, support program delivery, and ensure quality practice.

Training and Professional Development

Capacity building through training and professional development is essential. Legislation should invest in training for legal professionals, restorative justice facilitators, and other stakeholders. This training ensures that restorative processes are implemented competently and ethically.

Ongoing education keeps practitioners updated on best practices and emerging trends. Legislation should support continuing education and professional development, ensuring that restorative practice evolves with new knowledge and experience.

Monitoring and Evaluation

Regular assessment through monitoring and evaluation is essential for program effectiveness. Legislation should establish mechanisms for ongoing evaluation, including data collection, outcome measurement, and reporting requirements. These mechanisms ensure accountability and support continuous improvement.

Data collection and analysis should address program outcomes—victim satisfaction, recidivism rates, cost-effectiveness—to inform policy and practice. This evidence base demonstrates the value of restorative justice and guides ongoing development.

Challenges in Developing Legislative Frameworks

Developing legislative frameworks for restorative justice presents several challenges.

Resistance to Change

Cultural and institutional resistance is common. Stakeholders accustomed to retributive approaches may be skeptical of restorative alternatives. Overcoming this resistance requires education, demonstration of effectiveness, and gradual integration rather than abrupt replacement.

Building consensus among diverse stakeholders with differing perspectives on justice and conflict resolution is also challenging. Victims' advocates, offenders' rights groups, legal professionals, and community organizations may have different priorities and concerns. Finding common ground requires patience, dialogue, and compromise.

Balancing Flexibility and Consistency

Ensuring that legislative frameworks provide sufficient flexibility to address the unique needs of different cases and communities is important. Restorative processes must be adaptable to individual circumstances. Rigid legislation can undermine this flexibility.

At the same time, maintaining consistency and fairness requires clear standards. Balancing flexibility with consistency is a delicate task. Legislation must provide enough structure to ensure fairness while allowing enough flexibility to enable responsive practice.

Ensuring Equity and Access

Addressing potential disparities in access to restorative justice programs is essential. Marginalized and vulnerable populations may face barriers to participation—lack of information, lack of resources, lack of trust. Legislation must address these barriers.

Promoting inclusivity and cultural sensitivity in the design and implementation of restorative justice programs is equally important. Legislation should require cultural competence training, community engagement, and attention to diversity in program development.

Case Law and Precedents: Notable Legal Cases and Their Implications for Restorative Justice

Finally, we turn to the role of case law and judicial precedents in shaping restorative justice. Courts interpret legislation, apply principles, and set precedents that influence future practice.

Understanding Case Law and Precedents

Case law refers to the body of judicial decisions that interpret and apply laws in specific cases. Precedents established by higher courts are binding on lower courts within the same jurisdiction, shaping the application of legal principles and policies.

Role of Case Law in Restorative Justice

Courts play several important roles in relation to restorative justice. First, they interpret restorative justice legislation and policies, providing clarity on their application and scope. When legislation is ambiguous, judicial interpretation determines how it will be applied.

Second, judicial decisions set precedents that influence future cases. A court's ruling on the appropriateness of restorative justice in a particular context, or on the relationship between restorative and conventional processes, guides subsequent decisions.

Third, case law reflects evolving standards and practices in restorative justice. As restorative justice develops, courts respond, and their decisions contribute to its development and acceptance within the legal system.

Notable Legal Cases in Restorative Justice

Several notable legal cases have shaped the development of restorative justice.

R v. Gladue (1999) – Canada

The Supreme Court of Canada's decision in R v. Gladue addressed the overrepresentation of Indigenous people in the Canadian criminal justice system. The Court held that judges must consider the unique circumstances of Indigenous offenders and prioritize restorative justice principles, such as healing and rehabilitation, over incarceration.

The Court recognized that conventional sentencing practices had failed Indigenous communities and that restorative approaches offered a more appropriate response. It required judges to consider restorative alternatives and to explain their reasons when imposing custodial sentences.

This landmark decision led to the development of "Gladue reports"—pre-sentencing reports that provide information about an Indigenous offender's background and circumstances. It has increased the use of restorative justice practices for Indigenous offenders and influenced sentencing practices across Canada.

The theological significance of this decision is profound. It recognizes that justice must be attentive to context, to history, to the unique circumstances of communities. It embodies the biblical principle of justice that is responsive to the vulnerable and attentive to the particular.

R v. Proulx (2000) – Canada

In R v. Proulx, the Supreme Court of Canada clarified the application of conditional sentences, emphasizing the importance of restorative justice principles. The Court affirmed that conditional sentences should be used to promote restorative justice, focusing on reparation, rehabilitation, and community involvement.

The Court held that conditional sentences—sentences served in the community under supervision—can achieve restorative purposes that incarceration cannot. They allow offenders to make reparation, to maintain employment, to support their families, to participate in rehabilitative programs.

This decision reinforced the role of restorative justice in sentencing, encouraging the use of community-based alternatives to incarceration. It recognized that punishment and restoration are not mutually exclusive but can be combined in creative ways.

Mabo v. Queensland (No. 2) (1992) – Australia

The High Court of Australia's decision in Mabo v. Queensland (No. 2) recognized Indigenous land rights and emphasized the need for restorative justice in addressing historical injustices. The Court's recognition of native title—that Indigenous peoples had occupied and owned land before European settlement—challenged the legal fiction that Australia was terra nullius, land belonging to no one.

The Court's decision highlighted the importance of restorative justice principles in legal and social contexts. It acknowledged historical wrongs, recognized the rights of Indigenous peoples, and opened pathways for reconciliation.

This decision paved the way for greater integration of restorative justice approaches in addressing Indigenous rights and reconciliation efforts in Australia. It demonstrates that restorative principles can inform not only criminal justice but also broader legal and social issues.

South Africa's Truth and Reconciliation Commission – Post-Apartheid Era

While not a court case, the Truth and Reconciliation Commission's work has had profound implications for restorative justice. The TRC was established to address the atrocities committed during apartheid, using restorative justice principles to promote healing and reconciliation.

The TRC facilitated public hearings where victims and perpetrators could share their experiences, seek forgiveness, and agree on reparative actions. Perpetrators who fully disclosed their political crimes could receive amnesty; victims could tell their stories and receive acknowledgment and reparations.

The TRC's work set a global precedent for using restorative justice in post-conflict societies. It demonstrated the potential of restorative approaches to address systemic injustices and promote national healing, even in the aftermath of massive human rights violations.

R v. Restorative Justice Tribunal (Fictional Example)

Consider a hypothetical case involving the establishment of a Restorative Justice Tribunal to handle certain criminal cases in the United Kingdom. This tribunal would focus on restorative practices, including victim-offender mediation and community restitution, as part of its adjudication process.

Such a tribunal could complement traditional courts, offering alternative pathways for conflict resolution and harm reparation. It could handle cases where victims desire restorative encounter, where offenders are willing to take responsibility, where community involvement would be beneficial.

This example illustrates how specialized restorative justice bodies can be integrated into legal systems. They are not replacements for courts but supplements, offering options that courts cannot provide.

Analysis of Legal Precedents

These legal precedents have important implications for restorative justice.

Promoting Restorative Principles in Sentencing

Judicial decisions that emphasize restorative justice principles in sentencing guidelines encourage the use of non-custodial measures and reparative actions. They recognize that sentencing is not merely about punishment but about addressing harm, promoting accountability, and supporting rehabilitation.

Precedents that prioritize rehabilitation and community reintegration over punitive measures support the development of more humane and effective justice practices. They align with evidence about what works to reduce recidivism and promote public safety.

Addressing Systemic Injustices

Cases like R v. Gladue and Mabo v. Queensland (No. 2) highlight the role of restorative justice in addressing historical and systemic injustices. They recognize that conventional legal approaches have often failed marginalized communities and that restorative alternatives offer more appropriate responses.

The TRC's work in South Africa demonstrates the potential of restorative justice to facilitate healing and reconciliation in post-conflict societies. It provides a model for other nations grappling with legacies of violence and oppression.

Enhancing Victim Participation and Satisfaction

Judicial decisions that prioritize victim participation and satisfaction in restorative processes contribute to higher levels of victim empowerment and emotional healing. They recognize that victims are not merely witnesses but stakeholders whose needs and perspectives matter.

Encouraging reparative actions and community involvement in sentencing and dispute resolution promotes a more holistic approach to justice. It recognizes that justice is not only about what happens to offenders but also about what happens for victims and communities.

Challenges and Considerations

Despite these positive developments, several challenges remain.

Consistency in Application

Ensuring uniform application of restorative justice principles across different jurisdictions and cases is challenging. Courts may interpret legislation differently; practices may vary. Clear guidelines and ongoing training for legal professionals can help address this challenge.

Balancing the flexibility of restorative practices with the need for consistent and fair outcomes is essential to maintaining public trust and confidence in the justice system. This balance requires careful attention to both individual circumstances and systemic standards.

Integrating Restorative Justice with Formal Legal Systems

Overcoming resistance within traditional legal systems and institutions is necessary for the successful integration of restorative justice practices. Legal professionals accustomed to adversarial processes may be skeptical of restorative alternatives. Education, demonstration of effectiveness, and gradual integration can help overcome this resistance.

Developing collaborative approaches that involve legal professionals, restorative justice practitioners, and community members can enhance the integration and effectiveness of restorative justice. When all stakeholders work together, the whole is greater than the sum of its parts.

Protecting Participants' Rights

Ensuring that participation in restorative justice processes is voluntary and informed is critical to protecting the rights and well-being of participants. Coercion or pressure undermines the authenticity of the process and can cause additional harm.

Recognizing and addressing power imbalances between victims and offenders is essential to ensuring equitable and just outcomes. Facilitators must be trained to identify and mitigate these imbalances, creating conditions for genuine dialogue and mutual respect.

The Integration of Law, Psychology, Philosophy, and Theology

As we have explored the relationship between restorative justice and legal systems, we have seen how multiple disciplines inform our understanding.

Legal Perspectives

Law provides the framework within which restorative justice operates. Legal principles of due process, equal protection, and proportionality must be honored. Legal rights of victims and offenders must be protected. Legal institutions must be engaged if restorative justice is to be integrated into mainstream systems.

The legislative frameworks and case law we have examined demonstrate how law can support restorative justice. Legislation provides structure, resources, and legitimacy. Judicial decisions interpret and apply restorative principles, shaping their development.

Psychological Insights

Psychology illuminates why restorative justice produces its effects and what conditions are necessary for success. Research on trauma shows why safety and support are essential. Research on procedural justice shows why voice and respect matter. Research on moral development shows why empathy and accountability promote change.

The psychological dimensions of restorative justice are particularly relevant to its integration with legal systems. Legal processes that are trauma-informed, that provide voice and respect, that promote accountability and growth—these are more effective and more just.

Philosophical Foundations

Philosophy provides the ethical framework for restorative justice. Relational ethics explains why relationships matter. Communitarianism explains why community involvement is essential. Virtue ethics explains why character formation is important. Restorative ontology explains why healing is possible.

These philosophical foundations have implications for legal integration. They suggest that justice systems should be concerned not only with rules and punishments but with relationships, communities, character, and healing. They challenge purely retributive approaches and open space for restorative alternatives.

Theological Dimensions

For those who approach restorative justice from a faith perspective, theology provides deeper grounding. The biblical vision of *shalom*—peace, wholeness, right relationship—is what restorative justice seeks. The reconciling work of God in Christ is what restorative practices embody. The hospitality of God's kingdom is what restorative communities practice.

The theological dimensions of legal integration are significant. They remind us that justice is not merely a human construct but a divine calling. They ground our efforts in something larger than ourselves. They give us hope even when integration is difficult.

The biblical tradition offers rich resources for thinking about law and restorative justice. The Torah itself contains provisions for restitution, for sanctuary, for Jubilee—practices that embody restorative principles. The prophets call for justice that rolls down like waters, for mercy and faithfulness, for protection of the vulnerable. Jesus embodies and teaches reconciliation, forgiveness, and restoration. Paul proclaims that in Christ, God was reconciling the world to himself.

These biblical themes inform and enrich our understanding of restorative justice and its relationship to legal systems. They remind us that justice is ultimately about relationships—with God, with neighbor, with community. They call us to create legal systems that serve these relationships, not undermine them.

As we move forward into the remaining chapters, we will build on this exploration of restorative justice and legal systems. We will examine restorative justice in international contexts, including transitional justice and human rights. We will explore the intersection of restorative justice with social justice issues, including race, class, and gender. And we will look to the future, imagining how restorative justice might continue to transform our world.

The relationship between restorative justice and legal systems is complex and evolving. But the examples we have examined—from New Zealand to Canada, from South Africa to Australia—demonstrate that integration is possible. With thoughtful legislation, supportive judicial decisions, and committed practice, restorative justice can complement and enhance traditional legal systems, creating a more comprehensive and compassionate approach to justice.

CHAPTER 08

RESTORATIVE JUSTICE IN THE INTERNATIONAL CONTEXT

We have journeyed together through the philosophical foundations of restorative justice, explored its core principles and values, examined the practices and models that bring these principles to life, studied real-world applications across multiple domains, honestly assessed both the benefits and challenges, and considered the complex relationship between restorative justice and legal systems. Now, dear reader, we expand our视野 to the global stage. Restorative justice is not merely a Western phenomenon or a modern invention; it is a universal human response to harm that has emerged in diverse forms across cultures and throughout history.

In this chapter, we will explore restorative justice in international context, examining how different regions and cultures have developed and adapted restorative practices. We will then delve into the role of restorative justice in transitional societies—nations emerging from conflict, oppression, and mass violence. Finally, we will consider the relationship between restorative justice and human rights, exploring how these two frameworks can inform and strengthen one another.

Throughout this exploration, we will draw on insights from law, psychology, philosophy, and theology to illuminate the global dimensions of restorative justice. We will see how different cultural contexts shape restorative practice, and how universal principles can be adapted to local needs and traditions.

Global Perspectives: Restorative Justice Practices Around the World

Let us begin our global journey by examining how restorative justice is practiced in different regions. Each region has developed distinctive approaches, shaped by cultural traditions, historical experiences, and contemporary needs.

Restorative Justice in North America

North America offers a rich tapestry of restorative practices, from indigenous traditions that predate European contact to innovative contemporary programs.

Canada

Canada has a deep and diverse history of restorative justice, shaped significantly by Indigenous traditions. Indigenous peoples across Canada developed sophisticated restorative practices long before European colonization. The Cree concept of healing circles, for example, brings together community members to address harm, promote healing, and restore balance. These circles are not merely dispute resolution mechanisms but spiritual practices that engage the whole community in the work of restoration.

The Navajo peacemaking process, though originating in the southwestern United States, has influenced Canadian practice as well. This process involves respected community members who facilitate dialogue between parties in conflict, drawing on traditional teachings and cultural values. The goal is not to determine who is right or wrong but to restore harmony within the community.

These Indigenous practices have profoundly influenced modern restorative justice programs across Canada. The Truth and Reconciliation Commission, established to address the legacy of Indian Residential Schools, drew on restorative principles in its work. The Commission's calls to action include recommendations for incorporating Indigenous restorative practices into the mainstream justice system.

Canada's Youth Criminal Justice Act of 2003 incorporates restorative justice principles explicitly. The Act encourages the use of extrajudicial measures—including restorative justice programs—to address youth crime. It emphasizes the importance of repairing harm, involving victims and communities, and reintegrating young offenders. This legislative framework has supported the development of restorative programs across the country.

Community-based restorative justice programs are widespread in Canada. These programs, often run by non-profit organizations in partnership with the justice system, address a wide range of offenses. They focus on rehabilitation and community involvement, providing alternatives to conventional prosecution and incarceration.

The psychological dimensions of these programs are significant. Research shows that Indigenous restorative practices are particularly effective because they align with cultural values and community norms. When practices are culturally grounded, participants are more engaged, outcomes are more meaningful, and healing is more likely.

The theological dimensions are equally important. Many Indigenous traditions understand justice in spiritual terms—as the restoration of harmony with creation, with community, with the Creator. This understanding resonates with biblical themes of *shalom*—the peace that comes when all things are in right relationship.

United States

The United States has seen significant growth in restorative justice, particularly in juvenile justice and education. Several states have integrated restorative practices into their juvenile justice systems, using victim-offender dialogues, family group conferencing, and restorative circles. These programs offer alternatives to formal prosecution and incarceration, particularly for young offenders.

The psychological rationale for focusing on youth is compelling. Adolescence is a period of moral development, when young people are forming their identities and values. Restorative practices that engage youth in understanding harm, taking responsibility, and making amends can shape their development in positive directions. Research shows that restorative approaches are more effective than punitive measures in promoting pro-social development among young offenders.

School-based restorative justice programs have proliferated across the United States. These programs address bullying, reduce suspensions, and create positive school climates. They draw on the insight that schools are communities, and that conflicts within those communities are best addressed through processes that engage all affected parties.

The impact of school-based restorative justice has been remarkable. Schools that implement restorative practices report reductions in disciplinary incidents, improvements in school climate, and better academic outcomes. Students learn conflict resolution skills that serve them throughout life. Teachers report feeling more supported and effective.

Community restorative boards are another important innovation in the United States. These boards, composed of trained volunteers, address minor offenses and support offender reintegration. They represent the community's direct involvement in justice, embodying the principle of collective responsibility.

The philosophical foundations of these boards are significant. They reflect communitarian values—the belief that communities have a stake in justice and a role to play in its administration. They also reflect democratic values—the conviction that ordinary citizens can and should participate in governance, including the governance of justice.

Restorative Justice in Europe

Europe has developed distinctive approaches to restorative justice, shaped by its diverse legal traditions and cultural contexts.

United Kingdom

The United Kingdom has been a leader in promoting restorative justice through institutional support and integration with the criminal justice system. The Restorative Justice Council, established in the UK, promotes and regulates restorative practices. The Council provides training, accreditation, and resources to ensure high standards in restorative justice delivery. This institutional infrastructure has been crucial for the development of quality restorative programs.

Restorative justice is integrated into the UK's criminal justice system at various stages. Restorative conferencing and victim-offender mediation are used as diversion from prosecution, as conditions of probation, and as part of reentry planning. This integration ensures that restorative options are available throughout the justice process.

The education sector in the UK has also embraced restorative approaches. Many schools have adopted restorative practices to manage behavior, resolve conflicts, and improve school climates. These programs draw on the insight that schools are communities and that disciplinary issues are best addressed through processes that engage the whole school community.

Research on UK restorative programs has documented positive outcomes. Victims report high levels of satisfaction, offenders show reduced recidivism, and communities report improved relations with the justice system. These findings have supported continued investment in restorative approaches.

Norway

Norway has developed a distinctive approach to restorative justice through its conflict resolution boards, known as "konfliktråd." These boards handle minor offenses and disputes through restorative practices, involving community members in dialogue and reparation.

The Norwegian model is notable for its emphasis on community involvement. Board members are trained volunteers from the local community, not professional mediators or justice officials. This community engagement ensures that restorative processes are grounded in local values and have local support.

Restorative justice is a key component of Norway's juvenile justice system. The system emphasizes rehabilitation and reintegration over punishment, reflecting the broader Scandinavian approach to criminal justice. Young offenders are given opportunities to understand the impact of their actions, to make amends, and to be restored to community.

The philosophical foundations of the Norwegian approach are significant. They reflect a commitment to social solidarity and collective responsibility. They embody the belief that justice is not merely the business of the state but the concern of the whole community.

Germany

Germany has a well-established system of victim-offender mediation, known as "Täter-Opfer-Ausgleich." This practice is used for both juvenile and adult offenders, aiming to repair harm, promote understanding, and achieve mutually agreeable outcomes.

The German system is notable for its integration with the formal justice system. Mediation can be ordered by prosecutors or judges at various stages of the criminal process. Successful mediation can result in reduced charges, suspended sentences, or other favorable outcomes. This integration ensures that restorative options are available and accessible.

Community-based restorative justice programs in Germany address different types of offenses, focusing on victim support and offender accountability. These programs are often run by non-profit organizations in partnership with the justice system, drawing on community resources and volunteer involvement.

Research on German restorative programs has documented positive outcomes. Victims report high levels of satisfaction, offenders show reduced recidivism, and communities report improved confidence in the justice system. These findings have supported the continued expansion of restorative approaches.

The psychological dimensions of the German approach are significant. Mediation provides opportunities for empathy development, moral reflection, and behavioral change. Offenders who meet their victims, who hear about the impact of their actions, who take responsibility and make amends—these offenders are more likely to change than those who merely serve sentences.

Restorative Justice in Africa

Africa offers powerful examples of restorative justice, both in traditional practices and in innovative contemporary programs.

South Africa

South Africa's Truth and Reconciliation Commission is perhaps the most famous example of restorative justice in the world. Established in 1995 to address the atrocities committed during apartheid, the TRC embodied restorative principles on a national scale.

The TRC held public hearings where victims and perpetrators could share their experiences, seek forgiveness, and agree on reparative actions. Perpetrators who fully disclosed their political crimes could receive amnesty; victims could tell their stories and receive acknowledgment and reparations. The process was not about punishment but about truth, accountability, and reconciliation.

The philosophical foundations of the TRC drew on the concept of *Ubuntu*—the African philosophy that emphasizes interconnectedness and shared humanity. Archbishop Desmond Tutu, who chaired the commission, explained that Ubuntu means "my humanity is caught up, is inextricably bound up, in yours." This understanding shaped the TRC's restorative approach, emphasizing the interdependence of victims and perpetrators, the possibility of healing and reconciliation.

The theological dimensions of the TRC were equally significant. South Africa is a deeply religious society, and the TRC drew on Christian language and imagery. Forgiveness, reconciliation, redemption—these themes resonated with both victims and perpetrators, providing a framework for healing that transcended legal categories.

The TRC's work has been influential worldwide. It demonstrated that restorative approaches could address even the most severe human rights violations, that truth-telling and acknowledgment could promote healing, that amnesty could be conditional on accountability. Subsequent truth commissions in countries around the world have drawn on the South African model.

South Africa has also implemented numerous community-based restorative justice programs. These programs address local conflicts, promote social cohesion, and build community capacity. They draw on traditional African practices of community dialogue and consensus-building, adapting them to contemporary needs.

Kenya

Kenya's traditional justice systems offer rich examples of restorative practice. Elders' Councils, known by various names in different communities, have long resolved disputes and promoted community harmony through restorative processes. These councils bring together parties in conflict, listen to all sides, and work toward consensus and reconciliation.

The principles underlying these traditional practices are deeply restorative. The focus is on repairing relationships, not merely resolving disputes. The community is involved in the process, not merely as spectators but as participants. The goal is restoration of harmony, not victory of one party over another.

Efforts are being made to integrate restorative justice into Kenya's formal legal system, particularly for juvenile offenders and minor offenses. These efforts recognize that traditional practices have value and that formal justice systems can learn from them. They also recognize that restorative approaches may be more effective than conventional prosecution in addressing certain types of cases.

The psychological dimensions of traditional Kenyan justice are significant. These practices draw on community knowledge and relationships, ensuring that resolutions are grounded in local realities. They engage participants emotionally, promoting genuine understanding and reconciliation. They provide opportunities for healing that formal legal processes cannot offer.

Restorative Justice in Asia

Asia offers diverse examples of restorative justice, from pioneering statutory programs to traditional practices adapted for contemporary use.

New Zealand

New Zealand is a pioneer in restorative justice, particularly through its Family Group Conferencing program. Mandated for juvenile offenders under the Children, Young Persons, and Their Families Act 1989, FGC involves families, victims, and community members in the decision-making process.

The New Zealand model draws on Maori traditions of collective responsibility and community involvement. Maori concepts of justice—*whānau* (family), *hapū* (sub-tribe), *iwi* (tribe)—emphasize the interconnectedness of individuals and communities. Harm is not merely an individual matter but a breach in the fabric of community. Response to harm must involve the whole community in restoration.

The legislative framework for FGC is notable for its strength. The Act makes FGC mandatory for most youth offenses, with limited exceptions. It establishes procedures for conducting conferences, protecting participants' rights, and implementing agreements. It allocates resources for training, facilitation, and support.

The outcomes of New Zealand's FGC program have been impressive. Research shows high levels of victim satisfaction, reduced recidivism rates, and positive rehabilitation outcomes for young offenders. The program has been adapted for use with adult offenders and in other countries, demonstrating its replicability.

The philosophical foundations of FGC are significant. They reflect communitarian values—the belief that communities have a stake in justice and a role to play in its administration. They also reflect relational ethics—the understanding that harm damages relationships and that justice must repair those relationships.

Japan

Japan's legal system incorporates reconciliation committees that facilitate mediation between victims and offenders. These committees, composed of community volunteers and legal professionals, work to promote resolution and reparation. The process is informal and flexible, focused on dialogue and mutual understanding.

Community involvement is a key aspect of restorative justice in Japan. Local volunteers participate in the reconciliation process, bringing community knowledge and values to bear. This involvement ensures that outcomes are grounded in community norms and have community support.

The cultural context of Japanese restorative justice is significant. Japanese culture emphasizes harmony, consensus, and collective responsibility. These values align with restorative principles, making restorative approaches culturally resonant.

The emphasis on apology and forgiveness in Japanese culture also supports restorative processes.

Research on Japanese restorative programs shows positive outcomes. Victims report satisfaction with the process, offenders demonstrate accountability, and communities report improved relations. These findings suggest that restorative justice can be effective in diverse cultural contexts when adapted appropriately.

Singapore

Singapore has integrated restorative justice into its juvenile justice system, focusing on rehabilitation and reintegration. Practices such as family group conferencing and victim-offender mediation are commonly used, providing alternatives to formal prosecution and incarceration.

The Singaporean approach emphasizes the importance of family involvement. Families are engaged in restorative processes, providing support and accountability for young offenders. This involvement recognizes that families are essential to rehabilitation and reintegration.

Research on Singaporean restorative programs shows positive outcomes. Recidivism rates are reduced, victim satisfaction is high, and community confidence in the justice system is enhanced. These findings support continued investment in restorative approaches.

Restorative Justice in Latin America

Latin America has developed innovative restorative practices, often in challenging contexts of violence and inequality.

Brazil

Brazil has implemented restorative circles in various contexts, including schools, prisons, and community settings. These circles bring together affected parties to address conflicts, promote healing, and build community. They draw on both indigenous traditions and contemporary restorative practice.

Community-based restorative justice initiatives in Brazil focus on addressing local conflicts and building stronger, more cohesive communities. These initiatives often operate in marginalized neighborhoods affected by violence and crime, providing alternatives to both vigilantism and ineffective formal justice.

The psychological dimensions of Brazilian restorative circles are significant. Participants report feeling heard, respected, and valued. They develop empathy and understanding. They learn conflict resolution skills that serve them in multiple contexts. These outcomes contribute to individual healing and community resilience.

The theological dimensions are also important. Many Brazilian restorative programs are supported by faith-based organizations, drawing on Christian teachings about forgiveness, reconciliation, and community. The base communities of liberation theology, with their emphasis on participatory decision-making and social justice, have influenced restorative practice.

Argentina

Argentina has incorporated restorative justice principles into its juvenile justice system, emphasizing diversion, rehabilitation, and community involvement. Young offenders are offered opportunities to participate in restorative processes as alternatives to formal prosecution.

Victim-offender mediation programs in Argentina address various types of conflicts, supporting victim healing and offender accountability. These programs draw on both international best practices and local cultural contexts, adapting restorative approaches to Argentine realities.

Research on Argentine restorative programs shows promising outcomes. Victims report satisfaction, offenders demonstrate accountability, and communities report improved confidence in the justice system. These findings support continued development of restorative approaches.

Cultural Adaptations and Challenges

The global experience of restorative justice highlights both the universality of restorative principles and the importance of cultural adaptation.

Cultural Sensitivity and Relevance

Restorative justice practices must be adapted to fit the cultural context of the communities they serve. This includes respecting local customs, traditions, and values. A practice that works well in one cultural context may be ineffective or even harmful in another.

Adapting practices requires deep engagement with local communities. It means learning from traditional practices, understanding cultural norms, and respecting local knowledge. It means being humble about what outside experts know and open to learning from those with different perspectives.

Engaging local leaders and community members in the design and implementation of restorative justice programs enhances their cultural relevance and acceptance. When communities have ownership of restorative processes, they are more likely to trust them, participate in them, and support their outcomes.

The theological dimensions of cultural adaptation are significant. Different religious traditions offer resources for restorative practice—concepts of forgiveness, reconciliation, community, justice. Engaging these traditions respectfully can enhance the cultural relevance and spiritual depth of restorative programs.

Addressing Power Imbalances

Power imbalances between victims and offenders, and within communities more broadly, can affect restorative processes. Ensuring equitable participation requires attention to these dynamics. Facilitators must be skilled in recognizing and addressing power imbalances, creating conditions for genuine dialogue.

Providing support services, such as counseling and advocacy, can help vulnerable participants engage more fully in the restorative process. Victims may need support to articulate their needs; offenders may need support to manage shame and develop accountability. These services enhance equity and effectiveness.

The psychological dimensions of addressing power imbalances are significant. Trauma-informed practice recognizes that power imbalances can retraumatize victims and undermine healing. Creating safe, supportive environments is essential for restorative justice to achieve its goals.

Ensuring Sustainability

Securing funding and resources is essential for the sustainability of restorative justice programs. Governments, NGOs, and international organizations can play a role in providing financial support. But sustainability requires more than money—it requires institutional commitment, community engagement, and ongoing capacity building.

Investing in training and capacity building for practitioners and community members ensures the effective implementation and sustainability of restorative practices. Skilled facilitators are essential; communities that understand restorative principles can support programs over the long term.

The philosophical dimensions of sustainability are significant. Restorative justice is not a quick fix but a long-term commitment to transforming how communities respond to harm. Sustainability requires patience, persistence, and faith in the restorative process.

Transitional Justice: Restorative Approaches in Post-Conflict and Transitional Societies

We turn now to one of the most challenging and important applications of restorative justice: transitional justice. In societies emerging from conflict, oppression, and mass violence, restorative approaches offer pathways to healing and reconciliation that conventional justice cannot provide.

Understanding Transitional Justice

Transitional justice refers to the ways societies address legacies of mass violence, human rights abuses, and systemic injustices during periods of political transition. These transitions may follow the end of armed conflict, the fall of authoritarian regimes, or other fundamental political changes.

Key Principles of Transitional Justice

Transitional justice encompasses several key principles. Truth and acknowledgment involve establishing an accurate historical record of past abuses and ensuring public acknowledgment of the truth. This truth-telling is essential for victims, for communities, and for the nation as a whole.

Justice and accountability involve holding perpetrators accountable through legal and restorative processes. This accountability may take various forms—criminal prosecution, lustration (excluding perpetrators from public office), restorative processes that require truth-telling and reparation.

Reparation and redress involve providing reparations to victims, including material compensation, symbolic gestures, and community rebuilding. Reparations acknowledge the harm suffered and contribute to victims' recovery.

Reconciliation and healing involve promoting reconciliation between conflicting parties and fostering societal healing. This is the ultimate goal of transitional justice—not merely addressing past wrongs but building a foundation for peaceful coexistence.

Restorative Justice in Transitional Contexts

Restorative justice is particularly well-suited to transitional contexts. Its focus on repairing harm, promoting accountability, and fostering reconciliation aligns with the needs of societies emerging from conflict. Its emphasis on victim participation and community involvement addresses the marginalization that victims often experience.

In transitional societies, restorative approaches can address the needs of victims, reintegrate perpetrators, and rebuild trust within communities. They can provide alternatives to both impunity (ignoring past wrongs) and vengeance (seeking retribution that perpetuates conflict). They can create space for truth-telling, acknowledgment, and healing.

Mechanisms of Restorative Transitional Justice

Several mechanisms have been developed to implement restorative justice in transitional contexts.

Truth Commissions

Truth commissions investigate and document past human rights violations, providing a platform for victims and perpetrators to share their experiences. These commissions are not courts; they do not prosecute or punish. Their purpose is truth-telling, acknowledgment, and recommendation.

Truth commissions often incorporate restorative elements. Public hearings allow victims to tell their stories and be heard. Perpetrators may be invited to testify, to acknowledge their actions, to seek forgiveness. Commissions may recommend reparations, institutional reforms, and other measures to address the legacy of past abuses.

The psychological dimensions of truth commissions are significant. For victims, having their suffering acknowledged can be profoundly healing. For perpetrators, confronting the truth of their actions can be transformative. For society, establishing an accurate historical record can prevent denial and promote reconciliation.

Community-Based Restorative Practices

Community-based practices involve local communities in resolving conflicts and addressing past harms through dialogue, mediation, and collective decision-making. These practices draw on traditional conflict resolution mechanisms, adapting them to post-conflict contexts.

In Rwanda, for example, the Gacaca courts drew on traditional community-based justice to address the massive backlog of genocide-related cases. Community members participated in hearings, heard testimony, and contributed to decisions about accountability and reparation. This community involvement was essential for addressing the scale of the genocide and for promoting local reconciliation.

Community-based practices emphasize participation, empowerment, and community healing. They foster a sense of collective responsibility and solidarity, rebuilding the social fabric torn by conflict.

Victim-Offender Mediation and Dialogues

Facilitated dialogues between victims and perpetrators aim to address the harm, promote understanding, and develop reparative actions. These dialogues are not appropriate for all cases—they require careful preparation, skilled facilitation, and voluntary participation. But when they work, they can be profoundly healing.

In Colombia, for example, the Special Jurisdiction for Peace incorporates restorative dialogues as part of its process.

Perpetrators who acknowledge their responsibility and contribute to truth-telling may participate in restorative encounters with victims. These encounters provide opportunities for acknowledgment, apology, and reparation.

These processes encourage accountability, empathy, and mutual recognition. They contribute to personal and societal healing, transforming relationships that have been damaged by violence.

Reparations Programs

Reparations programs provide compensation and support to victims of human rights abuses, recognizing their suffering and contributing to their recovery. Reparations can take many forms—financial compensation, healthcare, education, housing, symbolic measures such as apologies and memorials.

Reparations are restorative in several ways. They acknowledge the harm suffered, validating victims' experiences. They provide material support for recovery, addressing practical needs. They contribute to a sense of justice, even when perpetrators cannot be prosecuted.

The psychological dimensions of reparations are significant. For victims, receiving reparations can be healing—a tangible acknowledgment that their suffering matters, that society cares about their recovery. For communities, reparations can contribute to rebuilding and reconciliation.

Institutional Reforms

Institutional reforms aim to address the root causes of conflict and prevent future abuses by transforming justice, security, and governance systems. These reforms may include vetting of personnel, changes in laws and policies, development of new institutions.

Institutional reforms are restorative in that they address systemic injustices and promote more just and equitable societies. They reflect the principle that preventing future harm is as important as addressing past harm.

Case Studies of Restorative Transitional Justice

Examining specific examples illuminates the potential and challenges of restorative transitional justice.

South Africa: Truth and Reconciliation Commission

The South African Truth and Reconciliation Commission, established in 1995, addressed the atrocities committed during apartheid. The TRC was a landmark experiment in restorative justice, seeking to promote national healing and reconciliation through truth-telling, accountability, and reparation.

The TRC held public hearings where victims and perpetrators could share their experiences. Victims told their stories, described their suffering, named those who had harmed them. Perpetrators testified about their actions, sometimes expressing remorse, sometimes seeking forgiveness. The hearings were televised, allowing the whole nation to witness the process.

The TRC provided amnesty to perpetrators who fully disclosed their political crimes. This provision was controversial—critics argued that it let perpetrators off too easily. But proponents argued that amnesty was necessary to secure testimony, to uncover the truth, to avoid endless prosecutions that could destabilize the transition.

The TRC recommended reparations for victims, including financial compensation, community rehabilitation, and symbolic measures. Implementation of these recommendations was imperfect—many victims felt that reparations were inadequate and delayed. But the recommendations themselves represented an acknowledgment of victims' suffering and a commitment to redress.

The TRC's work has been both praised and criticized. Supporters point to its role in uncovering truth, promoting reconciliation, and preventing a cycle of vengeance. Critics point to its limitations—incomplete truth, inadequate reparations, insufficient accountability. But whatever its limitations, the TRC demonstrated that restorative approaches could address even the most severe human rights violations.

The theological dimensions of the TRC were profound. South Africa is a deeply religious society, and the TRC drew on Christian language and imagery. Archbishop Desmond Tutu, who chaired the commission, spoke frequently of forgiveness, reconciliation, and redemption. The concept of *Ubuntu*—the African philosophy of interconnectedness—provided a framework for understanding justice in relational terms.

Rwanda: Gacaca Courts

Following the 1994 genocide, Rwanda faced an impossible challenge: how to address the crimes of hundreds of thousands of perpetrators through a justice system that had been destroyed. The conventional courts could not handle the caseload; imprisonment without trial was unsustainable; impunity was unacceptable.

The solution was the Gacaca courts—community-based tribunals drawing on traditional Rwandan justice practices. Gacaca courts were established in communities across the country, composed of locally elected judges (inyangamugayo) who heard testimony, determined guilt, and imposed sentences.

The Gacaca process was deeply restorative. Perpetrators were encouraged to confess their crimes, to acknowledge what they had done, to seek forgiveness from victims and communities. Those who confessed truthfully could receive reduced sentences, often involving community service rather than imprisonment. Victims could tell their stories, confront those who had harmed them, participate in determining appropriate outcomes.

The Gacaca courts resolved an enormous number of cases—over a million—in a relatively short period. They contributed to truth-telling, accountability, and community healing. They demonstrated that restorative approaches could work even in the aftermath of genocide.

But the Gacaca process was not without problems. Some perpetrators gave false confessions; some victims were pressured to forgive; some communities experienced tension and conflict. The quality of justice varied; the rights of defendants were not always protected. Critics raised concerns about due process, about the adequacy of defense, about the potential for bias.

Despite these limitations, the Gacaca courts represent a remarkable experiment in restorative transitional justice. They demonstrated that community-based processes could address mass atrocities, that truth-telling could promote healing, that accountability could take forms other than imprisonment.

Colombia: Special Jurisdiction for Peace

As part of the 2016 peace agreement between the Colombian government and the FARC guerrillas, the Special Jurisdiction for Peace (JEP) was established to address crimes committed during the armed conflict. The JEP incorporates restorative justice principles, offering reduced sentences to perpetrators who acknowledge responsibility, tell the truth, and contribute to reparations.

The JEP is a complex institution, combining restorative and retributive elements. Perpetrators who fully disclose their crimes, acknowledge responsibility, and contribute to truth and reparations may receive alternative sentences—restrictions on liberty rather than imprisonment. Those who do not cooperate may face conventional prosecution.

The JEP emphasizes victim participation. Victims can present information, participate in proceedings, and receive reparations. Their voices are central to the process, ensuring that their needs and perspectives shape outcomes.

The JEP also emphasizes truth-telling. Perpetrators must provide complete and truthful accounts of their actions. These accounts contribute to the historical record, to victims' understanding, to societal healing.

The Colombian process is ongoing, and its outcomes remain to be seen. But it represents an ambitious attempt to apply restorative principles to a complex conflict, to balance accountability and reconciliation, to address the needs of victims while reintegrating perpetrators.

Sierra Leone: Truth and Reconciliation Commission

Sierra Leone's Truth and Reconciliation Commission was established after the civil war to investigate human rights violations, promote reconciliation, and recommend reparations. The TRC held public hearings, gathered testimonies, and emphasized community involvement in the reconciliation process.

The Sierra Leone TRC drew on the South African model but adapted it to local circumstances. It emphasized community engagement, holding hearings in local communities and involving traditional leaders. It addressed not only the atrocities of the conflict but also the underlying social and economic conditions that contributed to violence.

The TRC's work contributed to a deeper understanding of the conflict's impact. It documented the experiences of victims, including the widespread use of child soldiers, the brutality of attacks on civilians, the destruction of communities. It provided a platform for victims to tell their stories and be heard.

The TRC recommended reparations for victims and reforms to prevent future conflict. Implementation of these recommendations has been uneven, limited by resources and political will. But the recommendations themselves represented an acknowledgment of victims' suffering and a commitment to address it.

Challenges and Considerations

Restorative transitional justice faces significant challenges.

Balancing Justice and Reconciliation

Balancing the need for justice and accountability with the goals of reconciliation and healing is challenging, particularly in contexts of widespread and severe abuses. Victims may demand punishment; perpetrators may resist accountability. Finding the right balance requires careful attention to context, to victims' needs, to the possibilities for reconciliation.

Integrating both retributive and restorative elements can help achieve a balanced approach. Criminal prosecution for the most responsible, restorative processes for lower-level perpetrators, truth commissions for historical clarification—these different mechanisms can complement one another. Ensuring that victims' needs and rights are prioritized is essential.

Ensuring Inclusivity and Participation

Ensuring the meaningful participation of all stakeholders, including marginalized and vulnerable groups, is essential for the legitimacy and effectiveness of restorative transitional justice. Women, children, ethnic minorities, and other marginalized groups must have voice and agency in transitional processes.

Engaging local communities, civil society organizations, and affected populations in the design and implementation of restorative processes enhances inclusivity and ownership. When people feel that they have a stake in transitional justice, they are more likely to support it and participate in it.

Managing Expectations and Outcomes

Managing the diverse and often high expectations of victims, perpetrators, and communities can be complex, particularly in volatile and rapidly changing environments. Victims may expect more than transitional processes can deliver; perpetrators may resist accountability; communities may be divided about what justice requires.

Setting realistic goals, communicating transparently, and being responsive to evolving needs and contexts can help manage expectations and achieve sustainable outcomes. Transitional justice is not a quick fix but a long-term process requiring patience and persistence.

Sustaining Long-Term Impact

Ensuring the long-term sustainability of restorative justice initiatives in transitional contexts requires ongoing commitment, resources, and institutional support. Truth commissions complete their work and disband; reparations programs may run out of funds; institutional reforms may be reversed.

Building local capacity, securing financial and political support, and integrating restorative practices into broader peacebuilding and development strategies can support sustainability. Transitional justice must be embedded in ongoing processes of social transformation, not treated as a one-time intervention.

Human Rights and Restorative Justice: The Relationship Between Human Rights and Restorative Practices

Finally, we turn to the relationship between restorative justice and human rights—two frameworks that share common principles and complementary goals.

Understanding the Relationship Between Human Rights and Restorative Justice

Human rights and restorative justice share a common foundation in promoting dignity, respect, and justice for all individuals.

Common Principles

Both human rights and restorative justice emphasize the inherent dignity and respect due to every individual, regardless of their actions or status. This principle is foundational in human rights law, enshrined in the Universal Declaration of Human Rights and subsequent treaties. It is equally foundational in restorative justice, which insists that even those who have caused harm retain their dignity and worth.

Both frameworks seek accountability and justice. Human rights law holds states and individuals accountable for violations; restorative justice holds offenders accountable to victims and communities. Both aim to repair harm and ensure that wrongdoers take responsibility.

Both prioritize participation and inclusion. Human rights law emphasizes the right to participate in decisions affecting one's life; restorative justice insists that victims, offenders, and communities must have voice in the justice process. Both frameworks recognize that justice cannot be imposed from above but must involve those affected.

Complementary Goals

Restorative justice focuses on healing and reparation, aligning with human rights principles that seek to address and remedy violations. The right to a remedy, enshrined in international human rights law, includes the right to reparation for harm suffered. Restorative practices offer one pathway to such reparation.

By addressing the root causes of conflict and harm, restorative justice contributes to the prevention of future human rights violations. When communities are strengthened, when conflicts are resolved constructively, when underlying grievances are addressed—human rights are better protected.

Restorative practices empower victims by giving them voice and active role in the justice process, aligning with human rights principles of victim-centered justice. Victims are not merely witnesses but participants, whose needs and perspectives shape outcomes.

How Restorative Justice Supports Human Rights

Restorative justice supports human rights in multiple ways.

Addressing Human Rights Violations

Truth and reconciliation commissions investigate and document human rights violations, providing a platform for victims and perpetrators to share their experiences and seek reconciliation. They help establish an accurate historical record and promote healing and justice. This truth-telling is itself a form of remedy, acknowledging violations and affirming victims' dignity.

In communities affected by human rights abuses, restorative practices can facilitate dialogue, understanding, and collective healing. Community-based restorative processes address the harm, promote social cohesion, and build resilience against future violations. They embody the principle that human rights are protected not only by law but by healthy communities.

Rehabilitation and Reintegration of Offenders

Restorative justice programs focus on the rehabilitation and reintegration of offenders, ensuring that they take responsibility for their actions and make amends to victims and communities. This approach aligns with human rights principles that emphasize the potential for rehabilitation and the humane treatment of offenders.

Human rights law prohibits cruel, inhuman, or degrading treatment or punishment. Restorative practices offer an alternative to harsh punishments that may violate this prohibition. They treat offenders as human beings capable of change, not as irredeemable monsters.

Empowering Marginalized Groups

Restorative justice practices can be designed to include and empower marginalized groups, ensuring that their voices are heard and their rights are respected. This approach helps address systemic inequalities and promote social justice.

Marginalized groups—racial and ethnic minorities, indigenous peoples, women, LGBTQ+ individuals, persons with disabilities—often experience discrimination in conventional justice systems. Restorative practices, when designed inclusively, can counter this discrimination and promote equity.

Reparations and Redress

Restorative justice emphasizes reparative measures, such as apologies, compensation, and community service, to address harm and support victims. These measures align with human rights principles that call for effective remedies for victims of violations.

The right to a remedy includes access to justice, reparation for harm suffered, and guarantees of non-repetition. Restorative practices contribute to all three elements—providing access to participatory processes, offering reparative outcomes, and addressing underlying causes to prevent recurrence.

Challenges in Integrating Human Rights and Restorative Justice

Integrating human rights and restorative justice presents several challenges.

Balancing Rights and Accountability

Ensuring that restorative justice processes hold perpetrators accountable while respecting their rights can be challenging. Offenders have rights—to due process, to avoid self-incrimination, to legal representation. These rights must be protected even as restorative processes proceed.

Voluntary participation is crucial. Ensuring that participation in restorative processes is voluntary and informed protects the rights and dignity of all participants. Coercion or pressure undermines both restorative goals and human rights principles.

Addressing Power Imbalances

Power imbalances between victims and offenders can affect the fairness and effectiveness of restorative processes. Facilitators must be skilled in recognizing and addressing these imbalances to ensure equitable participation.

Providing support services, such as counseling and advocacy, can help vulnerable participants engage fully in the restorative process. These services protect participants' rights and well-being while promoting restorative goals.

Cultural Sensitivity and Context

Restorative justice practices must be adapted to fit the cultural context and respect local customs and traditions. This adaptation helps ensure that practices are relevant and effective while upholding human rights principles.

Engaging local communities in the design and implementation of restorative justice programs enhances their cultural sensitivity and acceptance. When communities have ownership of restorative processes, they are more likely to respect human rights and support restorative outcomes.

Sustainability and Resources

Ensuring adequate funding and resources for restorative justice programs is essential for their sustainability and effectiveness. Under-resourced programs cannot deliver quality services or protect participants' rights.

Investing in training and capacity building for practitioners and community members ensures high-quality and consistent practice. Well-trained facilitators are better able to protect participants' rights and promote restorative outcomes.

Real-World Examples of Integration

Several real-world examples illustrate the integration of human rights and restorative justice.

South Africa: Truth and Reconciliation Commission

The TRC addressed gross human rights violations committed during apartheid. Its restorative approach—truth-telling, amnesty conditional on disclosure, reparations—aimed to promote healing and reconciliation while acknowledging violations and holding perpetrators accountable.

The TRC's work contributed to a national acknowledgment of past abuses, promoted forgiveness and reconciliation, and set a precedent for integrating human rights and restorative justice. It demonstrated that restorative approaches could address human rights violations at a national scale.

Canada: Indigenous Restorative Justice Programs

Canada has implemented restorative justice programs that incorporate Indigenous practices, addressing the historical injustices and human rights violations faced by Indigenous communities. Programs such as healing circles and peacemaking processes involve victims, offenders, and community members in dialogue and collective decision-making.

These programs promote healing, reconciliation, and the empowerment of Indigenous communities. They align with human rights principles by respecting Indigenous cultures, addressing historical wrongs, and promoting self-determination.

Rwanda: Gacaca Courts

The Gacaca courts addressed the massive backlog of genocide-related cases through community-based restorative processes. They emphasized truth-telling, accountability, and reparation, promoting community healing and reconciliation.

The Gacaca courts resolved a significant number of cases, facilitated local reconciliation, and promoted a sense of justice and closure for many victims and communities. They demonstrated that restorative approaches could address human rights violations even in the aftermath of genocide.

Colombia: Special Jurisdiction for Peace

The JEP incorporates restorative justice principles to address crimes committed during the armed conflict. Perpetrators receive reduced sentences in exchange for truth-telling, reparations, and contributions to community rebuilding. The process emphasizes victim participation and accountability.

The JEP aims to promote accountability, support victims, and foster reconciliation. It represents an ambitious attempt to integrate restorative and human rights principles in a complex transitional context.

Strategies for Effective Integration

Several strategies can support effective integration of human rights and restorative justice.

Policy and Legislative Support

Developing policies and legislation that support the integration of restorative justice and human rights principles is essential. Legal frameworks should recognize restorative justice as a legitimate response to human rights violations, establish standards for practice, and allocate resources for implementation.

Incentivizing participation—offering reduced sentences or other benefits for those who participate in restorative processes—can encourage engagement while respecting rights. These incentives must be carefully designed to ensure that participation remains voluntary and that outcomes are fair.

Training and Capacity Building

Providing comprehensive training for restorative justice practitioners on human rights principles and practices is essential. Practitioners must understand the rights of victims and offenders, the requirements of due process, the importance of voluntary participation.

Investing in capacity building for community members enhances their understanding of restorative justice and human rights. Communities that understand these principles are better able to support restorative processes and protect participants' rights.

Collaboration and Partnerships

Collaborating with human rights organizations, legal professionals, and community groups ensures the effective integration of restorative justice and human rights. These partnerships bring diverse expertise and resources to the table, enhancing program quality and legitimacy.

Facilitating collaboration between criminal justice agencies, human rights bodies, and restorative justice programs ensures coordinated and effective implementation. When different actors work together, restorative processes are more likely to respect rights and achieve restorative goals.

Monitoring and Evaluation

Implementing mechanisms for monitoring and evaluating restorative justice programs assesses their effectiveness and identifies areas for improvement. Monitoring should include attention to human rights impacts—whether participants' rights are respected, whether outcomes are fair, whether vulnerable groups are protected.

Collecting and analyzing data on program outcomes—victim satisfaction, recidivism rates, human rights impacts—informs policy and practice. This evidence base demonstrates the value of restorative justice and guides ongoing development.

The Integration of Law, Psychology, Philosophy, and Theology

As we have explored restorative justice in international context, we have seen how multiple disciplines inform our understanding.

Legal Perspectives

International law provides frameworks for restorative justice, particularly in transitional contexts. Human rights law establishes standards for treatment of victims and offenders. International humanitarian law governs accountability for war crimes. Transitional justice draws on multiple legal traditions to address past abuses.

The examples we have examined—truth commissions in South Africa, Gacaca courts in Rwanda, the JEP in Colombia—all operate within legal frameworks, whether domestic or international. They demonstrate that restorative justice can complement legal processes, not replace them.

Psychological Insights

Psychology illuminates the dynamics of trauma, healing, and reconciliation in transitional contexts. Victims of mass violence suffer profound psychological wounds; their healing requires acknowledgment, support, and opportunities to tell their stories. Perpetrators may carry their own trauma, their own need for accountability and restoration.

Restorative transitional justice, when trauma-informed, can promote psychological healing. Truth-telling provides validation; acknowledgment counters denial; reparation supports recovery. Community-based processes rebuild social connections that trauma has destroyed.

Philosophical Foundations

Philosophy provides frameworks for thinking about justice, accountability, and reconciliation in transitional contexts. Debates about the purposes of punishment, the nature of forgiveness, the meaning of reconciliation—all have philosophical dimensions that inform restorative practice.

The philosophical foundations of transitional justice draw on diverse traditions. Western philosophy contributes concepts of rights, justice, and accountability. African philosophy contributes *Ubuntu* and communal values. Indigenous philosophies contribute relational understandings of justice. These diverse traditions enrich restorative practice.

Theological Dimensions

Theology offers profound resources for restorative transitional justice. The biblical vision of *shalom*—peace, wholeness, right relationship—provides a framework for understanding what transitional justice seeks to achieve. The reconciling work of God in Christ models the reconciliation that transitional processes pursue.

In South Africa, the TRC drew explicitly on Christian theology. Archbishop Tutu spoke of forgiveness, reconciliation, and redemption. Churches provided support for victims and perpetrators. The process was infused with religious language and ritual.

In Rwanda, the Gacaca courts operated in a deeply Christian society. Forgiveness was a central theme; perpetrators sought it; victims offered it. The churches were involved in supporting both victims and perpetrators, in promoting reconciliation.

The theological dimensions of transitional justice remind us that these processes are not merely legal or political but deeply human and spiritual. They touch the deepest questions of meaning, hope, and possibility—questions that theology addresses.

As we move forward into the remaining chapters, we will build on this exploration of restorative justice in international context. We will examine the intersection of restorative justice with social justice issues, including race, class, and gender. We will explore how restorative principles can be applied to systemic injustice and historical wrongs. And we will look to the future, imagining how restorative justice might continue to transform our world.

The global experience of restorative justice demonstrates its universal appeal and adaptability. From the Indigenous healing circles of North America to the truth commissions of Africa, from the family group conferences of New Zealand to the restorative circles of Brazil, restorative practices are addressing harm, promoting healing, and building community across cultures and continents. This is the promise of restorative justice—a promise being fulfilled, one community at a time, around the world.

CHAPTER 09

RESTORATIVE JUSTICE AND SOCIAL JUSTICE

We have journeyed together through the philosophical foundations of restorative justice, explored its core principles and values, examined the practices and models that bring these principles to life, studied real-world applications across multiple domains, honestly assessed both the benefits and challenges, considered the complex relationship between restorative justice and legal systems, and expanded our视野 to the global stage. Now, dear reader, we arrive at one of the most critical intersections in our exploration: the relationship between restorative justice and social justice.

Restorative justice is not merely a set of techniques for resolving individual conflicts. It is a philosophy with profound implications for how we understand and address systemic injustice. When we apply restorative principles to issues of race, gender, class, and other dimensions of social inequality, we discover powerful resources for promoting equity, inclusion, and community empowerment.

In this chapter, we will explore three interconnected themes. First, we will examine intersectionality—how multiple social identities intersect to create unique experiences of privilege and oppression—and consider its implications for restorative practice. Second, we will explore social equity—the pursuit of fairness and justice in the distribution of resources, opportunities, and treatment—and consider how restorative justice can advance this goal. Third, we will examine community empowerment—the process of enabling communities to gain control over their lives and participate actively in their governance—and consider how restorative practices can build stronger, more resilient communities.

Throughout this exploration, we will draw on insights from law, psychology, philosophy, and theology to illuminate the relationship between restorative justice and social justice. We will see how these different perspectives can inform and enrich our understanding, and how restorative practices can contribute to the creation of a more just and compassionate society.

Intersectionality: Addressing Issues of Race, Gender, and Class in Restorative Justice

Let us begin with intersectionality—a framework that has transformed how we understand the complex ways that social identities shape human experience. Applying this lens to restorative justice is essential for ensuring that restorative practices address the full complexity of participants' lives.

Understanding Intersectionality

Intersectionality is a concept developed by legal scholar Kimberlé Crenshaw to describe how different social identities—

such as race, gender, class, sexuality, disability, and others—intersect and interact to produce unique experiences of marginalization or privilege. The metaphor of intersection captures something essential: just as a person standing at a crossroads may be struck by traffic from multiple directions, a person with multiple marginalized identities may experience harm from multiple sources simultaneously.

Definition and Origins

Crenshaw developed the concept of intersectionality in the late 1980s to address a gap she observed in both feminist theory and anti-racist activism. She noticed that Black women's experiences of discrimination were often invisible in discussions that treated race and gender as separate categories. When courts considered sex discrimination, they looked at whether Black women were being treated differently from men—but comparing Black women to Black men didn't capture discrimination based on gender, and comparing them to white women didn't capture discrimination based on race. Black women fell through the cracks.

The concept of intersectionality highlights the interconnected nature of social categorizations. These identities do not exist in isolation; they interact, overlap, and mutually constitute one another. A wealthy white woman experiences gender differently than a poor Black woman. A gay Black man experiences race differently than a straight Black man. These intersections produce unique experiences that cannot be understood by looking at any single identity in isolation.

The importance of intersectionality lies in its insistence on complexity. Human experience cannot be reduced to a single dimension. Addressing social inequality requires attending to the multiple, intersecting forms of discrimination and privilege that shape people's lives.

Relevance to Restorative Justice

Restorative justice aims to address harm, promote healing, and restore relationships. To do this effectively, restorative practices must attend to the full complexity of participants' lives—including the intersecting identities that shape their experiences of harm, their access to justice, and their possibilities for healing.

Consider a victim of crime who is also a member of a marginalized racial group, who has experienced discrimination in the past, who distrusts formal institutions, who has limited economic resources. These intersecting identities shape how they experience the harm, how they navigate the justice process, what they need for healing. A restorative process that ignores these dimensions will be less effective, perhaps even harmful.

Consider an offender who is also young, poor, a member of a marginalized group, with a history of trauma and limited educational opportunities. These intersecting identities shape why they offended, how they understand their actions, what they need to change. A restorative process that ignores these dimensions will miss opportunities for genuine accountability and transformation.

An intersectional approach promotes equity and inclusion by recognizing and addressing the specific needs and challenges faced by individuals based on their intersecting identities. It ensures that restorative justice does not simply reproduce the inequalities of the broader society but actively works to counter them.

The theological dimensions of intersectionality are significant. The biblical vision of justice consistently emphasizes God's concern for those who are marginalized—the widow, the orphan, the stranger, the poor. These categories are not isolated; they often intersect. A widow is likely poor; an orphan is vulnerable; a stranger is without protection. The Bible's repeated commands to care for these groups reflect an understanding that marginalization is complex and that justice must attend to those who are multiply disadvantaged.

Intersectionality in Restorative Justice Practices

Applying an intersectional lens to restorative justice requires attending to multiple dimensions of identity and experience.

Race and Ethnicity

Racial and ethnic minorities face systemic discrimination in many societies, including within the criminal justice system. In the United States, for example, African Americans and Latinos are disproportionately represented at every stage of the justice process—from arrest to incarceration to parole. This overrepresentation reflects not higher rates of offending but systemic bias in policing, prosecution, and sentencing.

Restorative justice must address these disparities to promote fairness and justice. This means being attentive to how race shapes participants' experiences—how a Black victim may experience harm differently because of its racial dimensions, how a Latino offender may have different pathways to accountability because of cultural factors.

It also means incorporating culturally relevant practices and perspectives into restorative justice processes. Practices that work well for white, middle-class participants may not resonate with participants from different racial or ethnic backgrounds. Adapting practices to fit cultural contexts—drawing on indigenous traditions, incorporating community values, using culturally appropriate language and symbols—enhances effectiveness and ensures that restorative processes are truly inclusive.

The psychological dimensions of race in restorative justice are significant. Racial identity shapes how people see themselves and how they are seen by others. Racial trauma—the cumulative impact of racism on mental health—affects how victims experience harm and how offenders understand their actions. Restorative practices that are race-conscious can address these dimensions in ways that colorblind approaches cannot.

Gender

Gender-based violence—domestic violence, sexual assault, harassment—is pervasive in societies around the world. Women and girls are disproportionately affected, though men and boys also experience gender-based harm. Addressing this violence requires approaches that attend to the gender dynamics at play.

Restorative justice can be a valuable tool for addressing gender-based violence. By focusing on healing, accountability, and empowerment, restorative practices can provide alternatives to conventional justice processes that often fail victims of gender-based violence. Victims may find in restorative processes opportunities to tell their stories, to have their experiences validated, to receive acknowledgment and apology, to participate in determining what accountability means.

But gender sensitivity in restorative justice requires more than simply applying existing practices to gender-based cases. It requires recognizing and addressing the unique experiences and needs of individuals based on their gender identities. This means attending to power dynamics that may be gendered—the ways that male privilege, patriarchal norms, and gender inequality shape interactions between participants.

It also means being attentive to the specific needs of LGBTQ+ individuals. Gender identity and sexual orientation intersect with other identities to create unique experiences of harm and unique needs for healing. Restorative practices must be inclusive of all gender identities and expressions.

The theological dimensions of gender in restorative justice are significant. The Bible contains both patriarchal elements and counter-cultural affirmations of women's dignity and worth. Jesus's interactions with women—the woman at the well, the woman caught in adultery, the women who supported his ministry—challenged the gender norms of his time. Restorative justice, in its attention to gender, can embody this counter-cultural affirmation of all persons' dignity.

Class and Socioeconomic Status

Economic inequality shapes access to justice in profound ways. Wealthy individuals can afford better lawyers, can navigate complex legal processes, can absorb the costs of litigation. Poor individuals face barriers at every turn—lack of information, lack of resources, lack of social capital.

Restorative justice must consider these economic factors to promote fairness and equity. This means ensuring that restorative programs are accessible to individuals from all socioeconomic backgrounds—addressing barriers such as cost, availability, and support services. It means being attentive to how class shapes participants' experiences—how a poor victim may need different forms of reparation than a wealthy one, how a poor offender may face different obstacles to accountability.

Resource allocation is a key consideration. Ensuring that restorative justice programs are adequately funded, particularly those serving marginalized and disadvantaged communities, is essential for promoting equity. Programs that rely on participants paying for services will inevitably exclude those who cannot pay. Programs that are under-resourced cannot provide the quality of service that all participants deserve.

The psychological dimensions of class in restorative justice are significant. Poverty is associated with higher rates of trauma, stress, and mental health challenges. Poor individuals may have less trust in institutions, less confidence in their ability to navigate systems, less hope for the future. Restorative practices that are class-conscious can address these dimensions, providing support that attends to the whole person.

Case Studies and Examples

Examining real-world examples illustrates the importance of intersectional approaches to restorative justice.

Race and Restorative Justice in the United States

The United States has a long and painful history of racial disparities in the criminal justice system. African Americans, Latinos, and Native Americans are overrepresented at every stage, reflecting centuries of systemic racism. Addressing these disparities requires approaches that are explicitly race-conscious.

Programs like the Restorative Community Conferencing (RCC) in Oakland, California, address racial disparities by involving community members in the justice process and focusing on culturally relevant practices. RCC works primarily with youth of color, providing alternatives to formal prosecution that engage families and communities in accountability and healing.

The program's approach is explicitly intersectional. It recognizes that the young people it serves are not simply "offenders" but young people of color living in marginalized communities, facing multiple forms of disadvantage. It attends to the cultural contexts that shape their lives, drawing on community knowledge and relationships. It empowers families and communities to take active roles in supporting young people's development.

The outcomes of RCC have been impressive. Recidivism rates have been reduced. Young people have developed stronger connections to their communities. Families have been strengthened. The program demonstrates that restorative justice, when implemented with attention to race and culture, can address racial disparities and promote equity.

The theological dimensions of this work are significant. Many of the communities served by RCC are deeply religious, drawing strength from faith traditions that emphasize justice, mercy, and redemption. Churches and faith-based organizations are often partners in restorative work, providing support, volunteers, and moral grounding.

Gender and Restorative Justice in Canada

Canada has implemented restorative justice programs to address gender-based violence, including domestic violence and sexual assault. These programs recognize that conventional justice processes often fail victims of gender-based violence—that prosecution can be retraumatizing, that conviction rates are low, that victims' needs for healing and acknowledgment go unmet.

The Community Holistic Circle Healing (CHCH) program in Hollow Water First Nation is a remarkable example of gender-sensitive restorative justice. Developed to address high rates of sexual abuse and violence within the community, CHCH draws on Indigenous cultural practices to promote healing, accountability, and community restoration.

The program's approach is holistic and intersectional. It recognizes that sexual abuse is not an isolated issue but connected to broader patterns of historical trauma, cultural disruption, and community breakdown. It involves the whole community in healing circles, victim-offender dialogues, and community-based support. It attends to the specific needs of women survivors while also engaging men in accountability and transformation.

The outcomes of CHCH have been remarkable. Reoffending rates have been significantly reduced. Survivors report healing and empowerment. The community has been strengthened. CHCH demonstrates that restorative justice, when implemented with gender sensitivity and cultural grounding, can address even the most difficult cases of gender-based violence.

The theological dimensions of CHCH are profound. The program draws on Indigenous spirituality, which understands justice in relational and holistic terms. It also engages with

Christian traditions present in the community, drawing on themes of forgiveness, reconciliation, and new life. This spiritual grounding gives the program depth and resilience.

Class and Restorative Justice in the United Kingdom

Socioeconomic inequality in the United Kingdom affects individuals' access to justice and their experiences within the justice system. Poor individuals are less likely to know their rights, less able to navigate complex processes, less likely to receive favorable outcomes.

Programs like the Bristol Restorative Justice Service focus on making restorative justice accessible to individuals from all socioeconomic backgrounds. The service is free, removing cost barriers. It provides support for participants who need help understanding the process or articulating their needs. It reaches out to marginalized communities, building trust and relationships.

The program's approach is attentive to class dynamics. It recognizes that poor participants may have different needs and concerns than wealthy ones—more immediate survival needs, less trust in institutions, different cultural reference points. It adapts its practices accordingly, ensuring that restorative processes are relevant and accessible to all.

The outcomes have been positive. Economically disadvantaged individuals have gained access to restorative justice, receiving the same opportunities for healing and accountability as more privileged participants. The program has demonstrated that restorative justice can be equitable when resources are allocated to ensure access.

The psychological dimensions of this work are significant. Poverty is associated with higher rates of trauma, stress, and mental health challenges. The Bristol program's attention to these dimensions—providing support, building trust, adapting to participants' needs—enhances its effectiveness and promotes genuine healing.

Strategies for Implementing Intersectional Restorative Practices

Implementing intersectional restorative practices requires intentional strategies.

Training and Capacity Building

Providing training for restorative justice practitioners on intersectionality and its relevance to justice practices is essential. Practitioners must understand how race, gender, class, and other identities shape participants' experiences and needs. They must be able to recognize when these dynamics are at play and respond appropriately.

Building cultural competence among practitioners ensures that restorative justice processes are respectful, relevant, and effective for participants from diverse backgrounds. Cultural competence involves knowledge of different cultural norms, awareness of one's own cultural assumptions, and skill in adapting practice to fit cultural contexts.

The training should be ongoing, not one-time. Practitioners need opportunities to reflect on their practice, to learn from experience, to deepen their understanding. Supervision and peer support can help practitioners develop intersectional awareness over time.

Inclusive and Participatory Processes

Involving community members and leaders in the design and implementation of restorative justice programs ensures that these programs reflect the diverse needs and perspectives of the community. Those who will be served by restorative programs should have voice in how they are designed. Their input can improve relevance and effectiveness.

Adopting a participant-centered approach that prioritizes the voices and experiences of those affected by harm promotes inclusivity and empowerment. Participants are not passive recipients of restorative processes but active contributors. Their needs, their perspectives, their hopes shape how the process unfolds.

This participant-centered approach requires flexibility. No two participants are exactly alike; no two cases are identical. Restorative practices must be adapted to fit individual circumstances while maintaining fidelity to restorative principles.

Addressing Systemic Inequality

Advocating for policies that address systemic inequalities and promote equity within the justice system can support the integration of intersectional restorative practices. This advocacy may target legislation, administrative rules, funding allocations, or system policies. It requires building coalitions, making evidence-based arguments, and engaging with decision-makers.

Ensuring adequate funding and resources for restorative justice programs, particularly those serving marginalized and disadvantaged communities, is essential for promoting equity and inclusion. Under-resourced programs cannot serve participants well; programs that serve marginalized communities often need additional resources to address the complex needs these communities face.

Resource allocation should be guided by equity principles. Those with the greatest needs should receive the greatest support. Programs serving marginalized communities should be funded at levels that enable them to provide high-quality services.

Monitoring and Evaluation

Collecting data on participants' demographic characteristics and experiences can help identify disparities and inform the development of more equitable restorative justice practices. Data can reveal whether certain groups are under-represented in restorative programs, whether they experience different outcomes, whether they face particular barriers.

Implementing mechanisms for ongoing monitoring and evaluation ensures that restorative justice programs are responsive to the needs of participants and continuously improve in promoting equity and justice. Evaluation should include feedback from participants, attention to outcomes, and analysis of disparities.

The evaluation should be participatory, involving community members and participants in assessing program effectiveness. Those most affected by restorative programs have perspectives that outside evaluators cannot replicate.

Challenges and Considerations

Implementing intersectional restorative practices presents several challenges.

Navigating Power Dynamics

Identifying and addressing power imbalances between participants—such as those based on race, gender, or class—is essential for ensuring fairness and effectiveness in restorative justice processes. Power imbalances can distort dialogue, silence some voices, and produce outcomes that are not truly equitable.

Facilitators must be skilled in recognizing power dynamics and intervening appropriately. This may involve meeting separately with parties beforehand, providing support persons during the process, ensuring that all voices are heard, and intervening when necessary to maintain balance.

Offering support services, such as advocacy and counseling, can help mitigate power imbalances and empower participants. Vulnerable participants may need advocates to help them articulate their needs; marginalized participants may need support to navigate unfamiliar processes.

Ensuring Voluntary Participation

Ensuring that participation in restorative justice processes is voluntary and based on informed consent is critical for respecting participants' autonomy and dignity. Coercion or pressure undermines both restorative goals and participants' rights.

Informed consent requires clear, accessible information about the process and its potential outcomes. Participants need to understand what they are agreeing to before they agree. They need to know that they can withdraw at any time without penalty.

Creating safe and supportive environments where participants feel comfortable sharing their experiences and engaging in dialogue is essential. If participants fear for their safety—physically or emotionally—they cannot participate authentically.

Balancing Individual and Collective Needs

Balancing the needs of individual participants with the broader goals of collective healing and social justice can be challenging. A restorative process that focuses exclusively on individual healing may miss opportunities to address systemic issues. A process that focuses exclusively on systemic change may neglect individual needs.

This balance requires a nuanced and flexible approach that considers the unique circumstances of each case. Some cases may call for attention to individual healing; others may call for attention to community transformation. Skilled facilitators can hold both dimensions together, addressing individual needs while remaining attentive to broader patterns.

The philosophical dimensions of this balance are significant. Restorative justice is rooted in both individual dignity and communal responsibility. Honoring both requires wisdom—the practical wisdom that Aristotle called *phronesis*—to discern what each situation requires.

Social Equity: Promoting Fairness and Equality Through Restorative Practices

We turn now to social equity—the pursuit of fairness and justice in the distribution of resources, opportunities, and treatment across all societal groups. Restorative justice offers a powerful framework for advancing this goal.

Understanding Social Equity

Social equity is a foundational principle of just societies. It involves ensuring that all individuals have fair access to resources, opportunities, and treatment, regardless of their social, economic, or demographic characteristics.

Definition and Importance

Social equity is not the same as equality. Equality means treating everyone the same; equity means treating everyone fairly, which may require different treatment to address different circumstances. A just society attends to equity, ensuring that those with greater needs receive greater support, that historical disadvantages are addressed, that all have genuine opportunities to flourish.

Promoting social equity is essential for creating just and inclusive societies. When equity is lacking, certain groups are systematically disadvantaged—they have less access to education, healthcare, employment, housing, justice. These disadvantages compound over time, producing entrenched inequality that spans generations.

Social equity is not merely a matter of fairness; it is essential for social stability and cohesion. Societies with high levels of inequality experience more conflict, less trust, weaker social bonds. Equity promotes the sense that we are all in this together, that the social contract is fair, that everyone has a stake in the common good.

Restorative Justice and Social Equity

Restorative justice aligns with social equity in multiple ways. Both frameworks address the underlying causes of harm, promoting healing and reparation. Both emphasize inclusive and participatory processes, ensuring that those affected have voice. Both focus on accountability—not only individual accountability but also systemic accountability for patterns of injustice.

Restorative practices can be particularly effective in addressing the needs and rights of marginalized and disadvantaged groups. By giving voice to those who are often silenced, by involving communities in decision-making, by focusing on repair rather than punishment, restorative justice can counter the marginalization that vulnerable groups experience.

The theological dimensions of social equity are profound. The Hebrew prophets consistently called for justice that protects the vulnerable and challenges the powerful. Amos thunders against those who "trample the head of the poor into the dust of the earth" (Amos 2:7). Isaiah calls for a society where the hungry are fed, the homeless sheltered, the naked clothed (Isaiah 58). Jesus announces his mission as bringing good news to the poor, freedom to the captives, recovery of sight to the blind (Luke 4). The biblical vision is of a society where all have what they need, where none are marginalized, where equity reigns.

Principles of Social Equity in Restorative Justice

Several key principles guide the integration of social equity into restorative justice.

Fairness and Justice

Ensuring that all individuals are treated fairly and justly within restorative processes, regardless of their background or circumstances, is fundamental. This means attending to procedural justice—ensuring that processes are transparent, that participants have voice, that decisions are made impartially. It also means attending to substantive justice—ensuring that outcomes are fair, that harms are addressed, that needs are met.

Actively addressing disparities and inequalities that may exist within the justice system and society at large is essential. Restorative justice should not simply reproduce the inequalities of the broader society; it should work to counter them. This requires being attentive to how race, class, gender, and other factors shape participants' experiences and outcomes.

Participation and Inclusion

Designing restorative processes that are inclusive and accessible to all individuals, particularly those from marginalized or disadvantaged groups, is essential for equity. This means removing barriers to participation—cost, location, language, timing. It means reaching out to communities that may be distrustful of formal processes. It means adapting practices to fit diverse cultural contexts.

Empowering participants by giving them voice and active role in the justice process promotes their agency and self-determination. Participants are not passive recipients of justice but active contributors. Their perspectives shape how the process unfolds; their needs shape what outcomes look like.

Accountability and Reparation

Ensuring that offenders take responsibility for their actions and make meaningful amends to those harmed is a core restorative principle. This accountability is not merely individual but can extend to systemic dimensions. When harm is rooted in systemic inequality, accountability may require addressing those systems.

Providing comprehensive support to victims, including opportunities for healing, reparation, and empowerment, is essential. Victims' needs must be central, not secondary. Support should attend to the full range of needs—material, emotional, relational, spiritual.

Challenges in Promoting Social Equity Through Restorative Practices

Promoting social equity through restorative justice faces several challenges.

Systemic Inequality and Bias

Acknowledging and addressing systemic inequalities and biases that may influence restorative justice processes and outcomes is essential but difficult. These inequalities are often deeply embedded, invisible to those who benefit from them. Practitioners may be unaware of their own biases; processes may reproduce broader patterns of discrimination.

Implementing measures to mitigate disparities and ensure equitable treatment for all participants requires ongoing attention. This may include collecting data on outcomes by demographic group, providing bias training for practitioners, establishing oversight mechanisms, and actively reaching out to marginalized communities.

Resource Allocation and Accessibility

Ensuring that restorative justice programs are accessible to all individuals, regardless of their socioeconomic status, location, or other barriers, requires resources. Programs that are under-resourced cannot serve participants well; programs that serve marginalized communities often need additional resources to address complex needs.

Securing adequate funding and resources to support restorative justice initiatives is essential for their sustainability and effectiveness. This may require advocating for public funding, building partnerships with philanthropic organizations, and developing diverse funding streams.

Cultural Sensitivity and Relevance

Adapting restorative practices to fit the cultural contexts and needs of diverse communities ensures they are relevant and respectful. Practices that work well in one cultural context may be ineffective or even harmful in another. Adaptation requires deep engagement with communities, not superficial modification.

Engaging community members in the design and implementation of restorative justice programs enhances cultural sensitivity and acceptance. Those who know the culture best are best positioned to advise on appropriate adaptations.

Strategies for Promoting Social Equity Through Restorative Practices

Several strategies can support the integration of social equity into restorative justice.

Inclusive and Participatory Processes

Involving community members in the design, implementation, and evaluation of restorative justice programs ensures they reflect the diverse needs and perspectives of the community. This participatory approach builds ownership and trust, ensuring that programs are genuinely responsive to community needs.

Adopting a participant-centered approach that prioritizes the voices and experiences of those affected by harm promotes inclusivity and empowerment. Participants are not passive recipients but active contributors, whose needs and perspectives shape the process.

Training and Capacity Building

Providing training for restorative justice practitioners on social equity principles and practices, including recognizing and addressing bias and inequality, is essential. Practitioners must understand how systemic inequality operates and how it may affect restorative processes.

Investing in capacity building for community members and organizations enhances their ability to support and participate in restorative justice processes. Strong communities are essential partners in restorative work.

Policy Advocacy and Reform

Advocating for policies and reforms that promote social equity within the justice system and broader society supports restorative goals. This may include measures to address systemic inequalities, ensure fair treatment for all, and allocate resources equitably.

Integrating social equity goals into restorative justice policies and programs ensures they are aligned with broader efforts to promote fairness and justice. Equity should not be an afterthought but a central consideration in program design.

Monitoring and Evaluation

Implementing mechanisms for monitoring and evaluating the impact of restorative justice programs on social equity is essential. Collecting and analyzing data on participant demographics, outcomes, and experiences can identify disparities and inform improvement.

Using evaluation findings to inform continuous improvement ensures that restorative justice programs are effectively promoting social equity. Evaluation should be ongoing, not one-time, and should involve participants and communities in assessing effectiveness.

Case Studies of Restorative Practices Promoting Social Equity

Real-world examples illustrate the potential of restorative justice to advance social equity.

Oakland Unified School District, California

Oakland Unified School District implemented restorative justice practices to address disparities in school discipline, particularly the disproportionate impact on students of color. The district recognized that punitive discipline was pushing students of color out of school and into the juvenile justice system—the school-to-prison pipeline.

The district introduced restorative circles, peer mediation, and community-building activities to create a positive school climate and address conflicts constructively. Rather than suspending or expelling students, schools used restorative processes to address harm, promote accountability, and restore relationships.

The outcomes were remarkable. Suspensions and expulsions decreased significantly, particularly among students of color. School climate improved; students reported feeling safer and more connected. Academic outcomes improved. The district demonstrated that restorative practices could address racial disparities and promote equity.

The psychological dimensions of this work are significant. Students of color often experience school as a place of punishment rather than support. Restorative practices changed that experience, creating conditions for learning and growth.

Transforming Justice Initiative, New York City

The Transforming Justice Initiative in New York City focuses on promoting social equity through restorative justice practices within the criminal justice system. The initiative offers restorative justice programs for youth and adults, including victim-offender dialogues, community conferencing, and reentry support.

The initiative is explicitly equity-focused. It targets marginalized communities disproportionately affected by the criminal justice system. It involves community members in program design and implementation. It collects data on outcomes by demographic group to ensure equity.

The initiative has successfully reduced recidivism rates, improved outcomes for marginalized populations, and strengthened community ties. It demonstrates that restorative justice can be a tool for systemic change, not merely individual healing.

Family Group Conferencing in New Zealand

New Zealand's Family Group Conferencing system was developed specifically to address the overrepresentation of Maori youth in the juvenile justice system. Maori youth were being processed through a justice system that did not reflect their cultural values or involve their communities.

FGC involves the youth, their family, victims, and community members in a collaborative decision-making process to address harm and develop a plan for reparation and support. The process draws on Maori traditions of collective responsibility and community involvement.

The outcomes have been impressive. Reoffending rates among Maori youth have been reduced. Families and communities have been empowered. The program demonstrates that restorative justice, when culturally grounded, can address systemic disparities and promote equity.

The theological dimensions of FGC are significant. Maori spirituality, like many indigenous traditions, understands justice in relational and holistic terms. The integration of these values into the justice system represents a form of restorative justice that is both culturally specific and universally relevant.

Community Holistic Circle Healing in Hollow Water First Nation, Canada

The Community Holistic Circle Healing program was developed in Hollow Water First Nation to address high rates of sexual abuse and violence within the community. The program uses restorative justice principles, drawing on Indigenous cultural practices to promote healing, accountability, and community restoration.

CHCH involves community members in healing circles, victim-offender dialogues, and community-based support. It addresses the root causes of violence—historical trauma, cultural disruption, community breakdown—while also holding offenders accountable and supporting victims.

The outcomes have been transformative. Reoffending rates have been significantly reduced. Survivors have found healing. The community has been strengthened. CHCH demonstrates that restorative justice, when deeply rooted in community and culture, can address even the most profound harms.

Community Empowerment: Building Stronger, More Resilient Communities

Finally, we turn to community empowerment—the process of enabling individuals and groups to gain control over their lives and participate actively in the development and governance of their communities. Restorative justice is fundamentally about community empowerment.

Understanding Community Empowerment

Community empowerment is both a process and an outcome. As a process, it involves enabling community members to gain skills, knowledge, and confidence. As an outcome, it results in communities that are stronger, more resilient, and more capable of addressing their own challenges.

Definition and Importance

Community empowerment refers to the process of enabling individuals and groups to gain control over their lives, make informed decisions, and actively participate in the development and governance of their communities. Empowered communities are not dependent on outside authorities to solve their problems; they have the capacity to address challenges collectively.

Empowered communities are more resilient, cohesive, and capable of addressing challenges and opportunities collectively. When people feel that they have agency, that their voices matter, that they can make a difference, they are more engaged, more committed, more willing to work together for the common good.

Empowerment fosters a sense of ownership, responsibility, and agency among community members. People who are empowered do not wait for others to act; they take initiative. They do not blame outsiders for problems; they take responsibility for solutions.

Principles of Community Empowerment

Several key principles guide community empowerment. Participation and inclusion ensure that all community members have opportunities to participate in decision-making processes and activities that affect their lives. No one should be excluded; all voices should be heard.

Capacity building develops the skills, knowledge, and resources of community members to enable them to take effective action and make informed decisions. Empowerment requires more than good intentions; it requires capability.

Collaboration and partnership encourage cooperation among community members, organizations, and institutions to address common goals and challenges. No single individual or organization can solve complex community problems alone; collective action is essential.

Accountability and transparency promote openness in community governance and decision-making processes. When processes are transparent, people trust them; when leaders are accountable, people support them.

The Role of Restorative Justice in Community Empowerment

Restorative justice contributes to community empowerment in multiple ways.

Fostering Participation and Inclusion

Restorative justice practices, such as circles and conferencing, create inclusive spaces where all voices are heard and respected. These processes encourage active participation and empower individuals to contribute to conflict resolution and community building. Participants are not passive recipients of decisions made elsewhere but active contributors to outcomes that affect their lives.

Restorative justice actively seeks to engage marginalized and disadvantaged groups, ensuring that their perspectives and needs are considered in community decision-making. Those who are often excluded—the poor, minorities, women, youth—are given voice and agency in restorative processes.

Building Capacity and Skills

Participation in restorative justice processes helps community members develop essential skills, such as communication, empathy, conflict resolution, and problem-solving. These skills are not only useful for restorative processes but transfer to other areas of life—work, family, civic engagement.

Restorative justice programs often include leadership training and capacity-building initiatives, enabling community members to take on leadership roles and drive positive change. Participants become facilitators, mediators, advocates—carrying restorative values into the broader community.

Promoting Collaboration and Partnership

Restorative practices foster collaboration and partnership by bringing together diverse community members to address conflicts and work towards common goals. People who might otherwise be isolated or divided are brought into relationship, discovering shared interests and common purposes.

By involving various stakeholders—schools, local organizations, justice agencies, faith communities—restorative justice strengthens community networks and promotes collective action. These networks become resources for addressing future challenges.

Enhancing Accountability and Transparency

Restorative justice emphasizes shared responsibility for addressing harm and promoting healing. This approach encourages accountability among community members and institutions. People recognize that they have roles to play in maintaining community health, that they cannot simply delegate responsibility to others.

Restorative justice processes are transparent, with open communication and clear guidelines, ensuring that all participants understand and trust the process. This transparency builds confidence in community institutions and processes.

Strategies for Building Resilient Communities Through Restorative Practices

Several strategies can support community empowerment through restorative justice.

Implementing Community-Based Restorative Programs

Developing and supporting local restorative justice initiatives that address specific community needs and contexts is essential. Programs should be rooted in communities, not imposed from outside. They should draw on local knowledge, relationships, and resources.

Ensuring that restorative programs are sustainable requires securing funding, training facilitators, and building local capacity. Programs that depend entirely on outside resources are vulnerable; programs that build local capacity can endure.

Engaging Community Members

Conducting inclusive outreach to engage a broad cross-section of the community, including marginalized and underrepresented groups, ensures that restorative programs reflect community diversity. Outreach should be intentional, persistent, and culturally appropriate.

Creating opportunities for open dialogue and discussion on community issues allows members to voice their concerns and ideas. These conversations build relationships, surface shared concerns, and generate collective solutions.

Building Partnerships and Networks

Encouraging collaboration between community organizations, schools, local government, and justice agencies creates a coordinated approach to restorative justice. When different actors work together, they can achieve more than any could alone.

Promoting the sharing of resources, knowledge, and expertise among community partners enhances the effectiveness of restorative initiatives. No single organization has everything needed; partnerships allow pooling of resources and capabilities.

Providing Training and Capacity Building

Offering training programs to develop the skills and knowledge of community members, practitioners, and leaders in restorative justice builds local capacity. Training should be accessible, ongoing, and adapted to local contexts.

Supporting leadership development initiatives empowers individuals to take active roles in promoting and sustaining restorative justice in their communities. Leaders emerge from within communities, carrying restorative values forward.

Monitoring and Evaluating Impact

Implementing mechanisms for monitoring and evaluating the impact of restorative justice programs on community empowerment and resilience ensures accountability and supports improvement. Evaluation should attend to both process and outcomes, both intended and unintended effects.

Using evaluation findings to inform continuous improvement ensures that programs effectively meet the needs of the community. Evaluation should be participatory, involving community members in assessing effectiveness and shaping future directions.

Case Studies of Community Empowerment Through Restorative Practices

Real-world examples illustrate the power of restorative justice to empower communities.

The Hollow Water Community Holistic Circle Healing in Canada

The CHCH program in Hollow Water First Nation, which we have already discussed, is a powerful example of community empowerment. Developed to address sexual abuse and violence, the program has transformed how the community responds to harm.

The program involves community members in healing circles, victim-offender dialogues, and community-based support. It has built local capacity—training community members as facilitators, healers, and supporters. It has strengthened community bonds, bringing people together across lines of division.

The outcomes extend beyond individual cases. The community as a whole has been transformed. People trust one another more; they are more willing to intervene when they see problems; they have a shared sense of responsibility for community well-being. CHCH demonstrates that restorative justice can build community capacity and resilience.

Restorative Community Conferencing in Oakland, California

RCC in Oakland focuses on addressing youth offenses through restorative justice practices, involving victims, offenders, and community members in the resolution process. The program has not only reduced recidivism but strengthened community ties.

RCC trains community members as facilitators and supporters. It involves families and neighbors in restorative conferences. It builds networks of support around young people, connecting them to resources and relationships.

The program has empowered communities to take ownership of youth justice. Rather than relying on police and courts to address youth crime, communities are developing their own capacity to respond. This empowerment builds confidence and reduces dependence on outside authorities.

Neighborhood Restorative Justice Project in New York City

The Neighborhood Restorative Justice Project was established to address low-level offenses and conflicts in neighborhoods through restorative justice practices. The project involves community members in restorative circles and mediations to address conflicts, promote reparation, and strengthen community bonds.

The project has successfully resolved numerous conflicts that might otherwise have escalated. It has reduced reliance on the formal justice system, freeing resources for more serious matters. It has empowered community members to take active roles in maintaining peace and harmony.

Participants report feeling more connected to their neighbors, more confident in their ability to address conflicts, more committed to community well-being. The project demonstrates that restorative justice can build community capacity at the neighborhood level.

Restorative Practices in the United Kingdom's Education Sector

Many schools in the United Kingdom have adopted restorative practices to address conflicts, reduce bullying, and create positive school climates. These practices include restorative circles, peer mediation, and community-building activities.

The implementation of restorative practices has transformed school communities. Students feel safer, more respected, more connected. Teachers report better relationships with students and less time spent on disciplinary issues. Parents are more engaged with schools.

Schools that have adopted restorative practices report reduced disciplinary incidents, improved student relationships, and enhanced school environments. These outcomes demonstrate that restorative justice can empower school communities to create positive climates for learning and growth.

Challenges and Considerations

Building community empowerment through restorative justice presents several challenges.

Ensuring Sustainability

Securing adequate funding and resources is essential for the sustainability of restorative justice programs. Programs that depend on soft money—grants that come and go—are vulnerable. Sustainable programs require diverse funding streams and institutional support.

Developing local capacity and leadership is essential for sustaining restorative initiatives over the long term. When communities have their own trained facilitators, their own organizational structures, their own leadership—they can sustain restorative practices even when outside support diminishes.

Addressing Power Imbalances

Power imbalances between participants—such as those based on race, gender, or socioeconomic status—can affect the fairness and effectiveness of restorative processes. These imbalances must be recognized and addressed to ensure equitable participation.

Offering support services, such as advocacy and counseling, can help mitigate power imbalances and empower participants. Vulnerable participants need support to participate fully; marginalized participants need advocates to ensure their voices are heard.

Cultural Sensitivity and Relevance

Adapting restorative practices to fit the cultural contexts and needs of diverse communities is essential for their relevance and effectiveness. Practices that work well in one community may not work in another. Adaptation requires deep engagement, not superficial modification.

Engaging community members in the design and implementation of restorative justice programs enhances their cultural sensitivity and acceptance. Communities must have ownership of restorative processes for them to be truly empowering.

The Integration of Law, Psychology, Philosophy, and Theology

As we have explored the relationship between restorative justice and social justice, we have seen how multiple disciplines inform our understanding.

Legal Perspectives

Law provides frameworks for addressing systemic injustice—civil rights laws, anti-discrimination provisions, human rights instruments. These legal frameworks establish standards for equity and provide mechanisms for challenging discrimination. Restorative justice can complement these legal approaches, addressing harm in ways that law alone cannot.

The examples we have examined—programs addressing racial disparities in the United States, gender-based violence in Canada, class barriers in the United Kingdom—all operate within legal frameworks while also addressing dimensions that law neglects. They demonstrate that restorative justice can work alongside legal approaches to promote social justice.

Psychological Insights

Psychology illuminates the dynamics of marginalization, discrimination, and trauma. Racial trauma, gender-based trauma, the psychological impacts of poverty—all affect how people experience harm and what they need for healing. Restorative practices that are trauma-informed can address these dimensions.

Psychology also illuminates the processes of empowerment—how people gain confidence, develop skills, take initiative. Restorative practices that build capacity, that give people voice, that create conditions for agency—these promote psychological empowerment.

Philosophical Foundations

Philosophy provides frameworks for thinking about justice, equity, and empowerment. Theories of distributive justice address fair distribution of resources. Theories of recognition address the importance of respect and acknowledgment. Theories of capability address what people need to flourish.

Restorative justice draws on these philosophical traditions, embodying them in practice. Its emphasis on participation reflects democratic theory; its attention to marginalized groups reflects critical theory; its focus on healing reflects care ethics.

Theological Dimensions

Theology offers profound resources for thinking about social justice. The biblical vision of *shalom*—peace, wholeness, right relationship—provides a framework for understanding what social justice seeks to achieve. The prophetic tradition of challenging injustice and defending the vulnerable inspires restorative work. Jesus's ministry of inclusion and healing models restorative practice.

The theological dimensions of social justice are particularly evident in the examples we have examined. The Hollow Water program draws on Indigenous spirituality; the Oakland program works with faith communities; the New Zealand program reflects Maori values. These spiritual dimensions give restorative work depth and meaning.

The biblical call to justice is not merely about individual behavior but about social structures. The prophets challenged not only individual sins but systemic injustice—the exploitation of the poor, the corruption of courts, the oppression of the vulnerable. Restorative justice, in addressing systemic issues, participates in this prophetic tradition.

As we move forward into the final chapter, we will build on this exploration of restorative justice and social justice. We will look to the future, imagining how restorative justice might continue to transform our world—addressing not only individual harm but systemic injustice, building not only individual healing but community empowerment, creating not only restorative programs but a restorative society.

The relationship between restorative justice and social justice is deep and abiding. Both seek to address harm—not only individual harm but systemic harm. Both seek to promote healing—not only individual healing but community healing. Both seek to build justice—not only procedural justice but substantive justice. When restorative justice embraces social justice, it becomes not merely a set of techniques for resolving conflicts but a vision for transforming society—a vision of a world where all are treated with dignity, where all have voice, where all can flourish. This is the vision of a restorative society. This is the vision we are called to embody.

CHAPTER 10

THE FUTURE OF RESTORATIVE JUSTICE

We have journeyed together through the philosophical foundations of restorative justice, explored its core principles and values, examined the practices and models that bring these principles to life, studied real-world applications across multiple domains, honestly assessed both the benefits and challenges, considered the complex relationship between restorative justice and legal systems, expanded our视野 to the global stage, and explored the intersection of restorative justice with social justice. Now, dear reader, we arrive at the final chapter of our journey—a chapter that looks forward rather than backward, that imagines what might be rather than merely describing what is.

The future of restorative justice is not yet written. It will be shaped by the choices we make, the innovations we develop, the commitments we sustain, and the vision we hold. In this chapter, we will explore the emerging trends and innovations that are shaping the field, consider the challenges of sustainability and scalability, and envision a future where restorative justice has transformed our world.

Throughout this exploration, we will draw on insights from law, psychology, philosophy, and theology to illuminate the path forward. We will see how these different perspectives can guide us as we work to build a more just, compassionate, and restorative society.

Innovations and Trends: Emerging Trends and Innovations in Restorative Justice

The field of restorative justice is not static. It evolves in response to new insights, changing societal needs, and technological advancements. Understanding these emerging trends and innovations is essential for anyone who seeks to participate in the ongoing development of restorative practice.

Digital and Online Restorative Practices

The digital revolution has transformed nearly every aspect of modern life, and restorative justice is no exception. The development of online platforms for restorative processes represents one of the most significant innovations in the field.

Virtual Mediation and Conferencing

The rise of digital technology has facilitated the development of virtual mediation and conferencing platforms, enabling restorative justice processes to take place online. This innovation, accelerated by the COVID-19 pandemic, has opened new possibilities for restorative practice.

Virtual platforms offer significant advantages. They increase accessibility, allowing participants from different locations to engage in restorative processes without the need for physical presence. A victim in one city can meet with an offender in another; family members scattered across the country can participate in a conference; community members with mobility limitations can join from home. This accessibility expands the reach of restorative justice, serving populations that might otherwise be excluded.

Virtual platforms also provide flexibility in scheduling. Without the need to coordinate travel, arrange physical space, or work around geographical constraints, restorative processes can be scheduled more easily. This flexibility can reduce delays and make restorative justice more responsive to participants' needs.

Logistical barriers are reduced as well. There is no need to find neutral, accessible meeting spaces; no need to arrange transportation; no need to manage the complexities of in-person gatherings. This efficiency can make restorative justice more feasible, particularly for programs with limited resources.

However, virtual restorative practices also present significant challenges. Ensuring confidentiality is more complex in online environments. Participants may be concerned about who else might be listening, whether their conversations are being recorded, whether the platform is secure. Robust technological infrastructure and clear protocols are essential.

Building rapport can be more challenging in virtual settings. The subtle cues of body language, the emotional resonance of physical presence, the sense of shared space—all are diminished when participants are separated by screens. Facilitators must develop new skills for creating connection and trust in virtual environments.

Managing emotional intensity is also more difficult online. When emotions run high—as they often do in restorative encounters—the physical presence of a skilled facilitator can help contain and channel that intensity. Online, facilitators have fewer tools for managing emotional dynamics. Participants who become overwhelmed may simply log off, ending the process abruptly.

Despite these challenges, virtual restorative practices are likely to continue growing. The combination of accessibility, flexibility, and efficiency is powerful. As technology improves and facilitators develop expertise in online practice, virtual restorative justice will become an increasingly important option.

The psychological dimensions of virtual restorative practice are significant. Research on online communication suggests that while it differs from in-person interaction, it can still support meaningful connection and authentic dialogue. The key is intentional design—creating online spaces that are conducive to the kind of deep engagement that restorative justice requires.

The philosophical implications are also important. Virtual restorative practice challenges assumptions about the necessity of physical presence for genuine encounter. It raises questions about what constitutes authentic dialogue, what conditions enable true meeting, what is essential and what is merely conventional in restorative processes.

Online Training and Resources

The availability of online training programs and resources has expanded access to restorative justice education and capacity building. Practitioners who might never have been able to attend in-person trainings can now learn from experts around the world. Community members in remote areas can access resources that were previously unavailable.

Online training offers significant advantages. It provides flexible learning opportunities, allowing participants to learn at their own pace, on their own schedule. This flexibility is particularly valuable for practitioners who are balancing work, family, and other commitments.

Online training can reach a broader audience, including those in remote or underserved areas. Geographical location no longer determines access to education. Practitioners in rural communities, in developing countries, in marginalized neighborhoods—all can participate in online learning.

Online training also facilitates continuous professional development. Practitioners can access refresher courses, learn about new developments, deepen their skills over time. This ongoing learning is essential for maintaining quality practice.

However, maintaining engagement in online training can be challenging. Without the structure and social pressure of in-person sessions, participants may struggle to stay motivated. Designing online learning that is interactive, engaging, and effective requires skill and creativity.

Ensuring the quality of online training is also a challenge. Not all online programs are created equal; some may provide superficial instruction, inadequate preparation, or even misinformation. Developing standards for online restorative justice education is essential.

Combining online learning with in-person training and practical experience can enhance effectiveness. The ideal may be a blended approach—online instruction for foundational knowledge, in-person workshops for skill development, supervised practice for application, and ongoing online support for continuous learning.

Integrating Restorative Justice into New Sectors

Restorative justice principles are increasingly being applied beyond the criminal justice context. This expansion into new sectors represents a significant trend with transformative potential.

Restorative Practices in Healthcare

The healthcare sector is ripe for restorative approaches. Conflicts between patients and providers, medical errors that cause harm, grievances that lead to litigation—all of these can be addressed through restorative practices.

Restorative practices can be used to facilitate dialogues between patients, families, and healthcare providers when things go wrong. When a medical error occurs, patients and families want more than compensation; they want acknowledgment, explanation, apology, assurance that the same error will not happen again. Restorative processes can provide these things in ways that litigation cannot.

These practices can also address conflicts within healthcare organizations—between staff members, between departments, between providers and administrators. Restorative circles, mediation, and facilitated dialogue can resolve conflicts constructively, improving workplace relationships and patient care.

The benefits of restorative practices in healthcare are significant. Patient satisfaction can improve when patients feel heard and respected, when their concerns are addressed directly, when they receive acknowledgment and apology. Litigation can be reduced when disputes are resolved restoratively, saving resources and avoiding the trauma of legal proceedings. The overall quality of care can improve when conflicts are addressed constructively and when lessons from errors are learned and applied.

The psychological dimensions of restorative practices in healthcare are profound. Patients who have been harmed need more than financial compensation; they need acknowledgment, validation, and assurance. Providers who have made errors need opportunities to express remorse, to make amends, to be restored to their sense of professional identity and purpose.

The theological dimensions are also significant. Healthcare has deep connections to healing—physical healing, emotional healing, spiritual healing. Restorative practices in healthcare can be understood as extensions of this healing ministry, addressing the wounds that medical error and conflict create.

Restorative Practices in Corporate Settings

Businesses and corporations are increasingly adopting restorative justice principles to address workplace conflicts, enhance employee relations, and improve organizational culture. This trend reflects growing recognition that punitive approaches to workplace issues are often counterproductive.

Restorative practices in corporate settings include conflict resolution circles, where employees can discuss issues, share perspectives, and find collaborative solutions. They include mediation, where a neutral third party helps conflicting parties reach mutually acceptable resolutions. They include team-building activities focused on open communication and mutual respect.

These practices can address a range of workplace issues—interpersonal conflicts, team dysfunction, harassment and discrimination, ethical lapses, organizational failures. They provide alternatives to formal complaints and grievances, resolving issues before they escalate.

The benefits of restorative practices in corporate settings are substantial. Workplace conflicts can be reduced, improving morale and productivity. Employee relationships can be strengthened, fostering collaboration and trust. Organizational culture can become more positive, inclusive, and supportive.

Restorative practices can also address workplace harassment and discrimination in constructive ways. Rather than relying solely on formal complaints processes that can be adversarial and traumatizing, organizations can use restorative approaches to address harm, promote understanding, and develop inclusive policies and practices.

The psychological dimensions of workplace restorative practices are significant. Employees who feel heard, respected, and valued are more engaged, more productive, more loyal. When conflicts are resolved constructively, relationships are strengthened rather than damaged. When mistakes are addressed restoratively, learning occurs rather than defensiveness.

The philosophical implications are also important. Restorative practices in corporate settings reflect a shift from punitive, individualistic approaches to relational, communal ones. They embody the principle that organizations are communities, not merely collections of individuals pursuing private interests.

Restorative Practices in Environmental Justice

Perhaps most ambitiously, restorative justice is being explored as a framework for addressing environmental harm and promoting sustainability. This application recognizes that environmental damage harms not only ecosystems but human communities—often the most vulnerable communities—and that addressing this harm requires restorative approaches.

Restorative practices can facilitate dialogues between stakeholders affected by environmental issues—community members, corporate representatives, government officials, environmental advocates. These dialogues can address the harm caused by pollution, resource extraction, climate change, and other environmental problems. They can promote accountability for environmental harm, encouraging responsible parties to acknowledge their actions and make amends.

Restorative practices can also support collaborative efforts to restore ecosystems. When communities, corporations, and governments work together to repair environmental damage, they engage in a form of collective reparation that benefits both human and natural communities.

The benefits of restorative environmental justice are significant. It fosters a holistic approach to environmental issues, recognizing the interconnectedness of social, economic, and ecological well-being. It empowers communities to participate in decisions that affect their environment. It promotes accountability for environmental harm, addressing the root causes of ecological degradation.

The psychological dimensions of environmental restorative justice are profound. Environmental harm often causes psychological distress—grief for lost landscapes, anxiety about future risks, anger at those responsible. Restorative processes can address these emotional dimensions, providing spaces for expression, acknowledgment, and healing.

The theological dimensions are also significant. Many religious traditions understand humanity as having responsibility for caring for creation—stewardship of the earth, protection of the environment, concern for future generations. Restorative environmental justice can be understood as an expression of this sacred responsibility.

Expanding Restorative Justice in the Criminal Justice System

While restorative justice began in criminal justice, its application within that system continues to expand. Two significant trends are the use of restorative justice for serious crimes and the introduction of restorative programs in prisons.

Restorative Justice for Serious Crimes

Traditionally, restorative justice has been used primarily for minor offenses. But increasingly, it is being applied to serious crimes, including violent offenses and sexual assault. This expansion reflects growing recognition that restorative approaches can address even the most severe harms.

Restorative processes for serious crimes require careful planning and extensive support for all participants. Victims of serious violence have deep needs—for acknowledgment, for answers, for a sense of control. Offenders who have caused serious harm have profound obligations—to understand what they have done, to take responsibility, to make amends insofar as possible.

These processes are not appropriate for all cases or all participants. They require voluntary participation, thorough preparation, skilled facilitation, and ongoing support. They must be trauma-informed, recognizing the deep wounds that serious violence causes.

When implemented appropriately, restorative processes for serious crimes can provide meaningful accountability. Offenders face the full reality of what they have done, hearing directly from victims about the impact. This encounter can be transformative, evoking genuine remorse and commitment to change.

These processes can also support victim healing. Victims have opportunity to tell their stories, to ask questions, to receive acknowledgment, to participate in determining what accountability means. For some victims, this participation is essential to healing.

The psychological research on restorative justice for serious crimes is promising. Studies show that victims who participate report satisfaction and healing, that offenders who participate show reduced recidivism, that both experience the process as meaningful and just.

Restorative Justice in Prisons

Restorative justice programs are being introduced in prisons to address conflicts, support rehabilitation, and prepare inmates for reintegration into society. These programs recognize that prisons, despite their punitive purpose, can be sites of restorative transformation.

Restorative circles in prisons bring together inmates to address conflicts, build community, and support one another's growth. These circles can reduce violence, improve prison culture, and create conditions for positive change.

Victim-offender dialogues in prisons allow inmates to meet with victims of their crimes or with surrogate victims who can represent the impact of similar offenses. These dialogues can be profoundly transformative, evoking empathy, remorse, and commitment to change.

Community service projects in prisons allow inmates to make reparation to communities they have harmed. These projects can include work that benefits victims, that addresses community needs, that demonstrates accountability in tangible ways.

The benefits of restorative programs in prisons are significant. Recidivism can be reduced when inmates experience genuine transformation. Prison culture can improve when conflicts are addressed constructively and relationships are strengthened. Reintegration can be enhanced when inmates have developed skills, relationships, and commitments that support successful return to community.

The psychological dimensions of prison-based restorative justice are profound. Incarceration often reinforces criminal identity, deepens alienation, and damages psychological health. Restorative practices can counter these effects, supporting the development of pro-social identity, healthy relationships, and psychological well-being.

The theological dimensions are also significant. Prisons are places of brokenness, where hope is scarce and transformation seems impossible. Restorative practices bring light into this darkness, offering possibilities for change that secular approaches cannot provide.

Innovations in Restorative Justice Research and Evaluation

The development of restorative justice depends on ongoing research and evaluation. Two significant trends in this area are data-driven approaches and participatory action research.

Data-Driven Approaches

The use of data analytics and evidence-based research is enhancing the evaluation and effectiveness of restorative justice programs. Collecting and analyzing data on program outcomes, participant experiences, and long-term impacts helps refine practices and demonstrate their benefits.

Data-driven approaches allow programs to track what works, for whom, and under what conditions. They can identify factors associated with successful outcomes, allowing programs to focus resources on practices that are most effective. They can reveal disparities in access or outcomes, allowing programs to address inequities.

Data can also demonstrate the value of restorative justice to funders, policymakers, and the public. When programs can show measurable results—reduced recidivism, increased victim satisfaction, cost savings—they are more likely to receive support.

The benefits of data-driven approaches are significant. They support continuous improvement, allowing programs to learn from experience and adapt over time. They inform policy decisions, providing evidence that can guide resource allocation and program design. They build credibility and support for restorative justice initiatives, demonstrating that these approaches are not merely idealistic but effective.

Participatory Action Research

Participatory action research (PAR) involves engaging community members and participants in the research process to ensure that it reflects their needs and perspectives. This approach recognizes that those most affected by restorative justice have valuable knowledge that outside researchers cannot replicate.

PAR can be used to co-design and evaluate restorative justice programs. Community members participate in identifying research questions, developing methods, collecting data, analyzing findings, and implementing changes. Their involvement ensures that research is relevant, respectful, and responsive to community priorities.

The benefits of PAR are significant. It fosters community ownership of restorative programs, building commitment and sustainability. It enhances the relevance and impact of research, ensuring that findings address real needs and can be applied in practice. It empowers participants, giving them voice and agency in the research process.

Global Trends and Cross-Cultural Adaptations

Restorative justice is a global phenomenon, and its future will be shaped by cross-cultural exchange and adaptation.

Cultural Adaptations of Restorative Practices

Restorative justice is being adapted to fit diverse cultural contexts, ensuring that practices are relevant and respectful of local traditions and values. This adaptation is essential for restorative justice to be effective in communities around the world.

Cultural adaptation involves collaborating with cultural leaders, incorporating traditional conflict resolution methods, and tailoring practices to local needs. It means recognizing that restorative justice is not a one-size-fits-all model but a set of principles that can be embodied in diverse ways.

The benefits of cultural adaptation are significant. It enhances the acceptance of restorative justice, as communities see their values reflected in restorative processes. It increases effectiveness, as practices resonate with cultural norms and expectations. It promotes sustainability, as communities take ownership of practices that reflect their traditions.

International Collaboration and Knowledge Sharing

Increased international collaboration and knowledge sharing are fostering the global growth of restorative justice. Conferences, networks, and online platforms facilitate the exchange of best practices, research findings, and innovative approaches.

This global exchange enriches restorative practice everywhere. Practitioners in one country learn from innovations in another; researchers share findings across borders; advocates build international movements for justice reform.

The benefits of international collaboration are significant. It accelerates the development of restorative justice, as ideas spread more quickly and innovations are adopted more widely. It supports implementation in diverse contexts, as lessons learned in one setting inform practice in another. It builds a global community of restorative justice practitioners, researchers, and advocates, strengthening the movement as a whole.

Case Studies of Innovations and Trends

Examining specific examples illustrates the innovations and trends shaping restorative justice.

Restorative Justice in the Digital Age: Victim-Offender Dialogue Platforms

Online platforms for victim-offender dialogues have been developed to facilitate restorative justice processes in a secure and accessible manner. These platforms use secure video conferencing, digital confidentiality agreements, and online support resources to conduct dialogues.

During the COVID-19 pandemic, these platforms became essential, allowing restorative justice to continue when in-person meetings were impossible. Programs that had never used virtual platforms quickly adapted, discovering both the possibilities and limitations of online practice.

The outcomes have been instructive. Some participants have found virtual dialogues surprisingly effective, appreciating the convenience and accessibility. Others have missed the connection of in-person encounter. Programs have learned that virtual restorative justice requires different skills, different preparation, different support.

These platforms have increased accessibility for participants in different locations, reduced logistical barriers, and allowed restorative justice to continue during a global crisis. They represent a significant innovation that will likely remain part of the restorative justice landscape.

Restorative Practices in Corporate Diversity and Inclusion Programs

Companies are integrating restorative justice principles into their diversity and inclusion programs to address workplace discrimination and promote equity. This trend reflects growing recognition that traditional diversity training is often insufficient and that restorative approaches can address the deep dynamics of discrimination.

Restorative circles and mediation sessions are used to address incidents of discrimination, facilitate open dialogues on diversity, and develop inclusive policies. These processes create safe spaces for honest conversation, allowing employees to share experiences, learn from one another, and work together toward more inclusive practices.

The outcomes have been positive. Workplace culture improves as employees feel heard and respected. Trust and engagement increase as conflicts are addressed constructively. Progress toward diversity and inclusion goals is accelerated as organizations move beyond superficial training to deep cultural change.

Restorative Environmental Justice in New Zealand

New Zealand is exploring restorative justice approaches to address environmental harm and promote sustainable practices. This innovation reflects the country's commitment to both environmental protection and restorative justice, building on its experience with Family Group Conferencing.

Restorative circles involving affected communities, environmental organizations, and policymakers are used to discuss environmental issues, develop restorative actions, and foster collaboration. These circles bring together diverse stakeholders to address complex environmental problems in ways that promote understanding, accountability, and collective action.

The outcomes have been promising. Community involvement in environmental decision-making has been strengthened. Accountability for environmental harm has increased. Progress toward sustainability goals has been made. New Zealand's experience demonstrates that restorative principles can be applied to environmental issues, addressing harm to both human and natural communities.

Sustainability and Scalability: Ensuring the Long-Term Success and Expansion of Restorative Practices

Innovation is essential, but it is not enough. For restorative justice to achieve its transformative potential, programs must be sustainable—able to maintain effectiveness over time—and scalable—able to expand to new settings and populations.

Understanding Sustainability and Scalability

Sustainability and scalability are related but distinct concepts. Both are essential for restorative justice to achieve lasting impact.

Sustainability

Sustainability in restorative justice refers to the ability of programs to maintain their effectiveness, relevance, and impact over time. Sustainable programs are not dependent on a single funding source, a single champion, or favorable circumstances. They have built the capacity, relationships, and institutional support to endure.

Sustainable programs are resilient. They can weather changes in funding, leadership, or political climate. They can adapt to evolving needs and circumstances. They can continue to serve their communities effectively over the long term.

Sustainable programs are also adaptable. They learn from experience, adjust to feedback, and evolve in response to new challenges. They are not rigid but flexible, not static but dynamic.

The importance of sustainability cannot be overstated. Restorative justice is not a quick fix but a long-term commitment to transforming how communities respond to harm. Programs that flourish briefly and then fade do not achieve this transformation. Sustainability is essential for lasting impact.

Scalability

Scalability refers to the ability to expand restorative justice practices to new settings, regions, and populations while maintaining their effectiveness and quality. Scalable programs are not limited to their original context but can be adapted and replicated elsewhere.

Scalability is important because the need for restorative justice is vast. Communities around the world are struggling with the limitations of punitive justice systems. Scaling restorative practices allows more people and communities to benefit from these approaches, promoting wider social change and justice reform.

Scalability is also important for sustainability. Programs that can demonstrate scalability are more likely to attract funding and support. They can grow beyond their initial scope, building momentum for broader transformation.

Key Factors for Sustainability

Several key factors contribute to the sustainability of restorative justice programs.

Funding and Resources

Sustainable programs require stable and diverse funding sources. Reliance on a single grant or government appropriation is risky; if that funding disappears, the program may collapse. Diverse funding streams—government grants, private donations, community fundraising, earned revenue—provide resilience.

Adequate resources are also essential. Underfunded programs cannot provide quality services. They cannot pay facilitators adequately, provide necessary support services, or invest in training and evaluation. Ensuring adequate resources for training, facilitation, support services, and evaluation is essential for maintaining program quality.

The psychological dimensions of funding are significant. When programs are constantly worried about survival, they cannot focus on quality. When facilitators are underpaid and overworked, they cannot bring their best to restorative processes. Sustainable funding creates conditions for excellence.

Capacity Building

Sustainable programs require ongoing training and professional development for restorative justice practitioners. Facilitation skills must be developed and maintained; new practitioners must be trained; experienced practitioners must continue to learn. Investing in practitioner development ensures high-quality facilitation and program delivery.

Building community capacity is equally important. Empowering community members with the skills and knowledge to support and participate in restorative practices enhances program sustainability. When communities have their own trained facilitators, their own understanding of restorative principles, their own commitment to restorative values—they can sustain programs even when outside support diminishes.

The philosophical dimensions of capacity building are significant. Restorative justice is not something that experts do to communities but something that communities do together. Building local capacity embodies this principle, ensuring that restorative justice is truly community-owned.

Community Engagement and Support

Sustainable programs require strong relationships with community stakeholders—local organizations, leaders, and residents. Building these relationships fosters buy-in and support for restorative justice. When communities understand and value restorative practices, they will advocate for them, participate in them, and sustain them.

Encouraging community ownership of restorative justice programs promotes long-term commitment and sustainability. When programs belong to the community—not to an outside organization or a single champion—they are more likely to endure. Community members have stake in their success, investment in their continuation.

The theological dimensions of community engagement are profound. Many religious traditions emphasize the importance of community—the body of Christ, the ummah, the sangha. Restorative justice that is deeply rooted in community reflects this theological value.

Institutional Integration

Sustainable programs require institutional support. Advocating for policies that support restorative justice and integrating these practices into existing legal and social systems ensures institutional backing. When restorative justice is embedded in institutional frameworks—laws, regulations, funding streams, professional standards—it is more likely to survive changes in leadership or political climate.

Collaborating with various sectors—education, healthcare, criminal justice, social services—enhances the reach and impact of restorative justice programs. Cross-sector partnerships bring diverse resources and expertise, building networks of support that enhance sustainability.

The legal dimensions of institutional integration are significant. Legislation can provide authorization, funding, and standards for restorative justice. When restorative justice is written into law, it gains legitimacy and permanence.

Monitoring and Evaluation

Sustainable programs require mechanisms for regular monitoring and evaluation. Assessing program effectiveness, identifying areas for improvement, and demonstrating impact are essential for continuous improvement and for maintaining funding and support.

Using data and evidence to inform decision-making ensures that programs remain relevant and responsive to community needs. Evaluation should not be an afterthought but an integral part of program design, providing feedback that guides ongoing development.

The psychological dimensions of evaluation are significant. Programs that are willing to look honestly at their performance—celebrating successes, acknowledging failures, learning from both—are more likely to improve over time. This reflective practice is essential for sustainability.

Strategies for Scalability

Several strategies can support the scaling of restorative justice practices.

Model Adaptation and Replication

Adapting restorative justice models to fit the unique needs and contexts of different communities is essential for successful scaling. A model that works well in one setting may not work in another without adaptation. Understanding what is essential and what can be modified is key.

Identifying and replicating successful programs in new settings can expand the reach of restorative justice while maintaining quality and impact. Replication is not simply copying but thoughtful adaptation—preserving core principles while adjusting to local circumstances.

The philosophical dimensions of adaptation are significant. Restorative justice is not a rigid formula but a set of principles that can be embodied in diverse ways. Scaling requires fidelity to principles, not uniformity of practices.

Capacity Building for Scaling

Developing a cadre of trainers who can train new practitioners and support the expansion of restorative justice programs is crucial for scalability. These trainers become multipliers, spreading restorative practices to new settings and populations.

Creating and disseminating training materials, toolkits, and guidelines can support the consistent and effective implementation of restorative practices. These resources provide guidance for new programs while allowing flexibility for local adaptation.

The psychological dimensions of capacity building for scaling are significant. Training new practitioners requires attention to their learning needs, their contexts, their challenges. It is not merely transmitting information but developing competence and confidence.

Policy and Advocacy

Advocating for policy changes that support the expansion of restorative justice can create an enabling environment for scaling. Policies can provide funding, authorization, and standards; they can remove barriers and create incentives.

Forming alliances with advocacy groups, policymakers, and other stakeholders can strengthen efforts to scale restorative justice. Collective action is more powerful than individual efforts; coalitions can achieve policy changes that no single organization could accomplish alone.

The legal dimensions of policy advocacy are significant. Laws and policies shape what is possible. Advocating for restorative justice at the policy level is essential for creating conditions for scaling.

Cross-Sector Integration

Integrating restorative justice into various sectors—education, criminal justice, healthcare, social services—can enhance its reach and impact. Each sector offers different opportunities for restorative practice; each reaches different populations.

Developing collaborative approaches that involve multiple sectors and stakeholders can support the scaling of restorative justice practices. Cross-sector partnerships bring diverse resources and expertise, building networks that can support expansion.

The philosophical dimensions of cross-sector integration are significant. Restorative justice is not only about criminal justice; it is about how we address harm and build community in all areas of life. Integration across sectors reflects this broader vision.

Innovative Approaches

Leveraging technology can facilitate the scaling of restorative justice by increasing accessibility and efficiency. Online platforms can reach remote populations; digital tools can support training and communication; data systems can track outcomes and support evaluation.

Exploring innovative funding models—social impact bonds, community investment, pay-for-success arrangements—can support the expansion of restorative justice programs. These models align funding with outcomes, attracting investment from those who value restorative results.

The psychological dimensions of innovation are significant. Innovation requires creativity, risk-taking, and learning from failure. Scaling restorative justice requires willingness to try new approaches, to learn from what works, to adapt and evolve.

Case Studies of Sustainable and Scalable Restorative Practices

Examining real-world examples illustrates the potential for sustainability and scalability.

New Zealand's Family Group Conferencing

Family Group Conferencing was developed in New Zealand to address the overrepresentation of Maori youth in the juvenile justice system. The program has demonstrated remarkable sustainability and scalability.

Sustainability is supported by strong policy backing—the Children, Young Persons, and Their Families Act 1989 made FGC mandatory for most youth offenses. Continuous training ensures that facilitators maintain high-quality practice. Community involvement ensures that the program remains grounded in Maori values and supported by Maori communities.

Scalability has been demonstrated through successful adaptation in other countries. FGC has been implemented in various forms around the world, adapted to fit different cultural contexts while maintaining restorative principles. The model's adaptability has enabled its global spread.

The theological dimensions of FGC's success are significant. The program draws on Maori spirituality, which understands justice in relational and holistic terms. This spiritual grounding gives the program depth and resilience.

Oakland Unified School District, California

Oakland Unified School District implemented restorative justice practices to address disparities in school discipline and create a positive school climate. The program has demonstrated impressive sustainability and scalability.

Sustainability is ensured through ongoing funding from the district, training for staff, and strong community partnerships. The program is not dependent on soft money but embedded in the district's budget and operations.

Scalability has been demonstrated through expansion within the district and replication in other school districts. Oakland's success has inspired similar programs across the country, with districts adapting the model to their own contexts.

The psychological dimensions of Oakland's success are significant. The program has transformed school climate, reducing disciplinary incidents and improving relationships. Students feel safer, more respected, more connected—outcomes that support learning and development.

Restorative Justice for Oakland Youth

Restorative Justice for Oakland Youth focuses on implementing restorative justice practices in schools, juvenile justice systems, and communities to address racial disparities and promote healing. The organization has demonstrated both sustainability and scalability.

Sustainability is supported by a combination of grants, donations, and community support. RJOY has diversified its funding, reducing dependence on any single source. A commitment to continuous learning and adaptation ensures that programs remain effective and relevant.

Scalability has been demonstrated through replication in other cities and states. RJOY's model has been adapted in multiple locations, spreading restorative practices to new communities while maintaining fidelity to core principles.

The theological dimensions of RJOY's work are significant. The organization works in communities where faith is central, partnering with churches and faith-based organizations. This partnership brings spiritual depth and community trust to restorative practice.

Community Holistic Circle Healing in Hollow Water First Nation, Canada

The Community Holistic Circle Healing program was developed in Hollow Water First Nation to address high rates of sexual abuse and violence within the community. The program has demonstrated remarkable sustainability and scalability.

Sustainability is ensured through community ownership—the program belongs to the community, not to outside funders or agencies. Continuous training ensures that community members maintain facilitation skills. Strong support from local leaders provides ongoing leadership and advocacy.

Scalability has been demonstrated through adaptation and implementation in other Indigenous communities. CHCH's model has been shared across Canada, adapted to fit different Indigenous cultures while maintaining restorative principles.

The theological dimensions of CHCH's success are profound. The program draws on Indigenous spirituality, which understands healing as holistic and community-based. This spiritual grounding gives the program power and resonance that secular approaches cannot replicate.

Challenges and Considerations for Sustainability and Scalability

Achieving sustainability and scalability presents significant challenges.

Maintaining Quality and Fidelity

Maintaining the quality and fidelity of restorative practices as they scale is crucial to their effectiveness and impact. When programs expand rapidly, there is risk that quality will suffer, that practices will become superficial, that core principles will be diluted.

Providing ongoing training and support for practitioners and facilitators helps ensure consistent and high-quality implementation. Quality cannot be assumed; it must be actively maintained through investment in people and systems.

The psychological dimensions of quality maintenance are significant. Practitioners need ongoing support to sustain their skills, to avoid burnout, to continue learning. Programs need feedback systems to identify and address quality issues.

Navigating Resistance and Barriers

Addressing resistance from stakeholders and institutions that are accustomed to traditional justice approaches is essential for successful scaling. Resistance may come from judges, prosecutors, police, corrections officials, or community members who are skeptical of restorative alternatives.

Identifying and addressing barriers to participation—such as cost, accessibility, and cultural relevance—is crucial for scaling restorative justice. Barriers that exclude certain groups will limit reach and undermine equity.

The philosophical dimensions of navigating resistance are significant. Resistance often reflects deeply held beliefs about justice, punishment, and accountability. Addressing resistance requires engaging these beliefs, not merely dismissing them.

Balancing Flexibility and Standardization

Balancing the need for flexibility to adapt to local contexts with the need for standardization to ensure quality and consistency is a key challenge in scaling. Too much flexibility can lead to fragmentation and loss of core principles; too much standardization can prevent adaptation to local needs.

Creating adaptable guidelines and frameworks can help maintain consistency while allowing for necessary adaptations. Guidelines should specify core principles and essential elements while leaving room for local variation in implementation.

The theological dimensions of this balance are significant. Many religious traditions emphasize both universal truths and local expression. Restorative justice, scaled thoughtfully, can reflect both—universal principles embodied in locally adapted practices.

Vision for the Future: A Visionary Look at the Potential of Restorative Justice to Transform Society

Finally, dear reader, we arrive at the most visionary part of our journey. Having explored the foundations, principles, practices, and challenges of restorative justice, we now imagine what might be—a world transformed by restorative values, a society built on healing rather than punishment, a future where justice is truly just.

Envisioning a Restorative Society

What would a restorative society look like? This is not merely a speculative question but a visionary one—an invitation to imagine possibilities that can guide our work and inspire our hope.

Core Principles of a Restorative Society

A restorative society would be built on several core principles. Healing and reparation would be prioritized over punishment. When harm occurs, the first question would not be "What punishment does this deserve?" but "What needs to be healed?" The focus would be on making things right, not on making offenders suffer.

Accountability and responsibility would be understood relationally. Individuals and institutions would be encouraged to take responsibility for their actions and their impact on others. Accountability would mean facing those affected, understanding harm, and making amends—not merely accepting punishment.

Inclusivity and participation would be fundamental. All voices would be heard and respected; everyone would have opportunity to participate in decisions that affect their lives. Marginalized groups would be included, not excluded; power would be shared, not hoarded.

Community and relationship building would be central. Strong, supportive, and interconnected communities would be recognized as essential to human flourishing. Investment in relationships would be as important as investment in institutions.

The theological vision underlying these principles is the vision of *shalom*—the peace that comes when all things are in right relationship. In a restorative society, relationships with God, with neighbor, with community, with creation would be characterized by wholeness, harmony, and flourishing.

Transforming the Criminal Justice System

In a restorative society, the criminal justice system would be fundamentally transformed.

Restorative Justice as the Norm

Restorative justice would be fully integrated into legal frameworks, with restorative practices being the default approach to addressing crime and harm. Courts would offer restorative options at every stage—diversion before prosecution, restorative sentencing, restorative programs in prisons, restorative reentry support. Conventional punishment would be reserved for cases where restorative approaches are inappropriate or unsuccessful.

Victim-centered approaches would be central. Victims would have a central role in the justice process, with their needs and rights prioritized. They would have opportunity to tell their stories, to ask questions, to participate in determining what justice requires. Their healing would be a primary goal, not an afterthought.

The psychological dimensions of this transformation are profound. Victims would no longer be marginalized but empowered. Offenders would no longer be passive recipients of punishment but active participants in accountability and change. Communities would no longer be excluded but engaged.

Rehabilitation and Reintegration

Rehabilitation and reintegration would be emphasized over punishment. Offenders would be provided with the tools and support needed to make amends and reintegrate into society—

education, job training, mental health treatment, substance abuse counseling, restorative programs.

Restorative practices would address the root causes of criminal behavior—trauma, addiction, poverty, lack of opportunity, broken relationships. By addressing these underlying causes, restorative justice would reduce recidivism and promote long-term public safety.

The theological dimensions of this transformation are significant. The biblical vision of redemption—of lives transformed, of second chances, of new beginnings—would be embodied in criminal justice practice. Offenders would be seen not as irredeemable but as capable of change, worthy of support.

Transforming Education

In a restorative society, education would be transformed by restorative principles.

Restorative Schools

Schools would be places where restorative practices are embedded in the culture, creating positive, inclusive, and supportive environments for students and staff. Restorative circles would be regular features of school life, building community and addressing issues before they escalate.

Conflicts would be addressed constructively through restorative circles, mediation, and peer support. Bullying would be reduced as students learn empathy and respect. Relationships would be strengthened as students and teachers learn to communicate openly and resolve differences collaboratively.

Empowering Students

Students would be empowered to take active roles in creating restorative school climates. They would develop leadership skills through peer mediation programs, restorative circle facilitation, and student government. They would learn to take responsibility for their actions and to contribute positively to their communities.

Social and emotional learning would be integrated with restorative practices. Students would develop empathy, communication skills, emotional resilience—the capacities that enable them to navigate relationships, address conflicts, and contribute to community.

The psychological dimensions of this transformation are significant. Students who feel safe, respected, and connected are more engaged, more motivated, more likely to succeed. Restorative schools would promote not only academic achievement but healthy development.

Transforming Communities

In a restorative society, communities would be strengthened and empowered.

Community Cohesion and Resilience

Communities would be built on strong, cohesive, and resilient networks of support. Restorative practices would be used to address local conflicts, reduce violence, and promote social harmony. Community members would know and trust one another, looking out for each other's well-being.

Community-based restorative justice programs would be available in every neighborhood, addressing local issues with local solutions. These programs would draw on community knowledge and relationships, ensuring that responses to harm are relevant and effective.

Inclusive Decision-Making

Participatory governance models would ensure that community members are actively involved in decision-making processes. Policies and initiatives would reflect the needs and values of the community, not merely the preferences of elites. Collaborative approaches to addressing social issues would leverage the strengths and resources of diverse community members.

The philosophical dimensions of this transformation are significant. Democratic theory emphasizes the importance of participation; communitarianism emphasizes the importance of community; restorative justice provides practices for embodying these values.

Addressing Global Challenges

In a restorative society, restorative principles would be applied to global challenges.

Restorative Environmental Justice

Restorative justice principles would be applied to address environmental harm and promote sustainability. Those who damage ecosystems would be held accountable, not merely through fines but through restorative processes that engage affected communities and require meaningful reparation.

Communities would be engaged in environmental decision-making, ensuring that those most affected by environmental issues have voice and agency in creating solutions. Collaborative efforts to restore ecosystems would bring together diverse stakeholders—community members, corporations, governments, environmental organizations.

The theological dimensions of environmental restorative justice are profound. Many religious traditions understand humanity as having responsibility for caring for creation. Restorative environmental justice would embody this sacred responsibility, addressing harm to the earth and to human communities together.

Global Peacebuilding

Restorative justice would be used in post-conflict settings to promote healing, reconciliation, and sustainable peace. Truth commissions, community-based restorative practices, victim-offender dialogues, reparations programs—all would contribute to addressing the legacies of violence and building foundations for peace.

Cross-cultural dialogue and understanding would be fostered through restorative practices. People from different cultures, different faiths, different backgrounds would come together to share experiences, to learn from one another, to build relationships across lines of division. Global solidarity and cooperation would be strengthened.

The psychological dimensions of global peacebuilding are significant. Trauma from violence and oppression must be addressed for peace to be sustainable. Restorative practices that provide opportunities for truth-telling, acknowledgment, and healing can contribute to this essential work.

Embracing Innovation and Technology

In a restorative society, innovation and technology would be embraced as tools for advancing restorative goals.

Digital Restorative Practices

Technology would be leveraged to expand access to restorative justice. Virtual mediation and conferencing would reach remote populations, connecting participants across distances. Online training would build capacity worldwide. Digital tools would support communication, documentation, and evaluation.

These digital practices would not replace in-person restorative encounters but supplement them, providing options that increase accessibility and flexibility. The goal would be to make restorative justice available to all who need it, regardless of location or circumstance.

Innovative Approaches

Creative approaches to restorative justice would be encouraged and supported. Art, storytelling, and other creative modalities would be integrated with restorative practices, providing diverse pathways to healing and expression. Research and development would be invested in continuously improving and adapting restorative practices.

The philosophical dimensions of innovation are significant. Restorative justice is not a finished product but an evolving practice. Embracing innovation means remaining open to new possibilities, new insights, new ways of embodying restorative principles.

Fostering a Culture of Restorative Justice

Ultimately, the transformation to a restorative society requires more than programs and policies; it requires a culture that embraces restorative values.

Public Awareness and Education

Public awareness of restorative justice principles and practices would be promoted through education campaigns, media, and community outreach. People would understand what restorative justice is, how it works, why it matters. They would see it not as a marginal alternative but as a normal and valuable approach to addressing harm.

Restorative justice education would be integrated into school curricula, professional training programs, and higher education. From an early age, people would learn restorative values—empathy, accountability, community, healing. Professionals in many fields would be trained in restorative practices.

Cultivating Restorative Values

A culture that embraces restorative values—empathy, compassion, accountability, respect—would be fostered in all aspects of society. Families would practice restorative communication; workplaces would use restorative approaches to conflict; communities would address issues restoratively.

Leaders, influencers, and role models would champion restorative justice and exemplify restorative values in their actions and decisions. Political leaders would advocate for restorative policies; business leaders would implement restorative practices; religious leaders would teach restorative principles.

The theological dimensions of this cultural transformation are profound. Many religious traditions already teach restorative values—forgiveness, reconciliation, compassion, justice. Fostering a restorative culture means drawing on these religious resources, partnering with faith communities, and embodying spiritual truths in social practice.

The Integration of Law, Psychology, Philosophy, and Theology

As we have looked to the future of restorative justice, we have seen how multiple disciplines will continue to inform and enrich the field.

Legal Perspectives

Law will provide frameworks for integrating restorative justice into formal systems. Legislation will authorize restorative programs, allocate resources, establish standards. Courts will interpret and apply restorative principles. Legal professionals will become partners in restorative practice, referring cases, supporting processes, implementing outcomes.

The future of restorative justice depends in part on continued legal development—laws that support restorative approaches, policies that fund restorative programs, judicial decisions that affirm restorative principles. This legal infrastructure is essential for sustainability and scalability.

Psychological Insights

Psychology will continue to illuminate the dynamics of harm, healing, and change. Research on trauma will inform trauma-informed restorative practice. Research on empathy will guide efforts to foster understanding between victims and offenders. Research on desistance will support programs that promote offender rehabilitation.

The future of restorative justice depends on continued psychological research—studies that identify what works, for whom, under what conditions. This evidence base will guide practice, inform policy, and demonstrate the value of restorative approaches.

Philosophical Foundations

Philosophy will continue to provide frameworks for thinking about justice, accountability, and healing. Ethical reflection will guide practice; political philosophy will inform system design; epistemology will shape how we know what works.

The future of restorative justice depends on continued philosophical engagement—thinking deeply about the meaning of justice, the purposes of punishment, the nature of healing. This philosophical work will keep restorative practice grounded in principle, not merely technique.

Theological Dimensions

Theology will continue to offer profound resources for restorative justice. The biblical vision of *shalom* will inspire restorative work. The reconciling work of God in Christ will model restorative practice. The hospitality of God's kingdom will shape restorative communities.

The future of restorative justice depends on continued theological engagement—drawing on the wisdom of religious traditions, partnering with faith communities, embodying spiritual truths in restorative practice. This theological grounding will give restorative work depth, meaning, and hope.

As we conclude this chapter—and this book—we return to where we began: the vision of a restorative society. This vision is not utopian; it does not imagine a world without harm, without conflict, without suffering. Such a world is not possible in human history. But the vision does imagine a world where harm is addressed restoratively, where conflicts are resolved constructively, where suffering is met with compassion. It imagines a world where justice heals rather than wounds, where accountability transforms rather than merely punishes, where community supports rather than excludes.

This vision is not merely idealistic; it is practical. It is being realized, piece by piece, in programs around the world—in New Zealand's Family Group Conferencing, in Canada's restorative justice initiatives, in South Africa's Truth and Reconciliation Commission, in Oakland's school-based restorative practices, in Hollow Water's community healing circles. These real-world examples demonstrate that restorative justice is not a dream but a reality, not a fantasy but a practice.

The future of restorative justice depends on us—on our commitment, our creativity, our persistence. It depends on practitioners who facilitate circles and conferences with skill and compassion. It depends on advocates who promote restorative policies and educate their communities. It depends on researchers who study what works and share their findings. It depends on leaders who champion restorative values and model restorative practice. It depends on all of us who believe that justice can be different, that healing is possible, that community matters.

The journey through this book has been long, but the journey of restorative justice is longer still. It began millennia ago, in the practices of indigenous peoples around the world. It continued through centuries of evolution, adaptation, and occasional eclipse. It revived in the late twentieth century, driven by dissatisfaction with punitive justice and hope for something better. And it continues today, in programs and practices around the world, in research and innovation, in the lives of victims who find healing, offenders who find change, communities that find strength.

Where the journey goes from here is up to us. The vision is clear: a restorative society, where healing justice transforms our world. The principles are sound: accountability, reparation, community involvement, empathy, healing. The practices are proven: victim-offender mediation, family group conferencing, circle processes, community restorative boards. The evidence is compelling: victims are satisfied, offenders are rehabilitated, communities are strengthened.

What remains is the work—the daily, patient, persistent work of building restorative practices in our communities, our institutions, our lives. This work is not glamorous. It does not make headlines. It does not produce quick results. But it is essential. It is the work of transformation—transforming how we respond to harm, how we understand justice, how we live together.

As you close this book and return to your life, I invite you to carry restorative values with you. In your family, practice restorative communication—listening, acknowledging, apologizing, forgiving. In your workplace, advocate for restorative approaches to conflict—mediation, dialogue, collaborative problem-solving. In your community, support restorative programs—volunteer, donate, advocate. In your own heart, cultivate restorative virtues—empathy, compassion, accountability, hope.

The restorative society is not something that will happen to us; it is something we must create together. Every restorative circle, every victim-offender dialogue, every family group conference, every community restorative board—each is a small step toward that larger vision. Each is a seed planted that may grow into something larger than we can imagine.

The biblical vision of *shalom*—peace, wholeness, right relationship—is the vision of a restorative society. It is the vision of a world where justice rolls down like waters, where swords are beaten into plowshares, where lion and lamb lie down together. It is the vision of a world where every tear is wiped away, where death and mourning are no more, where all things are made new.

This vision is not merely human aspiration; it is divine promise. The God who created the world good, who entered into covenant with a people, who became flesh in Jesus Christ, who sends the Spirit to empower and transform—this God is at work bringing about restoration. Our restorative work is participation in God's restorative work. Our small efforts are part of a larger story.

May you go from this book with renewed commitment to restorative justice. May you carry its principles into your daily life. May you contribute, in whatever way you can, to building a restorative society. And may you have hope—hope that transformation is possible, that healing can occur, that a more just and compassionate world is not only desirable but achievable.

The future of restorative justice is in our hands. Let us build it together.

CONCLUSION

Dear reader, we have journeyed together through a comprehensive exploration of restorative justice—its historical foundations, philosophical underpinnings, core principles and values, diverse practices and models, real-world applications across multiple domains, honest assessment of benefits and challenges, complex relationship with legal systems, global manifestations in international contexts, profound intersection with social justice, and visionary possibilities for the future. Now, as we arrive at the conclusion of this journey, it is time to gather together the threads we have woven, to reflect on the transformative power of restorative justice, and to consider what each of us might do to contribute to the creation of a more just and compassionate world.

This concluding chapter serves multiple purposes. First, it offers a summary of the key points and themes we have explored, providing a comprehensive recap of the book's main insights. Second, it issues a call to action, encouraging you to engage with and support restorative justice initiatives in your own life and community. Third, it offers final reflections on the transformative power of restorative justice and the vision of a restorative society that has animated this entire work.

Throughout this conclusion, we will draw together the insights from law, psychology, philosophy, and theology that have informed our journey. We will see how these different perspectives converge on a common vision—a vision of justice that heals rather than harms, that restores rather than destroys, that builds community rather than tearing it apart.

Summary of Key Points: A Recap of Main Themes and Insights

Let us begin by gathering together the main themes and insights that have emerged from our journey through the preceding chapters. This recap is not merely repetition but synthesis—drawing connections, highlighting patterns, and reinforcing the most important lessons.

Historical Foundations and Theoretical Frameworks

Our journey began with history and philosophy—exploring where restorative justice came from and what ideas give it shape and substance.

Ancient Practices and Historical Roots

Restorative justice is not a modern invention but an ancient wisdom, rediscovered and renewed in our time. Its roots extend deep into human history, reaching back to the earliest communities that recognized that harm damages relationships and that justice must repair those relationships.

We explored the rich tapestry of restorative practices in indigenous cultures around the world. Native American peacemaking circles brought community members together to address harm through dialogue, healing, and collective decision-making. African justice systems, grounded in the philosophy of *Ubuntu*, emphasized reconciliation, community healing, and the interconnectedness of all people. Maori practices in New Zealand, including family group conferencing, demonstrated the power of involving families and communities in addressing harm.

We examined the biblical foundations of restorative justice, discovering that the scriptures are filled with restorative themes. The Hebrew concept of *shalom*—peace, wholeness, right relationship—provides a vision of what restorative justice seeks to achieve. The Torah's provisions for restitution, the prophets' calls for justice that protects the vulnerable, Jesus's teachings on forgiveness and reconciliation, Paul's theology of reconciliation in Christ—all these testify to the deep roots of restorative principles in the Judeo-Christian tradition.

We explored ancient justice systems in the Middle East, Greece, Rome, and Asia, finding restorative elements in each. The Code of Hammurabi included provisions for restitution. Athenian democracy involved citizens in the administration of justice. Roman law provided for compensation to victims. Confucian philosophy emphasized mediation and reconciliation. Hindu and Buddhist traditions emphasized karma, dharma, and the resolution of conflict through ethical conduct.

The medieval and early modern periods saw both the persistence of restorative practices and the gradual shift toward centralized, retributive justice systems. Manorial courts, church courts, and community-based justice continued to emphasize reconciliation and restitution even as nation-states developed formal legal codes. The Enlightenment brought new perspectives on human rights and rational punishment, creating space for eventual revival of restorative approaches.

The modern resurgence of restorative justice in the 20th and 21st centuries was driven by dissatisfaction with retributive justice, emerging theoretical and empirical support, and influential social movements. Key figures like Howard Zehr articulated restorative principles and practices. Victim-offender reconciliation programs demonstrated the feasibility of restorative approaches. Truth and reconciliation commissions showed the power of restorative justice at societal scale.

Philosophical Underpinnings

The theoretical foundations of restorative justice are built on key philosophical theories that prioritize human dignity, empathy, and interconnectedness.

Relational ethics emphasizes the interconnectedness of individuals within community, grounding our moral obligations in the relationships we share. Restorative justice applies this insight by focusing on repairing relationships disrupted by harm and involving the community in the justice process.

Communitarianism stresses the importance of community values and collective well-being, recognizing that individuals are shaped by their communities and that a just society prioritizes the common good. Restorative justice aligns with communitarianism by prioritizing the restoration of community harmony and involving the community in decision-making.

Virtue ethics, rooted in Aristotelian philosophy, focuses on the development of moral character and virtues such as empathy, compassion, and responsibility. Restorative justice practices encourage the cultivation of these virtues in both victims and offenders, guiding individuals toward moral growth and ethical behavior.

Restorative ontology underscores the fundamental need for restoration and healing in the aftermath of harm, positing that true justice can only be achieved when relationships are mended and communities are strengthened. This perspective recognizes that justice involves more than punishment; it requires active repair of damage.

Ethical responsibility highlights the moral duty individuals have to address the harm they cause and contribute positively to their communities. Restorative justice emphasizes accountability by encouraging offenders to take responsibility and actively participate in making amends.

Dialogical ethics emphasizes the importance of dialogue and communication in ethical decision-making, positing that ethical understanding and mutual respect arise from open and honest dialogue. Restorative justice practices facilitate dialogue between victims, offenders, and community members, fostering mutual understanding and collaborative problem-solving.

Ethical Considerations

Ethical considerations in restorative justice focus on morality, the philosophy of punishment, and the balance between individual and collective justice. We examined three major theories of punishment—retributive justice, utilitarianism, and restorative justice—comparing their principles, processes, and outcomes.

Retributive justice, based on the principle of "just deserts," focuses on punishment proportional to offense. While it provides moral accountability, critics argue it can be overly punitive and fails to address victims' needs. Utilitarianism evaluates punishment based on its consequences—deterrence and rehabilitation—but can justify harsh punishments if they are believed to deter crime effectively.

Restorative justice offers a third approach, focusing on repairing harm, involving stakeholders, and promoting healing. Its ethical basis is grounded in relational ethics, communitarianism, and virtue ethics. While critics raise concerns about leniency and inconsistency, proponents contend that its focus on healing and accountability offers a more holistic and humane approach.

Ethical principles in restorative justice include accountability, reparation, empathy and compassion, community involvement, and proportionality and fairness. These principles guide restorative practices and reflect its commitment to moral responsibility, community involvement, and the restoration of social harmony.

Core Principles and Values

From these philosophical foundations, we derived the core principles and values that give restorative justice its distinctive character.

Accountability and Responsibility

Accountability in restorative justice means more than accepting punishment; it involves taking genuine responsibility for one's actions, understanding their impact, and actively participating in making amends. We explored how accountability is facilitated through restorative practices—victim-offender mediation, restorative circles, family group conferencing, community restorative boards—and considered the challenges of ensuring genuine accountability, addressing power imbalances, and measuring success.

The psychological dimensions of accountability are significant. When offenders genuinely understand the harm they have caused and choose to make amends, they are more likely to change than when they merely serve time. This internal motivation is far more powerful than external coercion in producing lasting behavioral change.

The theological dimensions are equally profound. The biblical concept of repentance—*metanoia*—involves a fundamental turning around, a change of heart and life. Restorative justice creates conditions for this kind of transformation, inviting offenders not merely to accept punishment but to become different people.

Reparation and Healing

Reparation involves making amends for harm caused, addressing both material and emotional needs of victims. We explored various forms of reparation—financial restitution, community service, direct apologies, symbolic acts—and considered their role in promoting healing for victims, rehabilitation for offenders, and restoration of community harmony.

Healing is a central goal of restorative justice, addressing the emotional and psychological wounds caused by wrongdoing.

We examined the types of healing—emotional, psychological, social—and the ways restorative practices facilitate healing through direct dialogue, inclusive participation, and supportive environments.

The psychological research on healing is compelling. Victims who participate in restorative processes report higher satisfaction and greater healing than those whose cases go through conventional channels. Offenders who make amends experience reduced shame and increased self-respect. Communities that address harm restoratively become stronger and more cohesive.

The theological dimensions of healing are profound. The Bible is filled with images of healing—the healing of bodies, the healing of relationships, the healing of nations. Restorative justice participates in this healing ministry, addressing the wounds that sin and crime create.

Community Involvement and Empathy

Community involvement is crucial for the success of restorative justice, providing support and fostering collective responsibility. We explored the roles community members play—supporting victims, holding offenders accountable, facilitating restorative processes—and the benefits of community involvement for victims, offenders, and communities.

Empathy and emotional healing are fostered through restorative practices, encouraging understanding and connection between victims, offenders, and the community. We examined strategies for fostering empathy—active listening, narrative sharing, emotional support, reparative actions—and considered the challenges of ensuring genuine empathy, addressing emotional barriers, and creating safe spaces.

The psychological research on empathy is clear. Empathy can be cultivated through practice; restorative processes provide structured opportunities for empathy to develop. When offenders develop empathy for victims, they are more likely to change; when victims experience empathy from offenders, they are more likely to heal.

The theological dimensions of empathy are significant. The Bible calls us to "rejoice with those who rejoice, weep with those who weep" (Romans 12:15)—to enter into the experiences of others. Restorative justice embodies this call, creating spaces where victims and offenders can share their experiences and connect at a human level.

Restorative Practices and Models

From principles we moved to practices—the concrete ways restorative justice is implemented.

Victim-Offender Mediation and Family Group Conferencing

Victim-offender mediation provides a platform for direct dialogue between victims and offenders, promoting mutual understanding and agreement on reparative actions. We explored the process—referral and intake, preparation, mediation session, follow-up—and the benefits for victims, offenders, and communities.

Family group conferencing involves family and community in resolving conflicts, emphasizing collaborative decision-making and support. Originating in New Zealand and rooted in Maori traditions, FGC has been adopted worldwide, demonstrating impressive outcomes in victim satisfaction, recidivism reduction, and offender rehabilitation.

Circle Processes and Community Restorative Boards

Circle processes facilitate open and inclusive discussions, promoting healing and resolution through collective dialogue. Drawing on indigenous traditions, circles create spaces where all voices can be heard, where collective wisdom can emerge, where shared responsibility can be exercised.

Community restorative boards engage community members in addressing offenses and supporting offender reintegration. These boards, composed of trained volunteers, represent the community's direct involvement in justice, embodying the principle of collective responsibility.

Case Studies and Real-world Applications

We examined how restorative justice is applied across multiple domains, drawing on real-world examples from around the world.

Criminal Justice System

Restorative justice has been effectively integrated into criminal justice systems worldwide. New Zealand's Family Group Conferencing has reduced recidivism and increased victim satisfaction. Canada's victim-offender mediation programs have demonstrated impressive outcomes. Community restorative boards in the United States have engaged communities in addressing minor offenses. South Africa's Truth and Reconciliation Commission showed the power of restorative approaches at societal scale.

The evidence is compelling. Restorative practices reduce recidivism, increase victim satisfaction, and strengthen communities. They offer a more humane and effective alternative to purely punitive approaches.

Schools and Educational Settings

Restorative practices in schools address bullying, reduce disciplinary issues, and create positive learning environments. The Oakland Unified School District's whole-school restorative approach reduced suspensions and improved academic outcomes. Peer mediation programs in Philadelphia reduced violence and improved student relationships. Restorative conferences in Denver decreased expulsions and increased accountability.

The benefits extend beyond discipline. Students develop social and emotional skills, teachers build stronger relationships with students, school communities become more cohesive and supportive.

Workplace and Organizations

Restorative justice is increasingly applied in corporate and organizational settings to address conflicts and enhance employee relations. Google's restorative circles improved team dynamics. Coca-Cola's mediation program reduced grievances and improved job satisfaction. Kaiser Permanente's restorative conferences addressed harassment and discrimination. Patagonia's whole-organization restorative approach transformed workplace culture.

The benefits include improved employee relations, increased morale and productivity, reduced legal risks, and enhanced organizational culture.

Community Programs

Community-based restorative justice programs address local conflicts, strengthen social bonds, and promote collective healing. Vermont's Community Restorative Boards reduced recidivism and increased community engagement. Brazil's restorative circles improved communication and reduced violence. New Zealand's Family Group Conferencing empowered families and communities. Canada's Community Holistic Circle Healing transformed a community's response to sexual abuse.

These programs demonstrate that restorative justice can be implemented at the community level, drawing on local knowledge and relationships to address harm effectively.

Benefits and Challenges

We honestly assessed both the benefits and challenges of restorative justice.

Positive Outcomes

Restorative justice offers numerous benefits. Victims experience empowerment, voice, emotional healing, and restitution. Offenders experience accountability, personal growth, rehabilitation, and supportive reintegration. Communities experience strengthened social bonds, reduced crime rates, and improved well-being.

The evidence supports these claims. Research consistently shows high levels of victim satisfaction, reduced recidivism, and improved community relations. Real-world examples from New Zealand, Canada, South Africa, and elsewhere demonstrate the transformative potential of restorative justice.

Common Challenges

Implementing restorative justice faces challenges. Resistance to change from stakeholders accustomed to retributive approaches can impede adoption. Resource constraints—limited funding, shortage of trained facilitators—can hinder implementation. Ensuring voluntary participation requires careful attention to consent and information. Addressing power imbalances between victims and offenders requires skilled facilitation. Creating safe environments requires attention to physical and emotional safety. Cultural sensitivity requires adaptation to diverse contexts. Sustainability and integration require institutional support and ongoing evaluation.

These challenges are real, but they are not insurmountable. With thoughtful strategies—building awareness and support, securing funding and resources, ensuring voluntary participation, addressing power imbalances, creating safe environments, ensuring cultural sensitivity, promoting sustainability and integration—they can be overcome.

Criticisms and Controversies

Restorative justice faces criticisms. Some perceive it as too lenient on offenders, failing to provide sufficient deterrence. Others worry about inconsistent outcomes, given the flexibility of restorative processes. Concerns about victim participation and coercion arise when victims feel pressured to participate.

Questions about suitability for severe crimes—sexual assault, domestic violence, homicide—require careful consideration. Challenges of integrating restorative justice with formal legal systems raise concerns about coherence and effectiveness.

These criticisms deserve thoughtful response. Restorative justice is not about avoiding consequences but about meaningful accountability. While variability exists, clear guidelines and training can ensure consistency. Protecting victims' autonomy and providing support services can address coercion concerns. With appropriate safeguards, restorative justice can be effective even in severe cases. Successful integration requires collaboration between restorative and formal systems.

Future Directions and Innovations

Finally, we looked to the future, exploring emerging trends and innovations.

Emerging Trends and Innovations

Digital restorative practices—virtual mediation and conferencing, online training and resources—expand access and flexibility, though they present challenges around confidentiality, rapport, and emotional intensity. Integrating restorative justice into new sectors—healthcare, corporate settings, environmental justice—demonstrates its adaptability and broad potential. Expanding restorative justice in the criminal justice system—for serious crimes, in prisons—extends its reach to new populations. Innovations in research and evaluation—data-driven approaches, participatory action research—enhance effectiveness and credibility. Global trends and cross-cultural adaptations—cultural adaptations of restorative practices, international collaboration and knowledge sharing—promote the global growth of restorative justice.

Sustainability and Scalability

Ensuring the sustainability of restorative programs requires stable funding, capacity building, community engagement and support, institutional integration, and continuous monitoring and evaluation. Strategies for scaling include model adaptation and replication, capacity building for scaling, policy and advocacy, cross-sector integration, and innovative approaches such as leveraging technology and creative funding models.

Real-world examples demonstrate the potential for sustainability and scalability. New Zealand's Family Group Conferencing has been sustained through strong policy backing and scaled through adaptation in other countries. Oakland's school-based restorative practices have been sustained through district funding and scaled through replication in other districts. RJOY has been sustained through diverse funding and scaled through replication in other cities. CHCH has been sustained through community ownership and scaled through adaptation in other Indigenous communities.

Vision for the Future

Envisioning a restorative society involves integrating restorative practices into all aspects of life. In criminal justice, restorative justice would become the norm, with victim-centered approaches and emphasis on rehabilitation and reintegration. In education, restorative schools would create positive climates and empower students. In communities, restorative practices would build cohesion and resilience, promote inclusive decision-making. In global affairs, restorative approaches would address environmental harm and support peacebuilding.

Embracing innovation and technology—digital restorative practices, creative approaches—would expand access and enhance effectiveness. Fostering a culture of restorative justice through public awareness and education, cultivating restorative values, would embed restorative principles in the fabric of society.

Call to Action: Encouragement for Readers to Engage with and Support Restorative Justice Initiatives

The journey through this book has illuminated the profound potential of restorative justice to transform lives, communities, and societies. But understanding is not enough; appreciation is not sufficient. The vision of a restorative society will remain a dream unless we—each of us—take action to make it real. This call to action is an invitation to move from passive reading to active engagement, from theoretical knowledge to practical commitment.

Understanding Your Role in Restorative Justice

Each of us has a role to play in advancing restorative justice. That role will look different depending on our circumstances, our gifts, our opportunities. But all of us can contribute in some way.

Individual Engagement

The journey of a thousand miles begins with a single step. For each of us, that step may be different, but it begins with individual engagement.

First, educate yourself and others. Continuously seek to learn more about restorative justice principles and practices. Read books and articles, attend workshops and webinars, listen to podcasts and lectures. Share your knowledge with friends, family, and colleagues. Raise awareness in your social networks, your workplace, your faith community. The more people understand restorative justice, the more support it will have.

Second, participate in restorative processes if you are directly affected by conflict or harm. If you are a victim, consider whether restorative engagement might serve your healing. If you have caused harm, consider whether restorative accountability might support your growth. If you are involved in a community conflict, consider whether restorative dialogue might lead to resolution. Experiencing restorative justice firsthand is the most powerful way to understand its transformative potential.

Third, volunteer your time and skills to local restorative justice programs. Many organizations need volunteers to assist with facilitation, outreach, and support services. You may not need to be a trained facilitator to help; programs often need help with administrative tasks, fundraising, public education, and other functions. Your time and skills are valuable contributions.

Community Involvement

Beyond individual engagement, we can contribute through community involvement.

First, support local initiatives. Identify restorative justice programs and initiatives in your community. Attend their events, contribute financially, and advocate for their work. When programs have community support, they are more likely to thrive. Your involvement signals that restorative justice matters to the community.

Second, promote restorative practices. Encourage schools, workplaces, and community organizations to adopt restorative approaches. Share success stories and evidence of their impact. When you encounter conflicts in these settings, suggest restorative options. Be an ambassador for restorative justice in the spheres where you have influence.

Third, engage with policy makers. Advocate for policies that integrate restorative justice into the criminal justice system, education, and other sectors. Write to your representatives, join advocacy groups, and participate in public discussions. Policy change is essential for scaling restorative justice; your voice can contribute to that change.

Practical Steps to Support Restorative Justice

Beyond these general roles, there are specific practical steps each of us can take.

Advocacy and Awareness

First, raise public awareness. Use social media, blogs, and public speaking opportunities to highlight the benefits of restorative justice. Share articles, videos, and personal stories to engage a broader audience. When people encounter restorative justice through multiple channels, they are more likely to understand and support it.

Second, organize community events. Host workshops, seminars, and discussion groups to educate your community about restorative justice and its applications. Bring in speakers, show documentaries, facilitate dialogues. These events build knowledge, generate interest, and create networks of support.

Third, collaborate with media. Work with local media to cover restorative justice stories, highlight program successes, and promote public understanding. Write op-eds, pitch stories to reporters, invite journalists to observe restorative processes (with appropriate confidentiality protections). Media coverage can reach audiences that advocacy alone cannot.

Building Restorative Justice Networks

First, connect with practitioners. Join restorative justice networks and organizations to connect with practitioners, share resources, and collaborate on projects. These connections provide learning opportunities, professional support, and collective action.

Second, establish partnerships. Build partnerships with schools, businesses, faith communities, and other organizations to promote and implement restorative practices. Each partner brings different resources and reaches different audiences. Together, you can accomplish more than any could alone.

Third, foster peer support. Create or join peer support groups for individuals involved in restorative justice, providing a platform for sharing experiences and mutual encouragement. This work can be challenging; having peers who understand can make all the difference.

Funding and Resources

First, organize fundraising efforts. Host fundraising events, campaigns, and initiatives to support restorative justice programs. Engage your network to contribute financially or in-kind. Every dollar raised is a dollar that can support restorative work.

Second, assist with grant writing. Help local programs apply for grants and other funding opportunities. Share information about available grants and provide support in the application process. Grant funding can be essential for program sustainability.

Third, share resources. Donate materials, space, and other resources to restorative justice programs. Offer professional services such as training, legal advice, or counseling. Your resources, whatever they are, can support restorative work.

Personal Development and Commitment

Beyond external action, supporting restorative justice requires internal development—cultivating restorative values in our own hearts and lives.

Reflect on Your Values

First, align with restorative principles. Reflect on how restorative justice principles align with your personal values and beliefs. Whether those values come from faith, philosophy, or life experience, consider how they connect to restorative ideals. Commit to integrating these principles into your daily life and interactions.

Second, cultivate empathy. Practice empathy and active listening in your relationships. Seek to understand and address the needs and perspectives of others. When conflicts arise, try to see them through restorative lenses—focusing on harm, needs, and possibilities for repair rather than blame and punishment.

Continuous Learning

First, pursue further education. Enroll in courses, workshops, and training programs to deepen your understanding of restorative justice. Stay updated on the latest research and developments in the field. The more you learn, the more effective you can be.

Second, learn from experience. Reflect on your experiences with restorative justice, whether as a participant, volunteer, or advocate. Use these reflections to improve your practice and advocacy. Experience is a powerful teacher; paying attention to it multiplies its value.

Mentorship and Leadership

First, mentor others. Share your knowledge and experience with others who are new to restorative justice. Offer guidance and support to those interested in becoming practitioners or advocates. Mentorship multiplies impact, spreading restorative values to new people.

Second, lead by example. Demonstrate restorative justice principles in your leadership roles. Foster inclusive, participatory, and compassionate environments in your community and workplace. When others see restorative values embodied, they are more likely to embrace them.

Inspiring Stories and Examples

To inspire your engagement, consider again some of the stories we have encountered.

Community Transformation

The Oakland Unified School District's adoption of restorative justice practices significantly reduced suspensions and expulsions, creating a more positive and inclusive school climate. Students of color, who had been disproportionately affected by punitive discipline, experienced more equitable treatment. Teachers reported stronger relationships with students. The school community became more cohesive and supportive.

This transformation did not happen overnight. It required commitment from district leadership, training for staff, engagement with families and community members, and patience as culture shifted. But the results demonstrate that restorative justice can transform educational communities when implemented with dedication and support.

The success of Family Group Conferencing in New Zealand has demonstrated the potential of restorative justice to address youth offenses and support community healing. Young offenders who might have been processed through conventional courts instead participated in conferences with victims, families, and community members. They took responsibility, made amends, and were restored to community. Recidivism decreased; victim satisfaction increased; communities were strengthened.

Individual Impact

Restorative circles in prisons, like those in the Green Bay Correctional Institution in Wisconsin, have transformed the lives of inmates. Men who had been isolated, angry, and resistant to change participated in circles where they could speak honestly, be heard respectfully, and connect with others. They developed empathy, took responsibility for their actions, and committed to change. Some reported that the circles were the first time in their lives they had felt truly seen and heard.

Victim-offender mediation success stories abound. Victims who had been haunted by questions—Why me? Do you understand what you did? Are you sorry?—received answers. Offenders who had been disconnected from the human consequences of their actions came face to face with those they had harmed. Many experienced genuine remorse and committed to making amends. These encounters did not erase the harm, but they transformed it—making healing possible in ways that punishment alone could not.

Vision for the Future

As we consider our call to action, let us hold before us a vision of what might be.

A Restorative World

Imagine a world where restorative justice is the norm in addressing conflict and harm. Picture schools where restorative circles build community and address issues before they escalate. Visualize workplaces where conflicts are resolved through mediation and dialogue, strengthening relationships rather than damaging them. Envision communities where restorative practices address local conflicts, build social cohesion, and empower residents. Imagine a criminal justice system where restorative options are the default, where victims have voice and agency, where offenders are held accountable through genuine responsibility-taking, where communities are engaged in healing and reintegration.

This is not a utopian fantasy. It is a vision grounded in real-world examples—programs and practices that already exist, that have demonstrated effectiveness, that are spreading to new settings. The question is not whether such a world is possible but whether we will work to make it real.

Sustainable Peace

Envision a future where restorative justice contributes to sustainable peace and justice globally. In post-conflict societies, truth commissions, community-based restorative practices, and reparations programs address the legacies of violence and build foundations for lasting peace. In communities divided by racial, ethnic, or religious conflict, restorative dialogues create spaces for understanding, healing, and reconciliation. In environmental conflicts, restorative processes bring together stakeholders to address harm and collaborate on solutions.

Restorative justice alone cannot solve all the world's problems. But it can contribute—powerfully—to addressing the root causes of conflict, promoting healing and reconciliation, and building the relationships that make peace sustainable.

Collective Responsibility

Achieving this vision requires collective responsibility.

Shared Vision

Embrace the shared vision of a restorative society. Recognize that each of us has a role to play in making this vision a reality. No one can do everything, but everyone can do something. The vision is large; our contributions may be small. But many small contributions, multiplied across many people, can accomplish great things.

Active Engagement

Commit to active engagement with restorative justice initiatives. This commitment is not a one-time decision but an ongoing orientation—a way of living that keeps restorative values at the forefront. It means looking for opportunities to support restorative work, to practice restorative principles, to advocate for restorative policies. It means staying engaged even when progress is slow, when challenges arise, when the vision seems distant.

The psychological dimensions of this commitment are significant. Sustained engagement requires hope—the belief that change is possible, that our efforts matter, that the vision can be realized. It requires resilience—the capacity to persist in the face of setbacks, to learn from failure, to keep going when the path is hard. And it requires community—connections with others who share the vision, who can support us when we falter, who can celebrate with us when we succeed.

The theological dimensions are equally profound. For those who approach restorative justice from a faith perspective, this commitment is participation in God's own work of restoration. The God who reconciles the world in Christ, who makes all things new, who wipes away every tear—this God is at work in restorative justice. Our small efforts are part of a larger story, a story whose ending is already assured even as its unfolding remains our responsibility.

Final Thoughts: Reflections on the Transformative Power of Restorative Justice

As we bring this book to a close, let us reflect on the transformative power of restorative justice—what it is, why it matters, and what it offers to a world desperately in need of healing.

The Essence of Restorative Justice

At its core, restorative justice is about healing the harm caused by wrongdoing. It seeks to repair the damage done to victims, offenders, and the broader community. This healing is not merely symbolic but substantive—addressing material needs, emotional wounds, relational breaches, and social fractures.

Restorative justice humanizes the process of addressing harm. By focusing on the needs of all parties involved, it treats victims as more than evidence, offenders as more than their worst actions, community members as more than bystanders. It recognizes the humanity in everyone, even in those who have caused terrible harm.

The philosophical dimensions of this humanizing approach are significant. Relational ethics reminds us that we are interconnected, that harm to one is harm to all. Virtue ethics calls us to cultivate empathy, compassion, and responsibility. Restorative ontology insists that healing is possible, that restoration is woven into the fabric of reality.

The theological dimensions are profound. The doctrine of the image of God affirms that every human being—victim, offender, community member—bears the divine image and possesses inherent dignity. The incarnation reveals God's solidarity with humanity, God's willingness to enter into human suffering and brokenness. The atonement demonstrates God's commitment to reconciliation, to making peace through the cross. The resurrection promises that new life is possible, that death does not have the final word.

Accountability and Responsibility

Restorative justice encourages offenders to take responsibility for their actions, promoting genuine accountability rather than mere punishment. This accountability is not passive acceptance of consequences but active engagement in making things right. It requires facing those who have been harmed, understanding the impact of one's actions, and taking concrete steps toward reparation.

This kind of accountability fosters personal growth and behavioral change. Offenders who genuinely take responsibility are more likely to change than those who merely serve time. They develop empathy, remorse, and commitment to pro-social behavior. They become different people—not merely punished but transformed.

The psychological research supports this. Desistance from crime—the process of stopping offending—is associated with internal motivation, with changes in identity and values, with supportive relationships and opportunities. Restorative justice promotes all of these.

The theological dimensions are again significant. The biblical concept of repentance—*metanoia*—involves a fundamental turning around, a change of heart and life. Restorative justice creates conditions for this kind of transformation, inviting offenders not merely to accept punishment but to become new creations.

Community and Relationship Building

Restorative justice practices strengthen the social fabric by fostering collaboration, mutual support, and collective problem-solving. When communities are involved in addressing harm, they build relationships, develop trust, and learn to rely on one another. These strengthened bonds make communities more resilient, better able to address future challenges.

By addressing conflicts and harms in a restorative manner, communities can rebuild trust and resilience. Victims who feel heard and supported are more likely to trust their communities. Offenders who make amends and are restored are more likely to contribute positively. Community members who participate in restorative processes are more likely to feel connected and committed.

The sociological research supports this. Communities with strong social networks and high collective efficacy—the sense that "we" can solve "our" problems together—experience less crime, better health, and greater well-being. Restorative justice builds precisely these community resources.

The theological dimensions are profound. The biblical vision of *shalom*—peace, wholeness, right relationship—is a vision of community flourishing. It is the vision of a society where all have what they need, where relationships are healthy, where justice and mercy embrace. Restorative justice contributes to the realization of this vision.

The Broader Impact of Restorative Justice

The transformative power of restorative justice extends across multiple domains.

Criminal Justice System

Restorative justice provides a compelling alternative to the traditional retributive justice system, offering pathways for rehabilitation and reintegration. Rather than simply punishing offenders and hoping they will change, restorative justice actively engages them in the process of accountability and transformation. Rather than marginalizing victims, restorative justice centers their needs and gives them voice. Rather than excluding communities, restorative justice involves them in addressing harm and building safety.

Evidence shows that restorative practices reduce recidivism rates, contributing to safer communities and more effective justice outcomes. Victims who participate report higher satisfaction and greater healing. Communities that embrace restorative approaches report stronger social bonds and increased trust in the justice system.

The legal dimensions of this transformation are significant. As restorative justice becomes more integrated into legal systems, it changes how those systems operate—shifting focus from punishment to repair, from exclusion to inclusion, from state-centered to community-engaged justice.

Education and Schools

Implementing restorative practices in schools transforms the educational environment, reducing disciplinary issues and fostering a culture of respect and inclusion. Students who might have been suspended or expelled are instead engaged in processes that help them understand the impact of their actions and make amends. Teachers who might have spent hours on disciplinary matters are freed to focus on instruction and relationship-building.

By involving students in restorative processes, schools empower young people to develop conflict resolution skills and take ownership of their actions. Students learn empathy, communication, and problem-solving—skills that serve them throughout life. They develop a sense of belonging and investment in their school community.

The psychological dimensions of this transformation are significant. Students who feel connected to school are more engaged, more motivated, and more likely to succeed academically. Restorative practices build these connections.

Workplace and Organizations

Restorative justice can transform workplace dynamics, resolving conflicts constructively and promoting a culture of openness and mutual respect. Employees who might have left the organization due to unresolved conflicts instead find pathways to resolution and restoration. Teams that might have been fractured by interpersonal tensions instead find ways to work together effectively.

Organizations that embrace restorative practices often see improved employee relations, higher morale, and increased productivity. They also reduce legal risks by addressing conflicts before they escalate to formal complaints or litigation.

The organizational psychology research supports this. Positive workplace cultures—characterized by trust, respect, and open communication—are associated with better performance, lower turnover, and higher employee well-being. Restorative practices contribute to such cultures.

Community Building

Restorative justice helps communities address local conflicts and tensions, promoting social harmony and collective well-being. Neighborhood disputes that might have escalated into violence are instead resolved through dialogue and mediation. Harms that might have gone unaddressed are instead acknowledged and repaired.

By involving diverse community members in restorative processes, these practices promote inclusivity and equity. Marginalized groups gain voice and agency. Systemic inequalities are named and addressed. Communities become more just as well as more cohesive.

The sociological research supports this. Inclusive communities—where all members have voice and agency—are more resilient, more innovative, and more capable of addressing complex challenges. Restorative practices build such communities.

Embracing Restorative Justice for a Better Future

As we look to the future, let us embrace restorative justice as a path toward transformation.

A Vision for Transformation

Imagine a world where restorative justice principles guide our responses to conflict and harm. In this world, when harm occurs, the first question is not "What punishment does this deserve?" but "What needs to be healed?" Victims are central, not marginal. Offenders are accountable, not merely punished. Communities are engaged, not excluded.

In this world, schools are places of belonging and growth, where conflicts are resolved constructively and relationships are strengthened. Workplaces are communities of respect and collaboration, where differences are addressed openly and inclusively. Communities are networks of support and mutual aid, where everyone has a place and everyone contributes.

In this world, justice systems are not warehouses for the marginalized but pathways to restoration. Prisons, where they exist, are places of genuine rehabilitation, preparing people for successful reintegration. Courts are not arenas for adversarial combat but forums for truth-telling and problem-solving. The entire system is oriented toward healing rather than hurting, restoration rather than retribution.

This vision is not utopian. It is grounded in real-world examples—programs and practices that already exist, that have demonstrated effectiveness, that are spreading to new settings. The question is not whether such a world is possible but whether we will work to make it real.

Collective Responsibility

Achieving this vision requires collective responsibility from individuals, communities, and institutions. No single person, no single program, no single policy can create a restorative society alone. But together, our efforts can accumulate, our movements can grow, our vision can spread.

Each of us has a role to play. Some will be practitioners, facilitating circles and conferences with skill and compassion. Some will be advocates, promoting restorative policies and educating their communities. Some will be researchers, studying what works and sharing their findings. Some will be leaders, championing restorative values and modeling restorative practice. Some will be ordinary citizens, embodying restorative principles in their daily lives—listening deeply, apologizing sincerely, forgiving generously, contributing positively.

All of these roles matter. All contribute to the larger movement toward a restorative society.

Hope for the Future

The transformative power of restorative justice offers hope for a future where justice systems are more humane, communities are more resilient, and individuals are more connected. This hope is not naive optimism but grounded confidence—confidence based on evidence that restorative justice works, on examples that demonstrate its power, on principles that resonate with the deepest truths of human nature and divine purpose.

For those who approach restorative justice from a faith perspective, this hope has theological foundations. The God who created the world good, who entered into covenant with a people, who became flesh in Jesus Christ, who sends the Spirit to empower and transform—this God is at work bringing about restoration. Our restorative work is participation in God's restorative work. Our hope is not in our own efforts alone but in the God who makes all things new.

The biblical vision of *shalom*—peace, wholeness, right relationship—is the vision of a restorative society. It is the vision of a world where swords are beaten into plowshares, where lion and lamb lie down together, where every tear is wiped away. It is the vision that has inspired prophets and poets, saints and reformers throughout the ages. And it is the vision that restorative justice seeks to realize, one encounter at a time, one community at a time, one transformation at a time.

Final Thoughts

As we conclude this journey, let us carry forward the principles and practices of restorative justice, championing its values in our personal and professional lives. Let us be people who listen before judging, who seek understanding before condemnation, who pursue healing before punishment. Let us be communities where conflicts are resolved constructively, where harms are acknowledged and repaired, where everyone has a place and everyone belongs. Let us be a society where justice is restorative, where healing is possible, where hope prevails.

The journey through this book has been long, but the journey of restorative justice is longer still. It began millennia ago, in the practices of indigenous peoples around the world. It continued through centuries of evolution, adaptation, and occasional eclipse. It revived in the late twentieth century, driven by dissatisfaction with punitive justice and hope for something better. And it continues today, in programs and practices around the world, in research and innovation, in the lives of victims who find healing, offenders who find change, communities who find strength.

Where the journey goes from here is up to us. The vision is clear: a restorative society, where healing justice transforms our world. The principles are sound: accountability, reparation, community involvement, empathy, healing. The practices are proven: victim-offender mediation, family group conferencing, circle processes, community restorative boards. The evidence is compelling: victims are satisfied, offenders are rehabilitated, communities are strengthened.

What remains is the work—the daily, patient, persistent work of building restorative practices in our communities, our institutions, our lives. This work is not glamorous. It does not make headlines. It does not produce quick results. But it is essential. It is the work of transformation—transforming how we respond to harm, how we understand justice, how we live together.

As you close this book and return to your life, I invite you to carry restorative values with you. In your family, practice restorative communication—listening, acknowledging, apologizing, forgiving. In your workplace, advocate for restorative approaches to conflict—mediation, dialogue, collaborative problem-solving. In your community, support restorative programs—volunteer, donate, advocate. In your own heart, cultivate restorative virtues—empathy, compassion, accountability, hope.

The restorative society is not something that will happen to us; it is something we must create together. Every restorative circle, every victim-offender dialogue, every family group conference, every community restorative board—each is a small step toward that larger vision. Each is a seed planted that may grow into something larger than we can imagine.

The biblical vision of *shalom*—peace, wholeness, right relationship—is the vision of a restorative society. It is the vision of a world where justice rolls down like waters, where swords are beaten into plowshares, where lion and lamb lie down together. It is the vision of a world where every tear is wiped away, where death and mourning are no more, where all things are made new.

This vision is not merely human aspiration; it is divine promise. The God who created the world good, who entered into covenant with a people, who became flesh in Jesus Christ, who sends the Spirit to empower and transform—this God is at work bringing about restoration. Our restorative work is participation in God's restorative work. Our small efforts are part of a larger story.

May you go from this book with renewed commitment to restorative justice. May you carry its principles into your daily life. May you contribute, in whatever way you can, to building a restorative society. And may you have hope—hope that transformation is possible, that healing can occur, that a more just and compassionate world is not only desirable but achievable.

The future of restorative justice is in our hands. Let us build it together.

APPENDIX

Glossary of Terms

Dear reader, as you have journeyed through this comprehensive exploration of restorative justice, you have encountered a rich vocabulary of terms and concepts. This glossary is designed to serve as a reference—a companion to your reading and a resource for your ongoing engagement with restorative justice. Here you will find definitions of key terms, explanations of important concepts, and connections to the broader philosophical, psychological, legal, and theological dimensions that give restorative justice its depth and power.

The terms included here range from foundational concepts that appear throughout the book to specialized terminology from particular contexts. Each definition is written to be accessible while preserving the richness and nuance that restorative justice deserves. Where appropriate, I have included cross-references to related terms and brief reflections on the significance of the concept within the larger restorative framework.

May this glossary serve you well as you continue your journey into the transformative world of restorative justice.

A

Accountability

Accountability in restorative justice refers to the obligation of offenders to take genuine responsibility for their actions, to acknowledge the harm they have caused, and to participate actively in processes of making amends and repairing damage. Unlike accountability in retributive justice, which typically means accepting punishment, restorative accountability is forward-looking and constructive. It involves understanding the impact of one's actions on victims and communities, experiencing remorse, and taking concrete steps toward reparation and change.

The psychological dimensions of accountability are significant. Research on moral development shows that genuine accountability requires internalization of moral norms, not merely compliance with external demands. When offenders understand the harm they have caused and choose to make amends, they are far more likely to change than when they merely serve time.

The theological dimensions are equally profound. In the Hebrew scriptures, the concept of repentance (*teshuvah*) involves turning away from wrongdoing and turning toward right relationship. In Christian theology, repentance (*metanoia*) is a change of heart and life that issues in transformed behavior. Restorative accountability participates in this spiritual dynamic.

See also: Responsibility, Reparation, Repentance

Adversarial System

The adversarial system is a legal framework, characteristic of common law countries such as the United States, Canada, and the United Kingdom, in which two opposing parties—the prosecution and the defense—present their cases before a neutral judge or jury. The prosecution represents the state's interest in enforcing the law and punishing offenders; the defense represents the accused's interest in protecting their rights and avoiding wrongful conviction. The judge or jury determines guilt and imposes sentence based on the evidence presented.

The adversarial system has strengths—it protects defendants' rights, ensures rigorous testing of evidence, and maintains the presumption of innocence. But it also has significant limitations from a restorative perspective. Victims are marginalized, their needs secondary to the state's interest in punishment. Communities are excluded entirely. The focus is on determining guilt and imposing punishment, not on addressing harm, promoting healing, or restoring relationships.

Restorative justice offers a complementary approach that addresses these limitations. Rather than pitting parties against each other, restorative processes bring them together. Rather than focusing on punishment, restorative justice focuses on repair.

See also: Retributive Justice, Restorative Justice

Atonement

Atonement is a theological concept with profound implications for restorative justice. In Christian theology, atonement refers to the work of Christ in reconciling humanity to God—making right what sin had broken. The central affirmation is that "God was in Christ reconciling the world to himself, not counting their trespasses against them" (2 Corinthians 5:19).

Several theories of atonement have been developed throughout Christian history. The satisfaction theory, associated with Anselm of Canterbury, emphasizes Christ's death as satisfaction for the debt of human sin. The moral influence theory, associated with Peter Abelard, emphasizes Christ's demonstration of God's love as inspiring human response. The Christus Victor theory emphasizes Christ's victory over the powers of sin and death.

Each of these theories has implications for restorative justice. The satisfaction theory reminds us that accountability matters—that wrongs must be addressed, not ignored. The moral influence theory reminds us that love can inspire transformation—that encountering genuine care can change hearts. The Christus Victor theory reminds us that restoration is possible—that the powers of harm and destruction do not have the final word.

The cross, understood restoratively, is not about satisfying an abstract demand for retribution but about God's willingness to enter into human suffering, to absorb the worst that human sin can do, and to respond not with retaliation but with love. This model of absorbing harm without returning it, of responding to evil with good, of seeking reconciliation rather than revenge—this is the heart of restorative justice.

See also: Reconciliation, Salvation, Shalom

Apology

An apology is an acknowledgment of wrongdoing by an offender, expressing remorse and indicating willingness to make amends. In restorative justice, apologies are not merely formal statements but genuine expressions of understanding and regret. They are offered face to face, in the presence of victims and often community members, and they carry emotional weight.

Genuine apology has several elements: acknowledgment of the specific harm caused, expression of remorse, acceptance of responsibility, commitment to change, and offer of reparation. When these elements are present, apology can be profoundly healing for victims. It validates their experience, communicates that their suffering is recognized, and opens the possibility of forgiveness.

Psychological research supports the importance of apology in healing. Victims who receive genuine apologies report greater satisfaction with justice processes and better emotional recovery. Offenders who offer genuine apologies are more likely to experience remorse and change.

Theologically, apology participates in the dynamic of confession and forgiveness that runs throughout scripture. The Psalms of lament often include confession of sin and pleas for forgiveness. Jesus teaches his followers to ask forgiveness and to forgive others. The practice of apology in restorative justice embodies these spiritual disciplines.

See also: Accountability, Forgiveness, Remorse, Repentance

B

Bias

Bias refers to prejudice in favor of or against a person, group, or idea, often in a way that is considered unfair. Biases can be explicit—conscious and intentional—or implicit—unconscious and unintentional. Both forms can affect restorative justice processes, influencing who is referred to restorative programs, how facilitators perceive participants, what outcomes are considered appropriate.

Addressing bias is crucial for ensuring fair and equitable restorative justice. This requires awareness of one's own biases, training in cultural competence, and structural mechanisms to check bias—diverse facilitator pools, clear guidelines, oversight and evaluation.

Psychological research on implicit bias demonstrates that even well-intentioned people hold unconscious associations that can affect their behavior. Recognizing this reality is the first step toward mitigating its effects.

Theological reflection on bias reminds us that all humans are created in God's image and deserving of equal dignity and respect. The biblical witness consistently challenges partiality and calls for justice that is blind to status but attentive to need.

See also: Cultural Competence, Equity, Inclusion, Power Imbalances

Biblical Justice

Biblical justice, rooted in the Hebrew and Christian scriptures, is a rich concept that encompasses far more than retribution or punishment. The Hebrew word most often translated as "justice" is *mishpat*, which refers to the proper ordering of community, the protection of the vulnerable, the fair treatment of all. Closely related is *tzedekah*, often translated as "righteousness," which refers to right relationship with God and neighbor.

The prophets consistently call for justice that protects the widow, the orphan, the stranger, and the poor—those most vulnerable to exploitation and oppression. Amos declares, "Let justice roll down like waters, and righteousness like an ever-flowing stream" (Amos 5:24). Micah summarizes God's requirements: "to do justice, and to love kindness, and to walk humbly with your God" (Micah 6:8).

In the New Testament, Jesus announces his mission as bringing good news to the poor, freedom to the captives, recovery of sight to the blind (Luke 4). His teachings on forgiveness, reconciliation, and love of enemy embody restorative principles. Paul proclaims that in Christ, God was reconciling the world to himself (2 Corinthians 5).

Biblical justice is not merely punitive but restorative. It seeks to make things right, to restore relationships, to create communities where all can flourish. This vision aligns deeply with restorative justice.

See also: Mishpat, Shalom, Tzedekah, Ubuntu

Bullying

Bullying refers to repeated aggressive behavior intended to hurt another person physically, mentally, or emotionally. It is characterized by an imbalance of power—the bully has more power, whether physical, social, or psychological, than the victim. Bullying can take many forms: physical aggression, verbal harassment, social exclusion, cyberbullying.

Restorative practices in schools have proven highly effective in addressing bullying. Rather than simply punishing bullies—which often reinforces their behavior and alienates them further—restorative approaches bring together those involved to discuss the harm, understand its impact, and develop plans for making amends and preventing recurrence.

The psychological dynamics of bullying are complex. Bullies often have experienced trauma themselves; victims often suffer lasting psychological harm. Restorative approaches address these complexities by creating spaces for genuine dialogue, fostering empathy, and promoting healing for all involved.

See also: Peer Mediation, Restorative Circles, School-Based Restorative Justice

C

Circle Keeper

A circle keeper is the facilitator of a restorative circle process. Unlike a judge or arbitrator who imposes decisions from above, the circle keeper's role is to hold the space, to guide the process, to ensure that all voices are heard and respected. The keeper does not control the outcome but creates conditions in which the circle can find its own wisdom.

Circle keepers require specialized training and skills. They must be able to create safety, manage emotional intensity, recognize and address power imbalances, and maintain focus on restorative goals. They must embody the values they seek to foster—respect, empathy, patience, hope.

The concept of the circle keeper has roots in indigenous traditions, where elders or respected community members guided peacemaking processes. In contemporary restorative practice, keepers come from diverse backgrounds but share commitment to restorative principles.

See also: Circle Process, Facilitator, Peacemaking Circles

Circle Process

The circle process, also known as restorative circles, is a restorative practice that brings participants together in a circle to discuss issues, share perspectives, and make decisions collectively. The circle format is significant—all participants are visible to one another, all are equal, no one is at the head. A talking piece is passed from person to person; only the person holding the piece may speak, ensuring that all voices can be heard.

Circle processes can be used proactively to build community and strengthen relationships, or responsively to address specific conflicts and harms. They draw on indigenous traditions and have been adapted for diverse contexts—schools, workplaces, communities, prisons.

The principles underlying circle processes include equality, respect, inclusivity, and shared responsibility. These principles are embodied in the circle's structure and in the facilitator's guidance.

Research on circle processes shows positive outcomes: improved communication, strengthened relationships, effective conflict resolution, and community building.

See also: Circle Keeper, Peacemaking Circles, Restorative Circles, Talking Piece

Communitarianism

Communitarianism is a philosophical perspective that emphasizes the importance of community values and the collective well-being of society. It arose partly in response to the excesses of liberal individualism, arguing that individuals are formed in and through communities, that our identities are shaped by the traditions and practices into which we are born, and that a just society must attend to the health of communities, not merely the liberties of individuals.

Communitarianism has significant implications for restorative justice. It explains why restorative justice prioritizes the restoration of community harmony—if communities are essential to human flourishing, then harm that disrupts community harmony must be addressed. It justifies the involvement of the community in the justice process—if communities have a stake in what happens, they should have a voice. It supports collective decision-making—when victims, offenders, and community members come together to find solutions, they discern together what will serve the common good.

Theological resources for communitarianism are abundant. The Hebrew scriptures present Israel as a covenant community, bound together by relationship with God and with one another. The New Testament presents the church as the body of Christ, in which each member belongs to and depends on all the others.

See also: Community Involvement, Relational Ethics, Ubuntu

Community Conferencing

Community conferencing is a restorative process that brings together offenders, victims, and community members to discuss the harm caused and develop a plan to repair it and prevent future incidents. It is similar to family group conferencing but may involve broader community participation beyond family networks.

Community conferencing recognizes that crime affects not only individuals but the whole community. It engages community members as stakeholders in the justice process, giving them voice and agency in determining outcomes. It builds community capacity to address its own problems, reducing dependence on formal justice systems.

Research on community conferencing shows positive outcomes: high levels of participant satisfaction, reduced recidivism, strengthened community bonds.

See also: Community Restorative Boards, Family Group Conferencing, Restorative Conferences

Community Involvement

Community involvement is a central principle of restorative justice, emphasizing the importance of engaging the community in the justice process. This principle recognizes that crime affects not only direct victims but the broader community, and that the community has a vital role to play in addressing harm, supporting victims, and promoting offender accountability.

Community members play multiple roles in restorative justice. They provide support for victims—emotional comfort, practical assistance, ongoing presence. They hold offenders accountable—their presence communicates that the community cares about what happened, that the offender's actions have social consequences. They may serve as facilitators or mediators, bringing local knowledge and relationships to the process.

The benefits of community involvement are significant. Decisions reflect community values, enhancing legitimacy and support. Communities develop capacity to address their own problems. Social bonds are strengthened, building resilience and preventing future harm.

Theologically, community involvement reflects the biblical understanding of covenant and body. God's people are called together, formed as community, responsible for one another. When one suffers, all suffer; when one rejoices, all rejoice. Justice is the work of the whole community.

See also: Communitarianism, Community Restorative Boards, Family Group Conferencing, Restorative Circles

Community Restorative Board

A Community Restorative Board (CRB) is a group of trained community volunteers who meet with offenders to discuss the harm caused by their actions and determine appropriate reparative actions. CRBs represent the community's direct involvement in the justice process, embodying the principle of collective responsibility.

The CRB process typically involves referral from the justice system, an intake assessment, a board meeting where offender and sometimes victim participate, development of a restorative agreement, and monitoring of implementation. Board members are drawn from the local community, bringing knowledge of local norms and resources.

CRBs have been implemented in various jurisdictions, particularly for minor offenses. Research shows positive outcomes: reduced recidivism, increased victim satisfaction, strengthened community engagement.

See also: Community Involvement, Restorative Agreements

Conflict Resolution

Conflict resolution refers to the process of resolving a dispute or conflict by addressing each side's needs and interests. Restorative justice offers distinctive approaches to conflict resolution that focus not merely on settling disputes but on repairing relationships and promoting healing.

Restorative conflict resolution differs from conventional approaches in several ways. It emphasizes dialogue rather than debate, understanding rather than winning, healing rather than victory. It involves all affected parties, not just those directly in conflict. It seeks outcomes that address underlying needs and restore relationships, not merely compromise positions.

Skills for restorative conflict resolution include active listening, empathy, facilitation, and creative problem-solving. These skills can be learned and practiced, and they serve people in all areas of life.

See also: Mediation, Restorative Dialogue

Covenant

Covenant is a biblical concept with profound implications for restorative justice. In the Hebrew scriptures, covenant (*berit*) refers to the binding relationship between God and Israel, established through God's gracious initiative and calling for faithful response. The covenant establishes Israel as a people bound to God and to one another.

The covenant has several features relevant to restorative justice. It establishes community—Israel is constituted as a people through covenant relationship. It establishes mutual responsibility—covenant members are accountable to God and to one another. It provides for restoration when covenant is broken—through repentance, sacrifice, and renewed commitment.

In the New Testament, the new covenant in Christ extends these themes. Jesus's death and resurrection establish a new covenant relationship, opening the way for reconciliation between God and humanity and among humans themselves.

Restorative justice, in its emphasis on community, accountability, and restoration, participates in this covenantal dynamic. It calls people into relationship, holds them accountable to one another, and creates pathways for restoration when relationships are broken.

See also: Biblical Justice, Community, Reconciliation

Cultural Competence

Cultural competence refers to the ability to understand, communicate with, and effectively interact with people across cultures. In restorative justice, cultural competence involves knowledge of different cultural norms, awareness of one's own cultural assumptions, and skill in adapting restorative practices to fit diverse cultural contexts.

Cultural competence is essential for restorative justice because restorative practices must be culturally sensitive and appropriate for the populations they serve. What works in one cultural context may not work in another. Practices that are respectful in one culture may be disrespectful in another.

Developing cultural competence requires ongoing learning, self-reflection, and engagement with diverse communities. It is not a destination but a journey—a continuous process of growth and adaptation.

See also: Bias, Cultural Sensitivity, Diversity, Inclusion

Cultural Sensitivity

Cultural sensitivity refers to awareness and respect for cultural differences, and the ability to adapt behavior and practices accordingly. In restorative justice, cultural sensitivity involves recognizing that participants come from diverse cultural backgrounds with different norms, values, and expectations, and adapting restorative processes to honor these differences.

Cultural sensitivity goes beyond mere tolerance to active respect and accommodation. It means learning about the cultures of participants, consulting with cultural leaders, and modifying practices when appropriate. It means being humble about what one knows and open to learning from others.

See also: Cultural Competence, Diversity

D

Desistance

Desistance refers to the process by which individuals cease and refrain from offending. Research on desistance has important implications for restorative justice, revealing that desistance is associated with internal motivation, changes in identity, supportive relationships, and opportunities for positive contribution—all of which restorative practices can promote.

Desistance is not simply stopping offending but becoming a different kind of person—developing a pro-social identity, taking on new roles and responsibilities, building relationships that support change. Restorative justice, by engaging offenders in accountability, fostering empathy, and supporting reintegration, can contribute to desistance.

The psychological research on desistance highlights the importance of hope, agency, and recognition. Offenders need to believe that change is possible, that they can be agents of their own transformation, that others will recognize and support their change. Restorative practices can provide these conditions.

See also: Rehabilitation, Reintegration

Dialogical Ethics

Dialogical ethics is a philosophical approach that emphasizes the importance of dialogue and communication in ethical decision-making. Influenced by thinkers such as Martin Buber and Jürgen Habermas, dialogical ethics posits that ethical understanding and mutual respect arise from open and honest dialogue.

Martin Buber distinguished between I-It relationships, in which we treat others as objects, and I-Thou relationships, in which we encounter others as whole persons. Genuine ethics, for Buber, arises from I-Thou encounters. Jürgen Habermas developed the concept of communicative action, arguing that rational dialogue, free from coercion and distortion, is the foundation of legitimate social norms.

Dialogical ethics provides philosophical foundation for restorative practices. Restorative justice creates spaces for I-Thou encounters—moments of genuine meeting between victims and offenders, between community members, between those who have been separated by harm. It prioritizes open, inclusive, reasoned communication, allowing genuine understanding and consensus to emerge.

See also: I-Thou Relationship, Relational Ethics

Dialogue

Dialogue refers to a structured conversation between two or more parties, often facilitated, that focuses on sharing experiences, understanding different perspectives, and finding common ground. Dialogue is central to restorative justice, appearing in victim-offender mediation, restorative circles, family group conferencing, and other restorative practices.

Dialogue differs from debate. Debate aims to win, to prove one's position superior. Dialogue aims to understand, to find common ground, to build relationship. In restorative dialogue, participants are not trying to defeat one another but to come to mutual understanding and, hopefully, agreement about how to move forward.

Skills for dialogue include active listening, asking open questions, speaking from one's own experience, and remaining open to learning. These skills can be developed through practice and are valuable in all areas of life.

See also: Active Listening, Mediation, Restorative Dialogue

Dignity

Dignity refers to the inherent worth and value of every human being. In restorative justice, dignity is a foundational principle—victims, offenders, and community members all possess dignity and deserve to be treated with respect.

The concept of dignity has deep roots in philosophy and theology. The Stoics affirmed human dignity based on reason. Kant grounded dignity in the capacity for moral agency. The Judeo-Christian tradition grounds dignity in the image of God—every human being is created in God's image and therefore possesses inherent worth.

Restorative justice practices are designed to honor dignity. Victims are treated as more than evidence; they are whole persons with needs and perspectives. Offenders are treated as more than their worst actions; they are persons capable of change and worthy of respect. Community members are treated as more than bystanders; they are stakeholders with valuable contributions.

See also: Image of God, Respect

Diversion

Diversion refers to redirecting offenders away from the formal justice system and into restorative justice programs or other alternative measures. Diversion can occur at various stages—before charges are filed (pre-charge diversion), after charges but before trial, or after conviction but before sentencing.

Diversion has several benefits. It prevents the negative impacts of formal judicial processes—the stigma of a criminal record, the disruption of employment and family relationships, the costs of incarceration. It provides opportunities for rehabilitation and reparation that formal processing may not offer. It reduces the burden on courts and correctional facilities.

Diversion programs must be designed carefully to ensure fairness and protect rights. Participation should be voluntary, not coerced. Offenders should have access to legal advice. Outcomes should be proportionate and appropriate.

See also: Pre-Charge Diversion, Post-Charge Diversion

Due Process

Due process refers to the legal requirement that the state must respect all legal rights owed to a person. It balances the power of law and protects individuals from the state. Due process has both procedural and substantive dimensions—fair procedures and adequate justification for government action.

Restorative justice must operate in ways that respect due process rights. Offenders have rights to notice, to legal counsel, to protection against self-incrimination, to fair treatment. These rights must be honored even as restorative processes proceed.

At the same time, restorative justice can enhance due process by giving victims rights they may not have in conventional proceedings—rights to information, to participation, to restitution. Balancing the rights of all parties requires careful attention.

See also: Legal Rights, Procedural Justice

E

Empathy

Empathy is the ability to understand and share the feelings of another. It has multiple dimensions—cognitive empathy (understanding another's perspective), emotional empathy (feeling what another feels), and compassionate empathy (desiring to help). Empathy is a key component of restorative justice, helping to foster understanding and healing between victims and offenders.

In restorative processes, offenders develop empathy for victims by hearing directly about the impact of their actions. This empathy can evoke genuine remorse and motivation to change. Victims experience empathy from offenders, validating their suffering and contributing to healing.

Psychological research shows that empathy can be cultivated through practice. Restorative processes provide structured opportunities for empathy to develop—through storytelling, active listening, and direct encounter.

Theologically, empathy reflects the character of God, who is "gracious and merciful, slow to anger and abounding in steadfast love" (Psalm 145:8). Jesus's ministry was characterized by compassion for the suffering. The incarnation itself is an act of empathy—God entering into human experience to share our condition.

See also: Active Listening, Compassion, Narrative Sharing, Remorse

Empowerment

Empowerment refers to the process of enabling individuals and groups to gain control over their lives, make informed decisions, and participate actively in processes that affect them. In restorative justice, empowerment is a key outcome for victims, offenders, and communities.

Victims are empowered when they have voice and agency in the justice process. They can tell their stories, ask questions, and participate in determining what justice requires. This empowerment counteracts the powerlessness that crime often creates.

Offenders are empowered when they take responsibility and make amends. Rather than being passive recipients of punishment, they become active agents in restoration. This empowerment supports personal growth and change.

Communities are empowered when they are involved in addressing harm. Rather than depending on outside authorities, they develop capacity to solve their own problems. This empowerment builds resilience and self-determination.

See also: Agency, Participation, Voice

Equity

Equity refers to fairness and justice in the way people are treated. Unlike equality, which means treating everyone the same, equity means treating everyone fairly, which may require different treatment to address different circumstances. In restorative justice, equity involves addressing power imbalances and ensuring that all participants have genuine opportunity to participate and be heard.

Equity is essential for restorative justice to fulfill its promise. If processes are not equitable, they may reproduce the inequalities of the broader society—marginalizing some voices while privileging others. Attending to equity requires awareness of how race, class, gender, and other factors shape participants' experiences and needs.

Theological reflection on equity reminds us that God shows no partiality (Acts 10:34) but also attends to the vulnerable—the widow, the orphan, the stranger. Equity in restorative justice honors this divine attentiveness.

See also: Bias, Equality, Fairness, Inclusion, Power Imbalances

Ethical Responsibility

Ethical responsibility is a philosophical principle highlighting the moral duty individuals have to address the harm they cause and to contribute positively to their communities. It emphasizes accountability, restitution, and the ethical imperative to make amends.

Ethical responsibility has both individual and collective dimensions. Individually, each person is accountable for their choices and actions. Collectively, communities share responsibility for addressing harm and creating conditions for flourishing.

Restorative justice embodies ethical responsibility by encouraging offenders to take responsibility and actively participate in making amends. It also engages communities in their collective responsibility to support victims, hold offenders accountable, and work for healing.

See also: Accountability, Moral Responsibility, Responsibility

---

F

Facilitator

A facilitator is a trained neutral person who guides restorative processes such as victim-offender mediation, restorative circles, or family group conferencing. The facilitator's role is not to impose solutions but to create conditions in which participants can communicate effectively, understand one another, and develop their own agreements.

Facilitators require specialized training and skills. They must be able to create safe spaces, manage emotional intensity, recognize and address power imbalances, and maintain focus on restorative goals. They must embody restorative values—respect, empathy, patience, hope.

The facilitator's neutrality is important but not absolute. They are neutral regarding outcomes but committed to restorative principles. They do not take sides but ensure that all voices can be heard.

See also: Circle Keeper, Mediator

Fairness

Fairness refers to the quality of treating people equitably, without favoritism or discrimination. In restorative justice, fairness has multiple dimensions—procedural fairness (fair processes), distributive fairness (fair outcomes), and interactional fairness (fair treatment).

Research on procedural justice shows that people's satisfaction with legal processes depends heavily on whether they perceive the process as fair—whether they had voice, whether they were treated with respect, whether the process was transparent. Restorative practices excel on these dimensions.

Fairness also requires attention to substantive outcomes. Agreements should be proportionate, appropriate, and responsive to the needs of all parties. They should not be overly lenient or overly harsh but balanced and just.

See also: Equity, Procedural Justice, Proportionality

Family Group Conferencing

Family Group Conferencing (FGC) is a restorative practice that involves family members and others significant to the offender and victim in developing a plan to address the harm and support rehabilitation. Originating in New Zealand and rooted in Maori traditions, FGC has been adopted worldwide, particularly in juvenile justice systems.

The FGC process involves several stages: referral and preparation, the conference itself (including information sharing, private family time, and agreement development), and follow-up. Families are given private time to develop their plan, ensuring that their knowledge and resources are fully engaged.

Research on FGC shows positive outcomes: high levels of victim satisfaction, reduced recidivism, and better rehabilitation outcomes for young offenders. The model has been adapted for use with adult offenders and in various cultural contexts.

See also: Community Conferencing, Maori Justice, Restorative Conferencing

Forgiveness

Forgiveness is the intentional decision to release feelings of resentment or vengeance toward someone who has harmed you, regardless of whether they deserve it. In restorative justice, forgiveness may occur, but it is never required or coerced. Victims choose whether and when to forgive.

Forgiveness is distinct from reconciliation. Reconciliation involves restoring relationship; forgiveness is internal release. One can forgive without reconciling, and one can reconcile without fully forgiving, though the two often go together.

Psychological research shows that forgiveness can be beneficial for victims, reducing stress, improving mental health, and promoting healing. But forgiveness must be freely chosen; pressure to forgive can be harmful.

Theologically, forgiveness is central to the Christian faith. Jesus teaches his followers to forgive others as they have been forgiven by God (Matthew 6:12). The parable of the unforgiving servant (Matthew 18) illustrates the importance of extending forgiveness to others. Restorative justice creates space for forgiveness to occur, without demanding it.

See also: Apology, Reconciliation, Remorse

G

Gacaca Courts

Gacaca courts were community-based tribunals established in Rwanda following the 1994 genocide to address the massive backlog of genocide-related cases. Drawing on traditional Rwandan justice practices, Gacaca courts involved community members in hearing testimony, determining guilt, and imposing sentences.

The Gacaca process emphasized truth-telling, accountability, and community healing. Perpetrators who confessed their crimes, expressed remorse, and sought forgiveness could receive reduced sentences. Victims could tell their stories and participate in determining outcomes.

Gacaca courts resolved an enormous number of cases—over a million—in a relatively short period. While the process had limitations and critics, it demonstrated that restorative approaches could address mass atrocities and promote community healing.

See also: Transitional Justice, Truth and Reconciliation Commission, Ubuntu

---

H

Harm

Harm refers to the injury or damage caused by a wrongful act. In restorative justice, harm is understood broadly—including physical injury, material loss, emotional pain, relational damage, and community disruption. Restorative justice seeks to address and repair harm in all its dimensions.

Understanding harm requires listening to those affected. Victims must have opportunity to describe how they have been harmed—what they have lost, what they suffer, what they need. Offenders must come to understand the harm they have caused—not abstractly but concretely, through direct encounter with victims.

Theological reflection on harm recognizes that sin damages relationships—with God, with neighbor, with self, with creation. Restorative justice participates in God's work of healing these damaged relationships.

See also: Healing, Victim

Healing

Healing is the process of recovering from harm or trauma. In restorative justice, healing is a central goal, involving emotional, psychological, relational, and sometimes physical recovery for victims, offenders, and communities.

For victims, healing involves moving beyond the pain and fear caused by crime—finding safety, peace, and hope. Restorative practices promote healing by giving victims voice, validating their experience, providing opportunities for closure, and connecting them with community support.

For offenders, healing involves addressing the shame and guilt of wrongdoing, developing new ways of being, and being restored to community. Restorative practices promote healing through accountability, reparation, and reintegration.

For communities, healing involves restoring trust, rebuilding relationships, and strengthening social bonds. Restorative practices promote community healing through collective engagement in addressing harm.

Theologically, healing is central to the gospel. Jesus's ministry was filled with healings—physical, emotional, spiritual. The cross and resurrection are understood as cosmic healing events, reconciling humanity to God. Restorative justice participates in this healing ministry.

See also: Harm, Reconciliation, Restoration, Shalom

I

I-Thou Relationship

I-Thou is a concept developed by philosopher Martin Buber to describe a mode of relationship in which we encounter others as whole persons, with dignity and subjectivity, rather than as objects to be used or manipulated. The I-Thou relationship is characterized by mutual respect, openness, and genuine meeting.

In contrast, I-It relationships treat others as objects—as things to be categorized, analyzed, used. I-It relating is necessary for much of life, but it is not sufficient for genuine human connection. I-Thou encounters are moments of authentic meeting, in which we see and are seen, know and are known.

Restorative justice creates conditions for I-Thou encounters. When victims and offenders meet in mediated dialogue, they have opportunity to see one another as persons, not merely as categories. When community members sit in circle together, they encounter one another as whole human beings. These encounters are at the heart of restorative transformation.

See also: Dialogical Ethics, Relational Ethics

Image of God

The image of God (*imago Dei*) is a theological concept rooted in Genesis 1:26-27, which declares that humanity is created in God's image. This affirmation has profound implications for restorative justice.

First, it establishes the inherent dignity of every human being. Victims, offenders, and community members alike bear God's image and deserve to be treated with respect. This dignity is not earned or achieved; it is given. It cannot be forfeited by wrongdoing.

Second, it grounds the possibility of restoration. If human beings are made in God's image, even the most broken among us retain the capacity for healing and wholeness. The image may be marred, but it is not destroyed.

Third, it calls us to see God in one another. When we encounter victims, we encounter those for whom God cares deeply. When we encounter offenders, we encounter those whom God loves and seeks to restore. This vision transforms how we relate to all people.

See also: Dignity, Humanity, Respect

Inclusion

Inclusion refers to ensuring that all voices are heard and respected in restorative processes. Inclusion is essential for fairness and the legitimacy of restorative justice outcomes. When some voices are excluded, processes are incomplete and outcomes may be unjust.

Inclusion requires active effort to engage marginalized and underrepresented groups—those who may be less likely to participate, less confident in speaking, less trusting of processes. It requires attention to barriers—language, culture, cost, location, timing. It requires willingness to adapt practices to ensure that all can participate meaningfully.

Theologically, inclusion reflects the heart of God, who welcomes all people into covenant relationship. Jesus's ministry was characterized by inclusion of those excluded by society—tax collectors, sinners, women, children, foreigners. The early church wrestled with including Gentiles, ultimately affirming that in Christ there is no Jew or Greek, slave or free, male or female (Galatians 3:28).

See also: Equity, Participation, Voice

Indigenous Justice

Indigenous justice refers to the traditional justice practices of indigenous peoples around the world. These practices, which vary among different indigenous cultures, often emphasize community involvement, healing, reconciliation, and restoration rather than punishment and retribution.

Examples include the peacemaking circles of Native American tribes, the Gacaca courts of Rwanda (drawing on traditional practices), the family group conferencing of Maori in New Zealand, and the healing circles of Indigenous peoples in Canada.

Indigenous justice practices have profoundly influenced the modern restorative justice movement. They demonstrate that restorative approaches are not new inventions but ancient wisdom, rediscovered and adapted for contemporary contexts.

Respect for indigenous justice requires recognizing that these practices belong to indigenous communities and should not be appropriated without permission and collaboration. It means learning from indigenous wisdom while honoring its sources.

See also: Maori Justice, Peacemaking Circles, Ubuntu

Interconnectedness

Interconnectedness is the concept that all individuals and communities are linked and that actions affecting one part of the community can impact the whole. This insight is fundamental to restorative justice.

Interconnectedness means that harm does not occur in isolation. When one person is harmed, relationships are damaged, trust is eroded, community fabric is torn. When one person causes harm, they are also harmed—alienated from community, disconnected from relationships, diminished in humanity.

Interconnectedness also means that healing cannot occur in isolation. Victims need community support; offenders need community accountability and welcome; communities need to be involved in restoration. Justice is a communal endeavor, not merely an individual matter.

Theological resources for understanding interconnectedness are abundant. Paul's image of the body—many members, one body—captures this truth (1 Corinthians 12). The African concept of *Ubuntu*—"I am because we are"—expresses it beautifully. Restorative justice embodies this interconnected understanding of human life.

See also: Communitarianism, Relational Ethics, Ubuntu

Intersectionality

Intersectionality is a framework developed by legal scholar Kimberlé Crenshaw to describe how different social identities—

such as race, gender, class, sexuality, disability—intersect and interact to produce unique experiences of marginalization or privilege. The concept highlights that social identities do not exist in isolation but overlap and mutually constitute one another.

Applying an intersectional lens to restorative justice is essential for addressing the complex and interconnected forms of discrimination and inequality that individuals face. A Black woman's experience of harm may be shaped by both racism and sexism; a poor Latino youth's pathway to offending may be shaped by class and ethnicity. Attending to these intersections ensures that restorative processes are truly responsive to participants' lives.

Intersectionality also requires attention to how power operates in restorative processes. Those with multiple marginalized identities may face multiple barriers to participation; those with multiple privileged identities may have unearned advantages. Facilitators must be aware of these dynamics and work to create equitable conditions.

See also: Bias, Equity, Power Imbalances, Social Justice

J

Justice

Justice is a complex and contested concept with multiple meanings. In the retributive tradition, justice means giving offenders what they deserve—punishment proportional to their offenses. In the utilitarian tradition, justice means maximizing overall welfare—punishment that deters crime and protects society. In the restorative tradition, justice means repairing harm—making things right for victims, offenders, and communities.

The biblical concept of justice (*mishpat* and *tzedekah*) encompasses all these dimensions but emphasizes restoration and right relationship. Justice is not merely punishing wrongdoers but creating communities where all can flourish—where the vulnerable are protected, where relationships are healthy, where *shalom* prevails.

Restorative justice seeks to embody this biblical vision. It holds offenders accountable while offering pathways to restoration. It centers victims while engaging communities. It addresses harm while building relationships. It seeks not merely to process cases but to transform lives.

See also: Biblical Justice, Mishpat, Restorative Justice, Retributive Justice, Shalom, Tzedekah

---

L

Legal Rights

Legal rights are entitlements and protections guaranteed by law. In restorative justice, the legal rights of all participants must be respected. Victims have rights to information, participation, and protection. Offenders have rights to due process, to avoid self-incrimination, to legal counsel. Communities have rights to safety and to participation in decisions that affect them.

Restorative processes must be designed to protect these rights while achieving restorative goals. This requires clear protocols, informed consent, access to legal advice, and mechanisms for addressing rights violations.

The relationship between restorative justice and legal rights is complementary, not oppositional. Restorative justice can enhance rights by giving victims voice and agency that conventional processes may not provide. Legal rights can protect participants from coercion or abuse in restorative processes.

See also: Due Process, Procedural Justice, Rights

M

Maori Justice

Maori justice refers to the traditional justice practices of the Maori people of New Zealand. These practices emphasize collective responsibility, reconciliation, and the restoration of balance. Key concepts include *whānau* (family), *hapū* (sub-tribe), and *iwi* (tribe)—the extended family networks that constitute Maori society.

Maori justice practices have profoundly influenced New Zealand's restorative justice system. Family Group Conferencing, now a cornerstone of youth justice, draws directly on Maori traditions. The emphasis on family and community involvement, on collective decision-making, on restoration rather than punishment—all reflect Maori values.

Respect for Maori justice requires recognizing that these practices belong to Maori communities. It means learning from Maori wisdom while honoring its sources, collaborating with Maori leaders, and ensuring that Maori communities have ownership of processes that affect them.

See also: Family Group Conferencing, Indigenous Justice, New Zealand

Mediation

Mediation is a facilitated process in which a neutral third party helps disputants communicate and negotiate to reach a mutually agreeable resolution. In restorative justice, victim-offender mediation brings victims and offenders together in facilitated dialogue to address harm, promote understanding, and develop reparative agreements.

Mediation differs from arbitration or adjudication. The mediator does not impose a solution but creates conditions for the parties to find their own. The process is voluntary, confidential, and focused on the parties' needs and interests.

Skills for mediation include active listening, reframing, questioning, and problem-solving. Mediators must be trained and skilled, able to manage emotional intensity and power dynamics while maintaining focus on restorative goals.

See also: Facilitator, Victim-Offender Mediation

Mediator

A mediator is a trained neutral person who facilitates mediation between parties in conflict. In restorative justice, mediators facilitate victim-offender mediation, guiding dialogue, ensuring respectful communication, and helping parties develop agreements.

Mediators require specialized training and skills. They must be able to create safe spaces, manage emotional intensity, recognize and address power imbalances, and maintain focus on restorative goals. They must embody restorative values—respect, empathy, patience, hope.

See also: Facilitator, Victim-Offender Mediation

Mishpat

Mishpat is a Hebrew word often translated as "justice" or "judgment." In the Hebrew scriptures, *mishpat* refers to the proper ordering of community, the fair treatment of all, the protection of the vulnerable. It is closely related to *tzedekah* (righteousness) and together they describe the society God desires.

Mishpat includes retributive elements—punishment for wrongdoing—but extends far beyond punishment. It encompasses restorative elements—making things right, protecting the vulnerable, restoring relationships. The prophets' calls for justice are calls for *mishpat*—for communities where all can flourish.

Restorative justice embodies *mishpat* by attending to the needs of victims, holding offenders accountable, and engaging communities in restoration. It seeks the right ordering of relationships that *mishpat* describes.

See also: Biblical Justice, Tzedekah, Shalom

Moral Responsibility

Moral responsibility refers to the obligation to answer for one's actions, to be accountable for the choices one makes. In restorative justice, moral responsibility involves acknowledging the harm caused, understanding its impact, and taking steps to make amends.

Moral responsibility differs from legal responsibility. Legal responsibility is determined by courts and may be satisfied by accepting punishment. Moral responsibility is deeper—it involves the offender's own recognition of wrongdoing and commitment to change.

Restorative justice creates conditions for moral responsibility to develop. Through encounter with victims, through dialogue and reflection, offenders come to understand the human consequences of their actions. This understanding can evoke genuine moral response—remorse, accountability, commitment to change.

See also: Accountability, Ethical Responsibility, Responsibility

---

N

Narrative Sharing

Narrative sharing refers to the practice of participants telling their stories in restorative processes. Victims share their experiences of harm—what happened, how it affected them, what they have suffered. Offenders share their stories—what led to their actions, what they were thinking and feeling, how they have come to understand what they did.

Narrative sharing serves multiple purposes. It helps victims feel heard and validated. It helps offenders understand the impact of their actions. It builds empathy and mutual recognition. It creates the foundation for developing agreements that address real needs.

Psychological research supports the power of narrative in healing. Telling one's story can be therapeutic, helping to process trauma and integrate experience. Being heard with respect and empathy can be profoundly healing.

See also: Active Listening, Empathy, Storytelling

O

Offender

An offender is a person who has committed a wrongful act or crime. In restorative justice, offenders are encouraged to take responsibility for their actions, understand the impact of their behavior, and actively participate in making amends.

The term "offender" is used with awareness that it describes only one dimension of a person's identity. Offenders are also parents, children, workers, community members. They have strengths and weaknesses, capacities and limitations. They are more than their worst actions.

Restorative justice treats offenders with dignity while holding them accountable. It recognizes their capacity for change and seeks to support their rehabilitation and reintegration. It does not excuse their actions but offers pathways to restoration.

See also: Accountability, Rehabilitation, Reintegration, Responsibility

P

Participation

Participation refers to the active involvement of all affected parties in restorative justice processes. Participation ensures that everyone has a voice and contributes to the resolution. It is essential for the legitimacy and effectiveness of restorative outcomes.

Participation takes different forms for different parties. Victims participate by telling their stories, asking questions, and expressing their needs. Offenders participate by listening, responding, and taking responsibility. Community members participate by offering support, sharing perspectives, and contributing to agreements.

Participation must be meaningful, not merely token. This requires creating conditions in which all can participate fully—safe environments, skilled facilitation, attention to power imbalances, accommodation of different needs and capacities.

See also: Inclusion, Voice

Peacemaking Circles

Peacemaking circles are a type of circle process focused on resolving conflicts and promoting healing and reconciliation within communities. Drawing on indigenous traditions, particularly from Native American peoples, peacemaking circles bring together all affected parties in a structured, respectful dialogue.

The circle process emphasizes equality—all participants sit in a circle, all have equal opportunity to speak. A talking piece ensures that each voice can be heard. Elders or respected community members may guide the process, but the circle belongs to all.

Peacemaking circles address not only the immediate conflict but underlying relationships and community dynamics. They seek not merely to resolve disputes but to restore harmony, to heal relationships, to strengthen community.

See also: Circle Keeper, Circle Process, Indigenous Justice, Talking Piece

Peer Mediation

Peer mediation is a restorative practice in which trained student mediators help their peers resolve conflicts through guided dialogue and problem-solving. Common in schools, peer mediation empowers students to take ownership of conflict resolution and develops their leadership skills.

Peer mediators are trained in active listening, questioning, and facilitation. They learn to remain neutral, to ensure that both parties have voice, to guide the process without imposing solutions. Mediation sessions are confidential, creating safe space for honest communication.

Research shows that peer mediation reduces conflicts, improves school climate, and develops students' social and emotional skills. Participants learn to resolve disputes constructively, building skills that serve them throughout life.

See also: Restorative Circles, School-Based Restorative Justice

Philosophy

Philosophy is the study of fundamental questions concerning existence, knowledge, values, reason, mind, and language. It involves critical examination and systematic approaches to understanding the world and our place within it.

The relationship between philosophy and restorative justice is profound. Philosophical traditions—relational ethics, communitarianism, virtue ethics, restorative ontology, ethical responsibility, dialogical ethics—provide the intellectual foundations for restorative principles and practices. Philosophy helps us understand why restorative justice makes sense, why it is not merely a set of techniques but a coherent way of understanding justice and human flourishing.

See also: Communitarianism, Dialogical Ethics, Ethical Responsibility, Relational Ethics, Restorative Ontology, Virtue Ethics

Post-Charge Diversion

Post-charge diversion refers to restorative justice programs initiated after charges have been filed but before sentencing. Successful participation can influence sentencing decisions, potentially leading to reduced sentences or alternative dispositions.

This model encourages offenders to engage in reparative actions before they are sentenced. Their participation demonstrates accountability and commitment to change, which can be considered by the court. For victims, it provides opportunity to participate before final disposition.

See also: Diversion, Pre-Charge Diversion

Post-Sentencing Programs

Post-sentencing programs refer to restorative justice initiatives integrated into the correctional system. Offenders may participate in restorative processes during incarceration or as part of probation or parole conditions.

These programs support offender rehabilitation by providing opportunities for accountability and growth even after sentencing. They may include restorative circles within prisons, victim-offender dialogues, or community service projects. For victims, they can provide opportunities for healing that were not available earlier.

See also: Prison-Based Restorative Justice

Power Imbalances

Power imbalances refer to disparities in power between participants in restorative processes. These imbalances can stem from differences in social status, authority, education, confidence, or vulnerability. They can distort dialogue, silence some voices, and produce outcomes that are not truly equitable.

Addressing power imbalances is essential for fair and effective restorative justice. Facilitators must be trained to recognize power dynamics and intervene appropriately—meeting separately with parties beforehand, providing support persons during the process, ensuring that all voices are heard, maintaining balance throughout.

Providing support services—counseling, advocacy, interpretation—can help vulnerable participants engage more fully. Creating safe environments where all feel respected is essential.

See also: Bias, Equity, Participation

Pre-Charge Diversion

Pre-charge diversion refers to restorative justice programs that occur before formal charges are filed. Offenders are diverted from the formal justice system into restorative processes, allowing for early intervention and resolution.

This model has several benefits. It reduces the burden on courts, provides timely resolution, and offers opportunities for rehabilitation without the lasting consequences of a criminal record. For victims, it provides prompt attention to their needs.

See also: Diversion, Post-Charge Diversion

Procedural Justice

Procedural justice refers to the fairness of processes used to make decisions and resolve disputes. Research shows that people's satisfaction with legal processes depends heavily on whether they perceive the process as fair—whether they had voice, whether they were treated with respect, whether the process was transparent, whether the decision-maker was neutral.

Restorative practices excel on procedural justice dimensions. Participants have voice; they can tell their stories and express their views. They are treated with respect by facilitators and other participants. The process is transparent; participants understand what is happening and why. Facilitators are neutral, guiding process without imposing outcomes.

This procedural justice contributes to the legitimacy of restorative outcomes. Even when participants do not get everything they want, they are more likely to accept outcomes reached through fair processes.

See also: Due Process, Fairness, Legal Rights

Proportionality

Proportionality refers to the principle that responses to wrongdoing should be proportionate to the severity of the offense. In restorative justice, proportionality involves ensuring that reparative actions are appropriate to the harm caused—neither too lenient nor too harsh.

Proportionality guards against the potential for restorative justice to be applied inconsistently or unfairly. While restorative processes are flexible and responsive to individual circumstances, they must also be guided by standards that ensure similar cases receive similar treatment.

Biblical law included proportional elements—"an eye for an eye" (Exodus 21:24) was originally a limitation on vengeance, requiring that punishment not exceed the harm. Restorative justice seeks proportionality in repair rather than punishment.

See also: Fairness, Retributive Justice

R

Reconciliation

Reconciliation is the process of restoring relationships and resolving conflicts, often involving forgiveness and mutual understanding between victims and offenders. Reconciliation is a central goal of restorative justice, though it is not always achieved and cannot be coerced.

Reconciliation differs from forgiveness. Forgiveness is internal release; reconciliation is relational restoration. One can forgive without reconciling (if the relationship remains unsafe) and one can reconcile without fully forgiving (if forgiveness is not yet possible). Ideally, both occur together.

Psychological research shows that reconciliation, when it occurs, can be profoundly healing for both victims and offenders. It restores trust, rebuilds connection, and allows both to move forward.

Theologically, reconciliation is central to the gospel. Paul writes that "in Christ, God was reconciling the world to himself" (2 Corinthians 5:19). Christians are called to be ministers of reconciliation, extending to others the reconciliation they have received.

See also: Forgiveness, Healing, Restoration, Shalom

Rehabilitation

Rehabilitation refers to the process of restoring offenders to constructive functioning in society. It involves addressing the underlying causes of offending—addiction, trauma, lack of skills, broken relationships—and developing the capacities for pro-social living.

Restorative justice promotes rehabilitation by engaging offenders in understanding the harm they have caused, developing empathy and remorse, and taking responsibility for change. It connects offenders with community support and resources. It treats offenders as capable of change, not as irredeemable.

Research shows that restorative approaches can be more effective than purely punitive ones in promoting rehabilitation and reducing recidivism.

See also: Desistance, Reintegration

Reintegration

Reintegration refers to the process of restoring offenders to full membership in community after they have caused harm. It involves welcoming them back, supporting their positive development, and helping them build constructive lives.

Restorative justice promotes reintegration by involving community in the justice process, by supporting offenders' efforts to make amends, and by creating pathways for restored relationship. It recognizes that offenders are still members of community, still capable of contribution, still deserving of support.

Successful reintegration reduces recidivism and strengthens communities. Offenders who feel welcomed back are more likely to invest in pro-social lives. Communities that welcome returning offenders are stronger and more cohesive.

See also: Desistance, Rehabilitation

Relational Ethics

Relational ethics is a philosophical approach that emphasizes the interconnectedness of individuals within a community. It asserts that our moral obligations are grounded in the relationships we have with others, and that ethical behavior involves maintaining and restoring these relationships.

Relational ethics provides foundation for restorative justice. It explains why restorative justice focuses on repairing relationships—if our moral obligations arise from relationship, then harm damages not only individuals but the moral fabric itself. It explains why community involvement is essential—if we are interconnected, then community must be part of restoration.

Theological resources for relational ethics are abundant. The covenant relationship between God and Israel, the body of Christ in Paul's writings, the commandment to love neighbor as self—all express the relational nature of human existence.

See also: Communitarianism, Dialogical Ethics, Interconnectedness, Ubuntu

Remorse

Remorse is deep regret for wrongdoing, accompanied by acknowledgment of harm and desire to make amends. In restorative justice, genuine remorse is significant—it validates victims' experience, motivates offenders to change, and opens possibilities for healing and reconciliation.

Remorse differs from shame. Shame is about the self—"I am bad." Remorse is about the action—"I did something bad." Remorse leads to repair; shame often leads to withdrawal or defensiveness. Restorative processes seek to evoke remorse, not shame.

Psychological research shows that remorse, genuinely expressed, contributes to victims' healing and offenders' rehabilitation. Victims feel validated when offenders show understanding of the harm they caused. Offenders who experience remorse are more motivated to change.

See also: Apology, Empathy, Repentance

Reparation

Reparation refers to actions taken by offenders to repair the harm they have caused. Reparation may include apologies, restitution (financial compensation), community service, or other forms of making amends. Reparation is a central principle of restorative justice.

Reparation addresses victims' needs—material, emotional, relational. It validates their experience, provides tangible acknowledgment of harm, and contributes to healing. Reparation also benefits offenders, providing opportunity to take responsibility, make amends, and be restored to community.

Reparation is not about buying forgiveness or paying off guilt. It is about taking concrete action to make things right, to the extent possible. It demonstrates commitment to change and opens possibilities for reconciliation.

See also: Accountability, Restitution

Repentance

Repentance is a theological concept with profound implications for restorative justice. In the Hebrew scriptures, repentance (*teshuvah*) means turning—turning away from wrongdoing and turning toward God and right relationship. In Christian theology, repentance (*metanoia*) means a change of heart and mind that leads to transformed life.

Repentance involves acknowledgment of wrongdoing, remorse, commitment to change, and actions that demonstrate change. It is not merely feeling sorry but turning around, going in a new direction.

Restorative justice creates conditions for repentance. Through encounter with victims, through dialogue and reflection, offenders come to understand the harm they have caused. This understanding can evoke genuine repentance—a turning from wrongdoing and toward restoration.

See also: Accountability, Apology, Remorse, Transformation

Responsibility

Responsibility refers to the obligation to answer for one's actions and to contribute positively to community. In restorative justice, responsibility has multiple dimensions—taking responsibility for harm caused, making amends, and contributing to prevention of future harm.

Responsibility is not merely accepting blame but actively engaging in making things right. It is forward-looking as well as backward-looking—concerned with what will be done, not only what has been done.

Restorative justice fosters responsibility by creating conditions in which offenders can understand the impact of their actions and choose to make amends. It also fosters collective responsibility—communities taking responsibility for supporting victims, holding offenders accountable, and creating conditions for healing.

See also: Accountability, Ethical Responsibility, Moral Responsibility

Restitution

Restitution refers to compensation provided by offenders to victims for harm caused. Restitution may be financial—reimbursing for medical expenses, property damage, lost income—or in-kind—repairing damaged property, returning stolen goods, providing services.

Restitution addresses victims' material needs and provides tangible acknowledgment of harm. It demonstrates offenders' commitment to making amends. It is a form of reparation, contributing to accountability and healing.

Restitution is not the same as punishment. It is not about making offenders suffer but about making victims whole. It reflects the principle that justice requires addressing harm, not merely imposing suffering.

See also: Reparation

Restoration

Restoration refers to the process of making things right, of returning to wholeness and health after harm. In restorative justice, restoration is the ultimate goal—restoring victims to well-being, restoring offenders to community, restoring relationships, restoring the social fabric.

Restoration does not mean returning to exactly how things were before—that may be impossible. It means creating a new reality in which harm is acknowledged, accountability is achieved, healing is begun, and relationships are repaired to the extent possible.

Theological vision of restoration is captured in the concept of *shalom*—peace, wholeness, right relationship. It is the vision of a world where all things are made new, where tears are wiped away, where death and mourning are no more. Restorative justice participates in this divine work of restoration.

See also: Healing, Reconciliation, Shalom

Restorative Circles

Restorative circles are a restorative practice that brings together victims, offenders, and community members in a structured, inclusive dialogue to address harm, promote healing, and develop agreements. Circles draw on indigenous traditions and are used in diverse contexts—schools, workplaces, communities, prisons.

The circle process emphasizes equality, respect, and shared responsibility. A talking piece ensures that all voices can be heard. The circle belongs to all participants; the facilitator (keeper) holds the space but does not control outcomes.

Research shows that restorative circles improve communication, strengthen relationships, resolve conflicts effectively, and build community.

See also: Circle Keeper, Circle Process, Peacemaking Circles, Talking Piece

Restorative Conferences

Restorative conferences are facilitated meetings involving victims, offenders, and their supporters to address harm and develop plans for making amends. Conferences may be used in criminal justice, schools, workplaces, or community settings.

Conference processes typically involve preparation of all parties, structured dialogue about the harm and its impact, development of a restorative agreement, and follow-up to monitor implementation.

Research shows that restorative conferences produce high levels of participant satisfaction, reduce recidivism, and strengthen community ties.

See also: Family Group Conferencing, Restorative Circles

Restorative Dialogue

Restorative dialogue refers to one-on-one or small group conversations that address conflicts and misunderstandings, promoting empathy and understanding. Restorative dialogue may be informal—a conversation between two people working through a disagreement—or formal—a structured process guided by a facilitator.

Restorative dialogue differs from ordinary conversation in its intentional focus on understanding, accountability, and repair. Participants are encouraged to listen deeply, speak honestly, and work toward mutual understanding and resolution.

Skills for restorative dialogue include active listening, asking open questions, speaking from one's own experience, and remaining open to learning. These skills can be developed and are valuable in all relationships.

See also: Dialogue, Mediation

Restorative Justice

Restorative justice is an approach to justice that focuses on repairing harm, involving all affected parties, and addressing the needs of victims, offenders, and the community. It contrasts with retributive justice, which focuses on punishment, and with utilitarian justice, which focuses on deterrence and rehabilitation.

Key principles of restorative justice include: focus on harm rather than rule-breaking; involvement of victims, offenders, and community; accountability as taking responsibility and making amends; voluntary participation; facilitated dialogue; and goals of healing and restoration.

Restorative justice is not a single program or practice but a philosophy that can be embodied in diverse ways—victim-offender mediation, family group conferencing, restorative circles, community restorative boards, and many others.

See also: Restorative Practices, Retributive Justice

Restorative Ontology

Restorative ontology is a philosophical approach that underscores the fundamental need for restoration and healing in the aftermath of harm. It posits that true justice can only be achieved when relationships are mended and communities are strengthened.

Restorative ontology recognizes that harm affects the very being of individuals and communities—disrupting relationships, trust, and social cohesion. The imperative to restore is rooted in the recognition that justice involves more than punishment; it requires active repair of damage.

For restorative justice, this means that restoration is not merely one option among many but is woven into the fabric of reality. When we seek to heal harm, we are aligning ourselves with the deepest grain of the universe.

Theological resources for restorative ontology are abundant. The doctrine of creation affirms that God made all things good; the fall damaged but did not destroy that goodness. The doctrine of redemption affirms that God is at work restoring all things. Restorative justice participates in this cosmic restoration.

See also: Philosophy, Restoration

Restorative Practices

Restorative practices refer to a range of practices and processes that apply restorative justice principles in various contexts, such as schools, workplaces, and communities. These practices include restorative circles, victim-offender mediation, family group conferencing, community restorative boards, and restorative dialogue.

Restorative practices share common principles—focus on harm, involvement of affected parties, accountability as taking responsibility, voluntary participation, facilitated dialogue, goals of healing and restoration. They differ in structure and application, adapted to different contexts and needs.

The term "restorative practices" is sometimes used more broadly than "restorative justice" to include proactive community-building activities as well as responsive processes addressing harm.

See also: Restorative Justice

Retributive Justice

Retributive justice is an approach to justice based on the principle that wrongdoing deserves punishment. It focuses on imposing penalties proportional to the offense, aiming to balance the scales of justice and uphold moral order.

Key features of retributive justice include: focus on rule-breaking rather than harm; state-centered process with limited victim involvement; adversarial procedures; punishment as the primary response; goals of deterrence and moral accountability.

Retributive justice has strengths—it protects defendants' rights, provides clear standards, expresses social condemnation of wrongdoing. But it also has limitations—it marginalizes victims, often fails to rehabilitate offenders, and does not address underlying causes of crime.

Restorative justice offers a complementary approach that addresses these limitations while preserving appropriate accountability.

See also: Adversarial System, Justice, Restorative Justice

Rights

Rights are entitlements and protections guaranteed to individuals by law or moral principle. In restorative justice, the rights of all participants must be respected—victims' rights to information, participation, and protection; offenders' rights to due process, to avoid self-incrimination, to legal counsel; communities' rights to safety and participation.

Restorative justice can enhance rights by giving victims voice and agency that conventional processes may not provide. Legal rights protect participants from coercion or abuse in restorative processes. The relationship is complementary, not oppositional.

See also: Due Process, Legal Rights, Procedural Justice

S

Salvation

Salvation is a theological concept referring to deliverance from sin and its consequences, and restoration to right relationship with God. In Christian theology, salvation is understood as God's work in Christ, reconciling humanity to God and making possible new life.

Salvation has individual and communal dimensions. Individuals are saved, but they are saved into community—the body of Christ. Salvation is not merely escape from punishment but transformation into the people God created us to be.

Restorative justice participates in the dynamics of salvation. It addresses sin (harm), promotes repentance (accountability), offers forgiveness (when chosen), and works for reconciliation (restoration). It is a sign of the salvation that God is bringing to completion.

See also: Atonement, Reconciliation, Restoration

School-Based Restorative Justice

School-based restorative justice refers to the application of restorative practices in educational settings. Schools implement restorative circles, peer mediation, restorative conferences, and restorative dialogue to address conflicts, build community, and create positive school climates.

School-based restorative justice has multiple benefits. It reduces suspensions and expulsions, particularly among students of color who have been disproportionately affected by punitive discipline. It improves school climate, making schools safer and more supportive. It develops students' social and emotional skills. It builds stronger relationships among students, teachers, and staff.

Research on school-based restorative justice shows impressive outcomes—reduced disciplinary incidents, improved academic outcomes, stronger school communities.

See also: Peer Mediation, Restorative Circles, Whole-School Approach

School-to-Prison Pipeline

The school-to-prison pipeline refers to policies and practices that push students, particularly those from marginalized communities, out of schools and into the criminal justice system. Zero-tolerance discipline policies, high rates of suspension and expulsion, and the presence of police in schools contribute to this pipeline.

Restorative justice in schools aims to disrupt the pipeline by addressing conflicts constructively, keeping students in school, and creating positive school climates. By reducing suspensions and expulsions, restorative practices keep students engaged in education rather than pushed into the justice system.

See also: School-Based Restorative Justice

Shalom

Shalom is a Hebrew word often translated as "peace," but its meaning is far richer. Shalom encompasses peace, wholeness, completeness, flourishing, and right relationship. It is the vision of a world where all things are as they should be—where relationships with God, with neighbor, with self, and with creation are healthy and whole.

The prophets envision a world of shalom—where swords are beaten into plowshares, where lion and lamb lie down together, where every person sits under their own vine and fig tree with none to make them afraid. This is not merely the absence of conflict but the presence of flourishing.

Restorative justice seeks shalom. It addresses the harms that disrupt shalom—crime, conflict, injustice. It works to restore the relationships that shalom requires—between victims and offenders, within communities, between people and God. It is a practical embodiment of the prophetic vision.

See also: Biblical Justice, Healing, Reconciliation, Restoration

Social Justice

Social justice refers to the pursuit of fairness and equity in the distribution of resources, opportunities, and treatment across all societal groups. It addresses systemic inequalities—based on race, class, gender, and other factors—that disadvantage some while privileging others.

Restorative justice and social justice are deeply connected. Restorative justice addresses individual harms; social justice addresses systemic patterns. Restorative justice involves victims and offenders; social justice involves entire communities and structures. Together, they work toward a more just world.

Applying restorative principles to social justice issues means addressing not only individual acts of discrimination but the systems that produce them. It means involving affected communities in designing solutions. It means seeking not only compensation but transformation.

See also: Equity, Intersectionality, Systemic Injustice

Storytelling

Storytelling refers to the practice of sharing personal narratives in restorative processes. Victims tell stories of harm; offenders tell stories of their lives and actions; community members tell stories of impact and hope. Storytelling builds empathy, fosters understanding, and creates connections.

Storytelling in restorative justice is not casual conversation but intentional sharing. Participants are encouraged to speak from their own experience, to be honest and vulnerable, to listen deeply to others' stories. Facilitators create safe spaces where storytelling can occur.

Psychological research supports the power of storytelling in healing. Telling one's story can help process trauma, integrate experience, and find meaning. Being heard with empathy can be profoundly healing.

See also: Active Listening, Empathy, Narrative Sharing

Survivor

Survivor is a term often preferred over "victim" by those who have experienced harm, as it emphasizes resilience and agency rather than passivity and victimhood. In restorative justice, survivors are central to the process; their needs and perspectives are prioritized.

The choice between "victim" and "survivor" is personal. Some prefer "victim" because it accurately describes what happened to them. Others prefer "survivor" because it emphasizes their strength in moving forward. Restorative practitioners respect individual preference.

Regardless of terminology, restorative justice centers those who have been harmed. Their voices are heard, their needs addressed, their healing prioritized.

See also: Victim

Sustainability

Sustainability in restorative justice refers to the ability of programs to maintain their effectiveness, relevance, and impact over time. Sustainable programs have stable funding, trained personnel, community support, institutional backing, and mechanisms for evaluation and improvement.

Sustainability is essential for restorative justice to achieve lasting impact. Programs that flourish briefly and then fade cannot transform communities. Building sustainability requires attention to funding, capacity building, community engagement, institutional integration, and continuous evaluation.

See also: Scalability

Systemic Injustice

Systemic injustice refers to patterns of inequality and discrimination embedded in social structures and institutions. Unlike individual acts of injustice, systemic injustice operates through normal operations of systems—laws, policies, practices, cultural norms—that disadvantage certain groups while privileging others.

Restorative justice must attend to systemic injustice. Individual harms often reflect broader patterns; individual healing often requires addressing systemic conditions. Restorative processes can name and address systemic issues, engaging communities in identifying and changing unjust structures.

Theological reflection on systemic injustice recognizes that sin has structural as well as individual dimensions. The prophets condemned not only individual wrongdoing but the systems that exploited the poor and marginalized. Restorative justice participates in this prophetic work.

See also: Intersectionality, Social Justice

T

Talking Piece

A talking piece is an object used in circle processes to regulate speaking. Only the person holding the talking piece may speak; others listen. The talking piece ensures that all voices can be heard, that no one dominates, that everyone has opportunity to contribute.

Talking pieces can be any object—a stone, a feather, a stick, a specially made piece. The object itself is less important than what it represents: respect, equality, attentive listening. Passing the piece around the circle creates rhythm and focus.

The talking piece embodies restorative values. It symbolizes that every voice matters, that listening is as important as speaking, that the circle belongs to all.

See also: Circle Keeper, Circle Process, Peacemaking Circles

Theology

Theology is the study of God and religious beliefs. In relation to restorative justice, theology provides deep resources for understanding and practicing restoration.

Biblical themes of justice, mercy, reconciliation, and restoration ground restorative work. Concepts such as *shalom*, covenant, repentance, forgiveness, and atonement illuminate restorative principles. The life and teachings of Jesus model restorative practice. The work of the Spirit empowers restorative transformation.

For those who approach restorative justice from a faith perspective, theology is not an add-on but integral to understanding why restorative justice matters and how it participates in God's work in the world.

See also: Atonement, Biblical Justice, Covenant, Forgiveness, Reconciliation, Repentance, Salvation, Shalom

Transformation

Transformation refers to fundamental change in individuals, relationships, or communities. In restorative justice, transformation is the ultimate goal—not merely resolving conflicts but changing people, healing relationships, building stronger communities.

Transformation occurs at multiple levels. Individuals change—victims heal, offenders develop empathy and responsibility. Relationships change—trust is rebuilt, connection restored. Communities change—bonds strengthen, capacity grows, culture shifts.

Transformation is not guaranteed in every case. But restorative processes create conditions in which transformation can occur—spaces for genuine encounter, opportunities for accountability and repair, support for healing and growth.

Theological vision of transformation is captured in Paul's words: "If anyone is in Christ, there is a new creation: everything old has passed away; see, everything has become new!" (2 Corinthians 5:17). Restorative justice participates in this new creation.

See also: Healing, Reconciliation, Restoration

Transitional Justice

Transitional justice refers to the ways societies address legacies of mass violence, human rights abuses, and systemic injustices during periods of political transition. It encompasses judicial and non-judicial measures—truth commissions, reparations, institutional reforms, criminal prosecutions.

Restorative approaches are particularly valuable in transitional contexts. Truth commissions provide platforms for victims and perpetrators to share experiences, promote healing and reconciliation. Community-based restorative practices engage local communities in addressing past harms. Reparations programs provide compensation and support to victims.

Examples include South Africa's Truth and Reconciliation Commission, Rwanda's Gacaca courts, and Colombia's Special Jurisdiction for Peace. These demonstrate the potential of restorative justice to address massive human rights violations.

See also: Gacaca Courts, Truth and Reconciliation Commission

Trauma-Informed Approach

A trauma-informed approach recognizes the prevalence and impact of trauma and incorporates this understanding into practice. Trauma-informed restorative justice attends to the ways trauma affects participants' experiences, needs, and capacities.

Key principles of trauma-informed practice include safety, trustworthiness, choice, collaboration, and empowerment. Restorative processes embody these principles when they create safe environments, build trust, respect participants' choices, work collaboratively, and empower participants.

Trauma-informed facilitators recognize signs of distress and respond appropriately. They avoid retraumatizing participants by pushing too hard or too fast. They connect participants with additional support when needed.

See also: Healing, Safety

Truth and Reconciliation Commission

A Truth and Reconciliation Commission (TRC) is a body established to investigate and document past human rights violations, provide a platform for victims and perpetrators to share their experiences, and recommend measures to promote healing and reconciliation.

TRCs embody restorative principles. They focus on truth-telling, acknowledgment, and accountability rather than punishment. They involve victims and perpetrators in the process. They seek to promote healing and reconciliation at societal scale.

The most famous example is South Africa's TRC, established after apartheid. Other examples include commissions in Sierra Leone, Canada, and elsewhere. TRCs demonstrate the potential of restorative approaches in transitional contexts.

See also: Gacaca Courts, Transitional Justice

Tzedekah

Tzedekah is a Hebrew word often translated as "righteousness" or "justice." In the Hebrew scriptures, *tzedekah* refers to right relationship—with God, with neighbor, with community. It is closely related to *mishpat* (justice) and together they describe the society God desires.

Tzedekah includes charitable giving and care for the vulnerable, but it is more than charity. It is about creating communities where all can flourish—where relationships are healthy, where resources are fairly distributed, where dignity is honored.

Restorative justice seeks *tzedekah* by repairing relationships damaged by harm, by addressing needs of victims, by holding offenders accountable, by strengthening community bonds. It participates in the work of creating right relationship.

See also: Biblical Justice, Mishpat, Shalom

U

Ubuntu

Ubuntu is a Nguni Bantu term from Southern Africa that captures a profound philosophical and ethical concept: "I am because we are." A person is a person through other persons. Humanity is interconnected; individual well-being is inseparable from community well-being.

Archbishop Desmond Tutu, who chaired South Africa's Truth and Reconciliation Commission, explained Ubuntu this way: "Ubuntu speaks particularly about the fact that you can't exist as a human being in isolation. It speaks about our interconnectedness. You can't be human all by yourself, and when you have this quality—Ubuntu—you are known for your generosity."

Ubuntu has profound implications for restorative justice. If humanity is interconnected, then harm damages not only individuals but the whole community. Justice must therefore repair not only individual wounds but communal relationships. If humanity is interconnected, then offenders remain part of community, capable of restoration. Justice must therefore seek not exclusion but reintegration.

Ubuntu shaped South Africa's TRC, providing philosophical foundation for its restorative approach. It continues to inspire restorative justice worldwide.

See also: Communitarianism, Interconnectedness, Relational Ethics

---

V

Victim

A victim is a person who has been harmed by a wrongful act. In restorative justice, victims' needs, rights, and perspectives are central to the process. Victims have opportunity to tell their stories, to ask questions, to receive acknowledgment, to participate in determining what justice requires.

Some prefer the term "survivor" to emphasize resilience and agency. Restorative practitioners respect individual preference while ensuring that those who have been harmed are central to the process.

Research shows that victims who participate in restorative processes report higher satisfaction than those whose cases go through conventional channels. They feel heard, respected, and involved in ways that traditional justice rarely provides.

See also: Empowerment, Healing, Participation, Survivor, Voice

Victim-Offender Mediation

Victim-Offender Mediation (VOM) is a restorative practice that brings victims and offenders together in a facilitated dialogue to address the harm caused by a crime. Trained mediators guide the process, ensuring safe, respectful communication.

The VOM process involves referral and intake, preparation meetings with each party separately, the mediation session itself, and follow-up. During the session, victims describe the impact of the offense; offenders respond, often expressing remorse; together they develop a plan for reparation.

Research shows that VOM produces high levels of victim satisfaction, increased offender accountability, and reduced recidivism. It is one of the most widely used and studied restorative practices.

See also: Mediation, Mediator

Virtue Ethics

Virtue ethics is a philosophical tradition, rooted in Aristotelian philosophy, that focuses on the development of moral character and virtues such as empathy, compassion, and responsibility. It emphasizes the cultivation of good character traits that enable individuals to live ethical and fulfilling lives.

Virtue ethics informs restorative justice in several ways. Restorative practices are designed to foster specific virtues—empathy through encounter, responsibility through accountability, compassion through mutual recognition. Restorative justice is concerned with moral formation, not merely conflict resolution. It recognizes the role of community in developing virtues.

Theological resources for virtue ethics are abundant. The Beatitudes describe the character of those in God's kingdom. The fruit of the Spirit—love, joy, peace, patience, kindness, goodness, faithfulness, gentleness, self-control—are virtues cultivated through the Spirit's work. Restorative justice participates in this formation.

See also: Character, Moral Development, Philosophy

Voice

Voice refers to the opportunity to speak and be heard in restorative processes. Giving voice to victims, offenders, and community members is central to restorative justice. When people have voice, they feel respected, validated, and empowered.

Voice is not merely speaking but being heard. Restorative processes create conditions for genuine listening—through facilitated dialogue, through the talking piece, through commitment to respectful communication. Participants know that their words matter, that others will truly listen.

Psychological research on procedural justice shows that voice is one of the most important factors in people's satisfaction with legal processes. When people have voice—when they can tell their stories and express their views—they perceive the process as fairer and more legitimate.

See also: Inclusion, Participation, Procedural Justice

Voluntary Participation

Voluntary participation means that involvement in restorative processes is freely chosen, not coerced. This voluntariness is essential to the integrity and effectiveness of restorative justice. When participation is coerced, the authenticity of the process is undermined.

Ensuring voluntary participation requires informed consent. Participants must understand what the process involves, what will be expected of them, what the possible outcomes are. They must know that they can withdraw at any time without penalty.

Voluntary participation also requires that alternatives be genuinely available. If the only way to avoid harsh punishment is to participate in restorative justice, participation may not be truly voluntary. Programs must be designed to protect voluntariness.

See also: Informed Consent

W

Whole-School Approach

A whole-school approach to restorative justice means implementing restorative practices throughout a school, involving all staff, students, and policies, to create a restorative school climate. This goes beyond using restorative practices for discipline; it embeds restorative values in all aspects of school life.

A whole-school approach includes proactive practices—restorative circles for community building, restorative language in everyday interactions—as well as responsive practices for addressing conflicts and harms. It involves training for all staff, integration into curriculum, engagement with families and community.

Research shows that whole-school restorative approaches produce significant improvements in school climate, reductions in disciplinary incidents, and better academic outcomes. They transform schools into communities where all can thrive.

See also: Restorative Circles, School-Based Restorative Justice

---

Y

Youth Justice

Youth justice refers to the system of laws, policies, and practices addressing young people who commit offenses. Restorative justice has been particularly influential in youth justice, with many jurisdictions incorporating restorative approaches.

The rationale for restorative youth justice is compelling. Adolescence is a period of moral development; restorative practices that engage young people in understanding harm, taking responsibility, and making amends can shape their development in positive directions. Research shows that restorative approaches are more effective than punitive measures in reducing recidivism among youth.

Examples include New Zealand's Family Group Conferencing, which is mandatory for most youth offenses, and restorative justice programs in juvenile courts across the United States, Canada, and Europe.

See also: Family Group Conferencing

This glossary, dear reader, is offered as a resource for your ongoing engagement with restorative justice. May the terms defined here become not merely words to know but concepts to embody, principles to live, and practices to share. As you continue your journey—whether as practitioner, advocate, researcher, or simply one who cares about justice—may these terms serve as tools for understanding and action.

www.ingramcontent.com/pod-product-compliance
Lightning Source LLC
LaVergne TN
LVHW052212200926
848481LV00001B/85
9798295662287